Olympiad Champs

LOGICAL REASONING

Workbook — Class 1

with **Chapter-wise Previous 5 Year** (2018 - 2022) Questions

DISHA™
Publication Inc

DISHA Publications Inc.

45, 2nd Floor, Maharishi Dayanand Marg,
Corner Market, Malviya Nagar, new Delhi –110017
Tel: 49842349/ 49842350

Typeset By

DISHA DTP Team

Buying books from DISHA

Just Got A Lot More Rewarding!!!

We at DISHA Publication, value your feedback immensely and to show our apperciation of our reviewers, we have launched a review contest.

To participate in this reward scheme, just follow these quick and simple steps:
- Write a review of the product you purchase on Amazon/Flipkart.
- Take a screenshot/photo of your review.
- Mail it to *disha-rewards@aiets.co.in*, along with all your details.

Each month, selected reviewers will win exciting gifts from
DISHA Publication. Note that the rewards for each month
will be declared in the first week of next month on our website.

https://bit.ly/review-reward-disha.

Write To
Us At
feedback_disha@aiets.co.in

Preface

We are pleased to launch the 2nd edition of **Olympiad Champs Logical Reasoning Class 1** which is the first of its kind book on Olympiad in many ways.

The Unique Selling Proposition of this new edition is the inclusion of past year questions till 2022 of different Olympiad exams held in schools.

The book is aimed at achieving not only success but deep rooted learning in children. It is prepared on content based on National Curriculum Framework prescribed by NCERT. All the text books, syllabi and teaching practices within the education programme in India must follow NCF. Hence, Olympiad Champs become an ideal book not only for the Olympiad Exams but also for strengthening the concepts for Class 1.

There is an exhaustive range of thought provoking questions in MCQ format to test the student's knowledge thoroughly. The questions are designed so as to test the knowledge, comprehension, evaluation, analytical and application skills. Solutions and explanations are provided for all questions. The questions are divided into two levels - Level 1 and Level 2. The first level, Level 1, is the beginner's level which comprises of questions like fillers, analogy and odd one out. When the child covers Level 1, it means his basic knowledge about the subject is clear and now it is ready for Level 2. The second level is the advanced level. Level 2 comprises of techniques like matching, chronological sequencing, picture, passage and feature based, statement correct/ incorrect, integer based, puzzle, grid based, crossword, venn diagram, table/ chart based and much more.

The first concern which each parent faces is how to make their children read a book especially when it is based on academics. Keeping this in mind interesting facts, real life examples, historical preview, short cut to problem solving, charts, diagrams, illustrations and poems are added. In addition to this, we have introduced comic strip which increases the readability quotient and make the reading experience for the children more exciting.

With the vision to remove all the misconception a child may have pertaining to the subject, to relate his knowledge to the real world and to develop a deeper understanding of the subject this book will cater all the requirements of the students who are going to appear in Olympiads.

While preparing this book, some errors might have crept in. We request our readers to identify those errors and send it across on **feedback_disha@aiets.co.in.**

We wish you all the best for your Olympiads and happy reading.......

Team Disha

For feedback : **feedback_disha@aiets.co.in.**

CONTENTS

Scan code to gain **FREE access** to **"Olympiad Champs"**, a unique page dedicated to prepare students of class 1-8 to ace all National Level Olympiad Exams.

Current Affairs Updates, Mock Tests, Past Papers, Quizzes, Interesting, Fun Facts, Parenting Articles & Free Courses

DISHA™
Publication Inc

10 Principles to CRACK ANY EXAM

1. Chase consistency, not intensity.

Doing intensive study makes your day. But it also exhausts you in the long run, leading to lesser output and added pressure. Toppers always focus on doing consistent work daily, for consistency is far more valuable than intensity.

Remember consistent study of 4 hours every day is more important and powerful than studying 12 hours a day and then not studying at all for next 2 days.

2. Go beyond the surface.

Most students only see a few reasons (teacher, coaching, books, etc) behind Toppers' success, which is only the tip of the iceberg. What they donot see is Toppers Mindset, self belief, habits and discipline and that is where the real problem is.

3. Focus on giving your best, not chasing the best.

We want the best coaching, the best teacher, best batch and the best books but we are not ready to give our BEST. Success comes only when we are ready to give our best. We must focus on giving our best than chasing excuses to cover up our failures.

4. Clarity of concept is the key

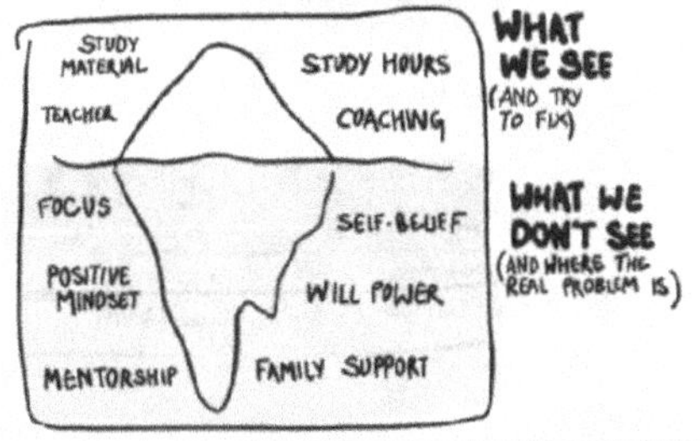

Concept clarity is critical. If you cannot solve a question, you must go back to the theory and thoroughly examine the concept instead of referring to the solutions. Remember question is one of the chehra(face) of the concept. When toppers get stuck in a problem, they go back and refer the theory(read the concept again and again on which the question is based)

5. Every failure should be a lesson learned.

Most students do not learn from their failures and repeat their mistakes. Toppers also face failures, but they learn from mistakes and elevate themselves. Making mistakes and learning from them is the key to success.

6 Choosing the quality of resources is more important than quantity.

More than 90% of the questions in most books are the same as their substitutes. Instead of practicing from four books and failing to complete them, it is best to prepare from two books and complete them with thorough revisions.

7 Difficult things become easy by taking it one day at a time.

The best way to take any preparation forward is by taking it one day at a time. It makes the impossible possible by taking small steps every day.

Starting a difficult subject. No worries. Keep on working session by session, day by day and week by week and one day you will become unstoppable force.

8. Everything is easy

Before starting everything looks difficult. Once you take a first step, it slowly starts looking easy and over a period of time you become master in the activity. This is toppers secret to become master in any subject.

9. Nobody is gifted

We think toppers are god gifted. We think toppers have high IQ. We think toppers are special/lucky. But the truth is every topper was once an average student (no body is born topper). What makes them different is their consistent and focused efforts

10. Believe in your journey and success will come to you.

There is never a straight path to success; hard work & patience is required for the results to show up. Keep on working hard without thinking too much about the results and success will come to you eventually.

Analogy

OBJECTIVES

- Students will understand how analogies are used.
- Students will be able to make comparisons between concepts and complete analogies.

INTRODUCTION

An analogy is a comparison between things which are basically not alike but which share some kind of striking similarity.

HOW TO "READ" ANALOGIES

The symbol (:) means "is to" and the symbol (: :) means "as." Thus, the analogy, "apple : fruit : : carrot : vegetable," should be read "apple is to fruit as carrot is to vegetable." Stated another way, the relationship between apple and fruit is the same as the relationship between carrot and vegetable.

Steps to Solve

Step 1: Look carefully at the first pair of examples.

Step 2: How are these two pairs connected?

Step 3: Complete the second pair in the same way as the first pair.

Step 4: Make sure that all the necessary changes are made.

Types of Analogy

(i) Picture Based Analogy

Directions (Examples 1-2): Choose the correct matching pair.

1.

Ans. (b)

The first figure is a part of second figure and the second image is the complete figure.

So, the correct answer is (b).

2.

Ans. (c)

Pair of figures on the left side of : : are vegetables. Pair of figures on the right side of : : are fruits.

(ii) Number Based Analogy

Direction (Example 3): Choose the correct matching pair.

3.   (2) : (4) : : (3) : (?)

(a) 4   (b) 1   (c) 6   (d) 7

Ans. (c)

$$2 \times 2 = 4$$

Similarly,

$$3 \times 2 = 6$$

So, the correct answer is (c).

(iii) Alphabet Based Analogy

Direction (Example 4): Choose the correct matching pair.

4. B : D : : X : ?

   (a) D   (b) Z   (c) Y   (d) U

Ans. (b)

Letter B of first pair is moved two steps forward i.e., $B \xrightarrow{+2} D$

Similarly,

Letter X of second pair is moved two steps forward i.e., $X \xrightarrow{+2} Z$

(iv) **Word Based Analogy**

Direction (Example 5): Choose the correct matching pair.

5. Birds : Fly : : Men : ?

   (a) Fly   (b) Walk   (c) Swim   (d) Hop

Ans. (b)

As, birds fly to move, similarly, men walk to move.

LEVEL-1

Direction (Qs. 1-25): Find the matching pair.

1.  :  ::  : ?

(a) 　　(b) 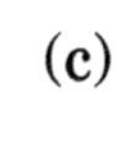 　　(c) 　　(d) 

2.  :  ::  : ?

(a) 　　(b) 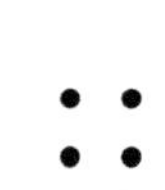 　　(c) 　　(d) 

3.  :  ::  : ?

(a) 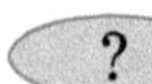　　(b) 　　(c) 　　(d)

4. (3) : (5) :: (5) : (?)

(a) 4　　　　(b) 6　　　　(c) 7　　　　(d) 2

5. (Ten) : (10) :: (Nine) : (?)

(a) 5　　　　(b) 9　　　　(c) 7　　　　(d) 2

6. 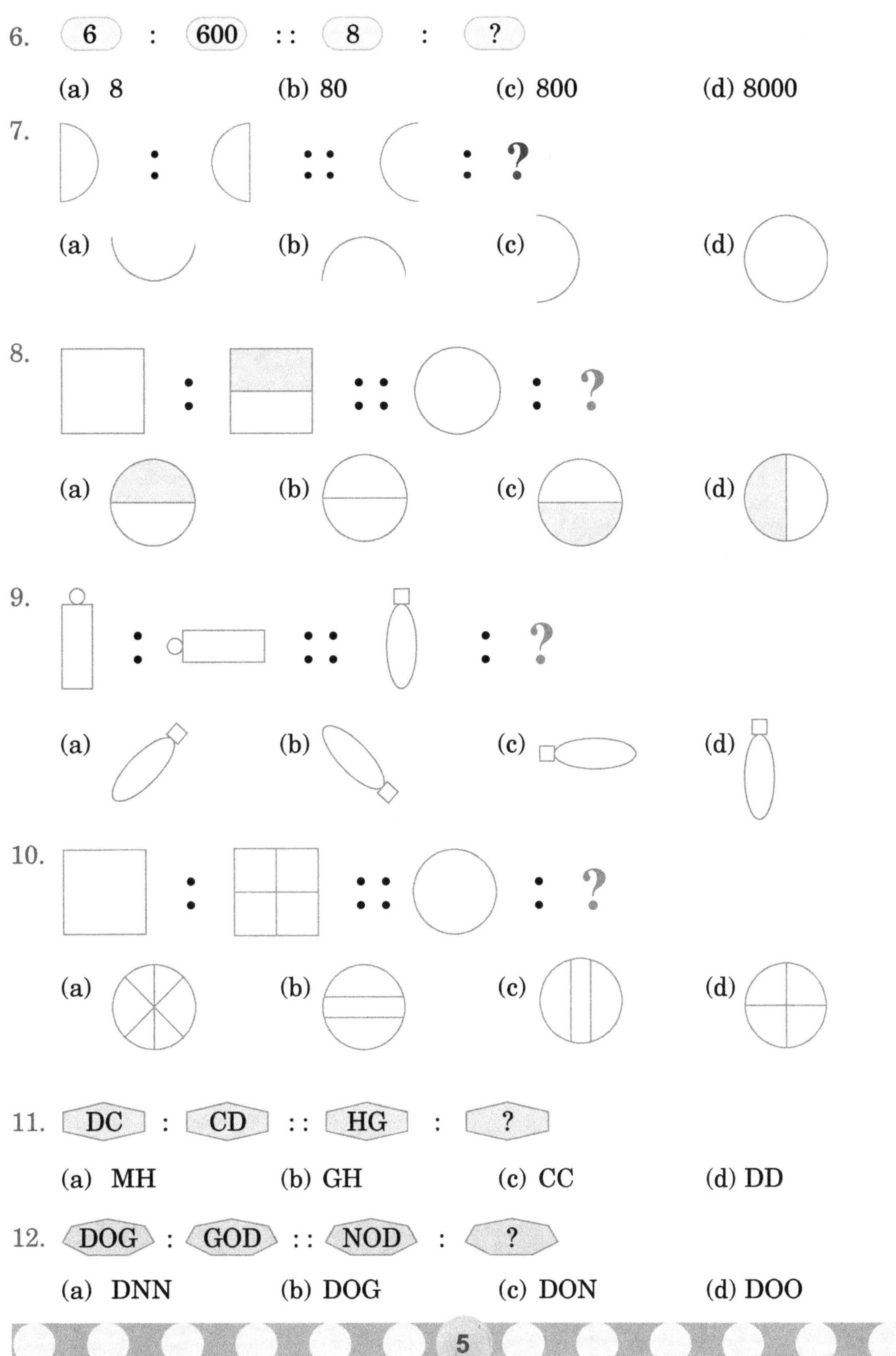 6 : 600 :: 8 : ?

(a) 8   (b) 80   (c) 800   (d) 8000

7. (a)   (b)   (c)   (d)

8. (a)   (b)   (c)   (d)

9. (a)   (b)   (c)   (d)

10. (a)   (b)   (c)   (d)

11. DC : CD :: HG : ?

(a) MH   (b) GH   (c) CC   (d) DD

12. DOG : GOD :: NOD : ?

(a) DNN   (b) DOG   (c) DON   (d) DOO

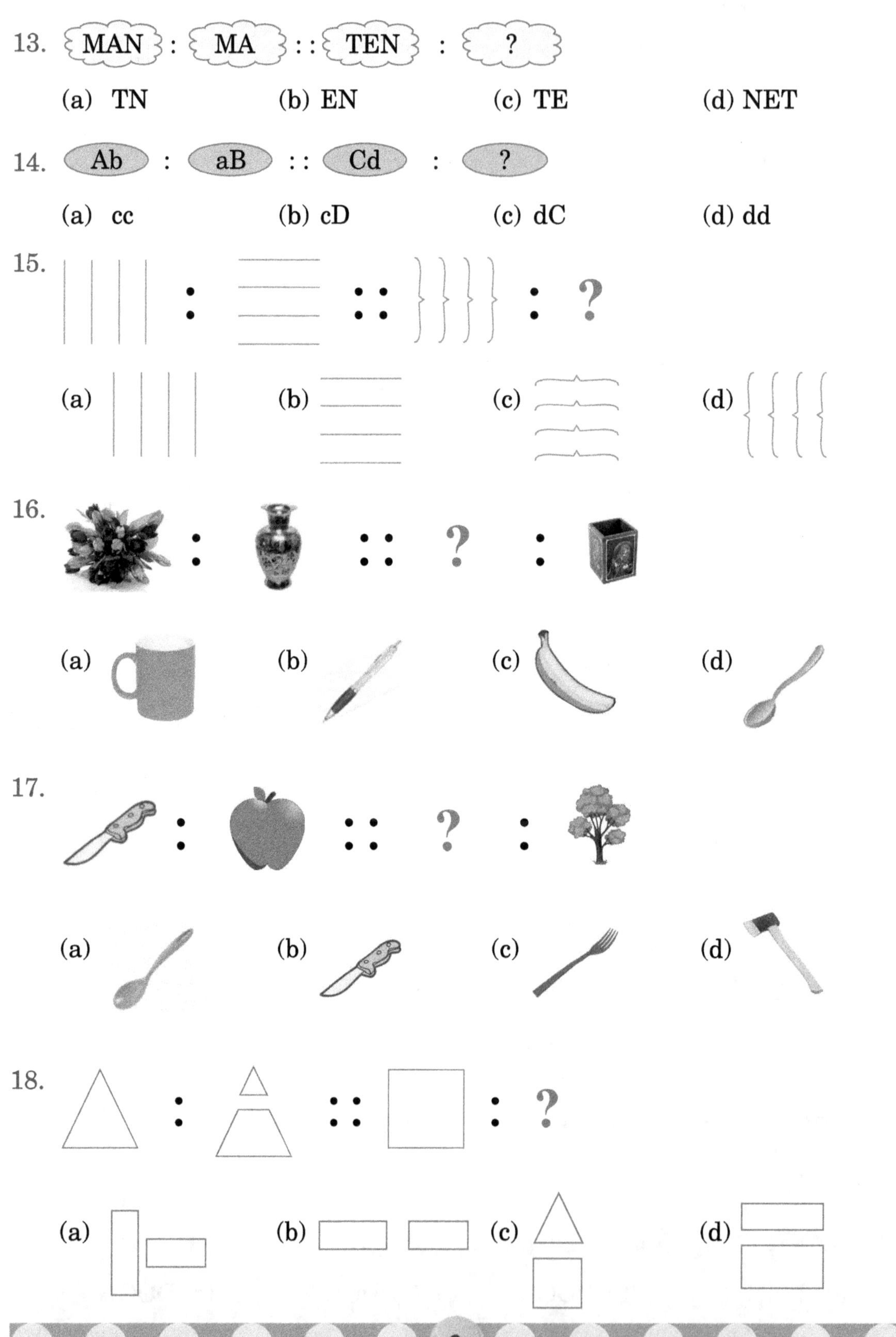

13. MAN : MA :: TEN : ?

   (a) TN   (b) EN   (c) TE   (d) NET

14. Ab : aB :: Cd : ?

   (a) cc   (b) cD   (c) dC   (d) dd

15.   (a)   (b)   (c)   (d)

16.   (a)   (b)   (c)   (d)

17.   (a)   (b)   (c)   (d)

18.   (a)   (b)   (c)   (d)

19. Up : Down :: Left : ?

(a) Over   (b) Close   (c) Right   (d) Before

20. Pen : Write :: Brush : ?

(a) Paint   (b) Erase   (c) Play   (d) Sleep

21. Milk : Cow :: Wool : ?

(a) Sheep   (b) Horse   (c) Tiger   (d) Dog

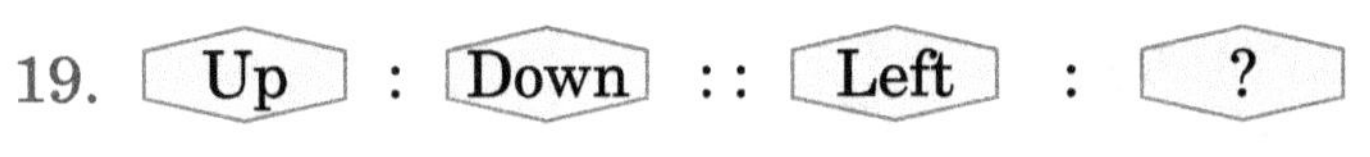

LEVEL-2

Direction (Qs. 1-17): Find the matching pair.

1. 9 : 8 :: 4 : ?

(a) 3   (b) 2   (c) 5   (d) 6

2. 1 : 11 :: 2 : ?

(a) 10   (b) 22   (c) 11   (d) 20

3. 8 : 4 :: 6 : ?

(a) 7   (b) 5   (c) 2   (d) 9

4. 13 : 31 :: 12 : ?

(a) 21   (b) 22   (c) 12   (d) 13

5.

6. 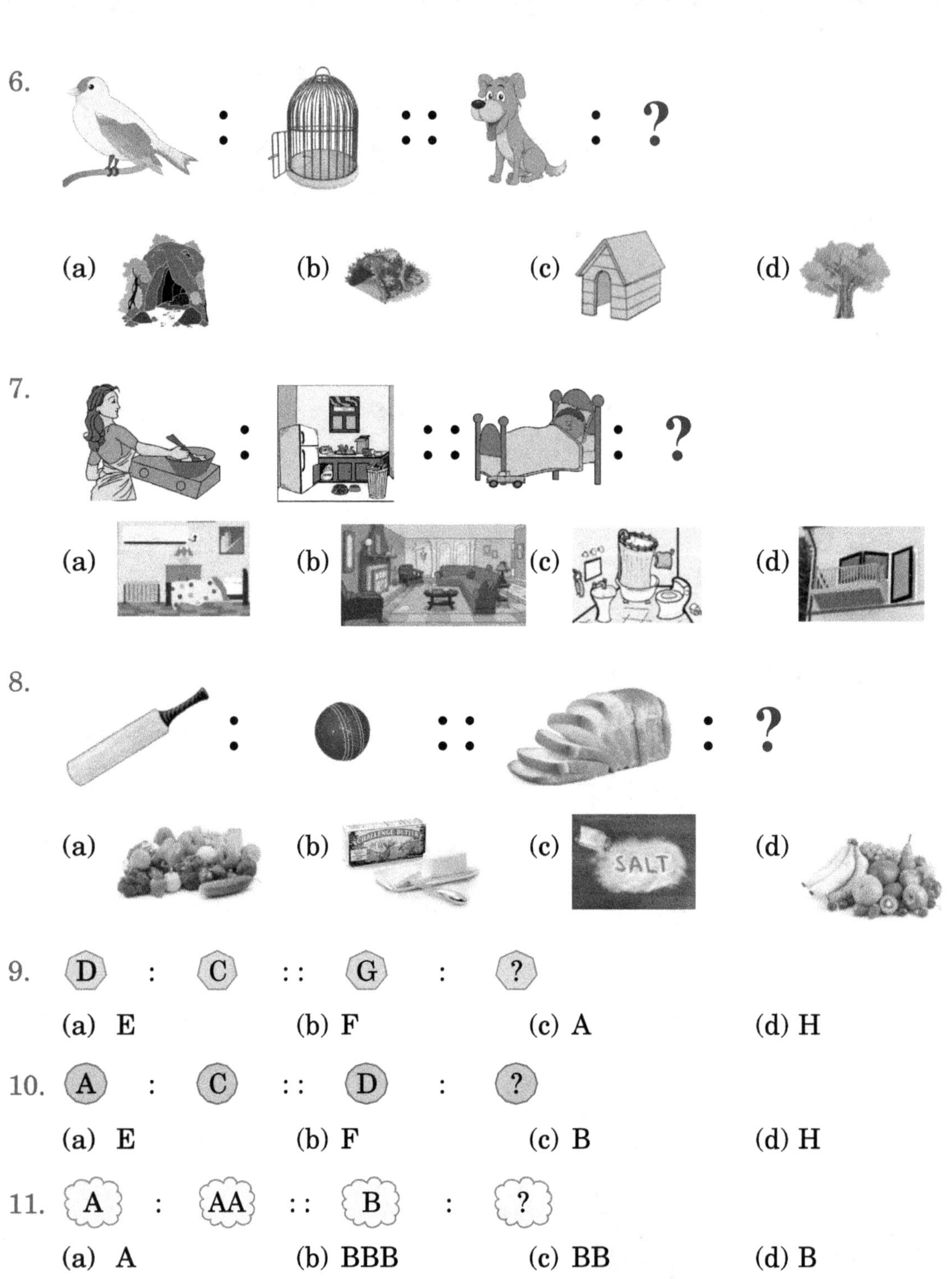

7.

8.

9. D : C :: G : ?
(a) E   (b) F   (c) A   (d) H

10. A : C :: D : ?
(a) E   (b) F   (c) B   (d) H

11. A : AA :: B : ?
(a) A   (b) BBB   (c) BB   (d) B

12. AB : BA :: CD : ?
(a) DC   (b) AC   (c) AD   (d) CD

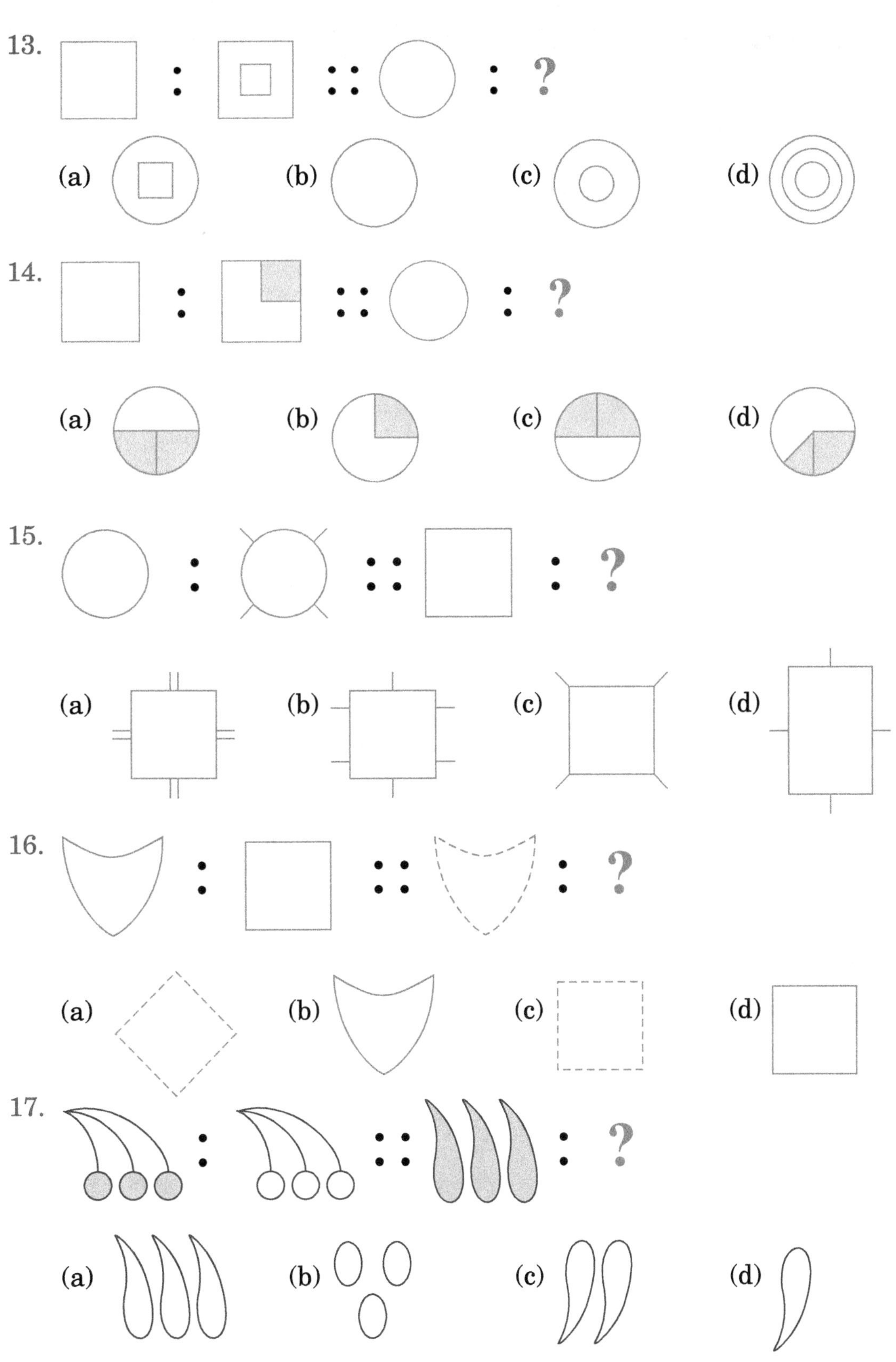

13.

(a)   (b)   (c)   (d)

14.

(a)   (b)   (c)   (d)

15.

(a)   (b)   (c)   (d)

16.

(a)   (b)   (c)   (d)

17.

(a)   (b)   (c)   (d)

Direction (Qs. 18 to 27): Find the matching word.

18. Rose : Flower :: Apple : **?**

(a) Vegetable   (b) Fruit   (c) Seed   (d) Tool

19. Tub : Bathroom :: Stove : **?**

(a) Bedroom   (b) Drawing room

(c) Kitchen   (d) Washroom

20. Banana : Yellow :: Apple : **?**

(a) Red   (b) Green   (c) Black   (d) White

21. October : November :: March : **?**

(a) April   (b) August   (c) May   (d) June

22. Eyes : See :: Ears : **?**

(a) Touch   (b) Smell   (c) Hear   (d) Taste

23.

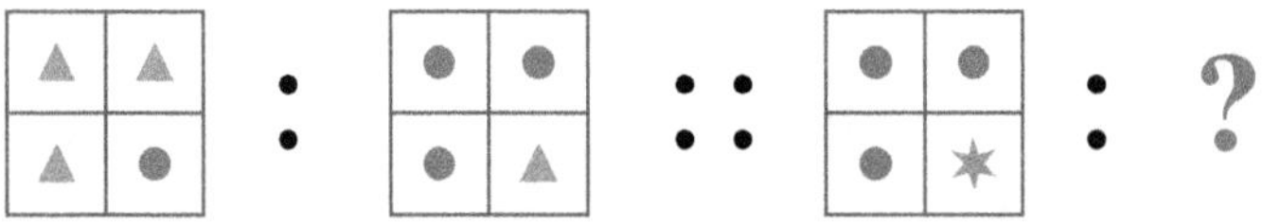

(a) 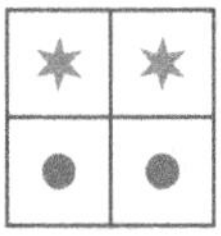   (b)

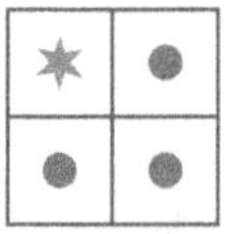

(c) 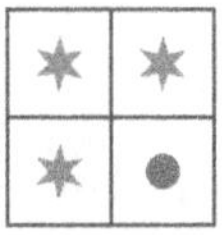   (d)

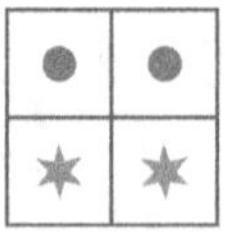

24. 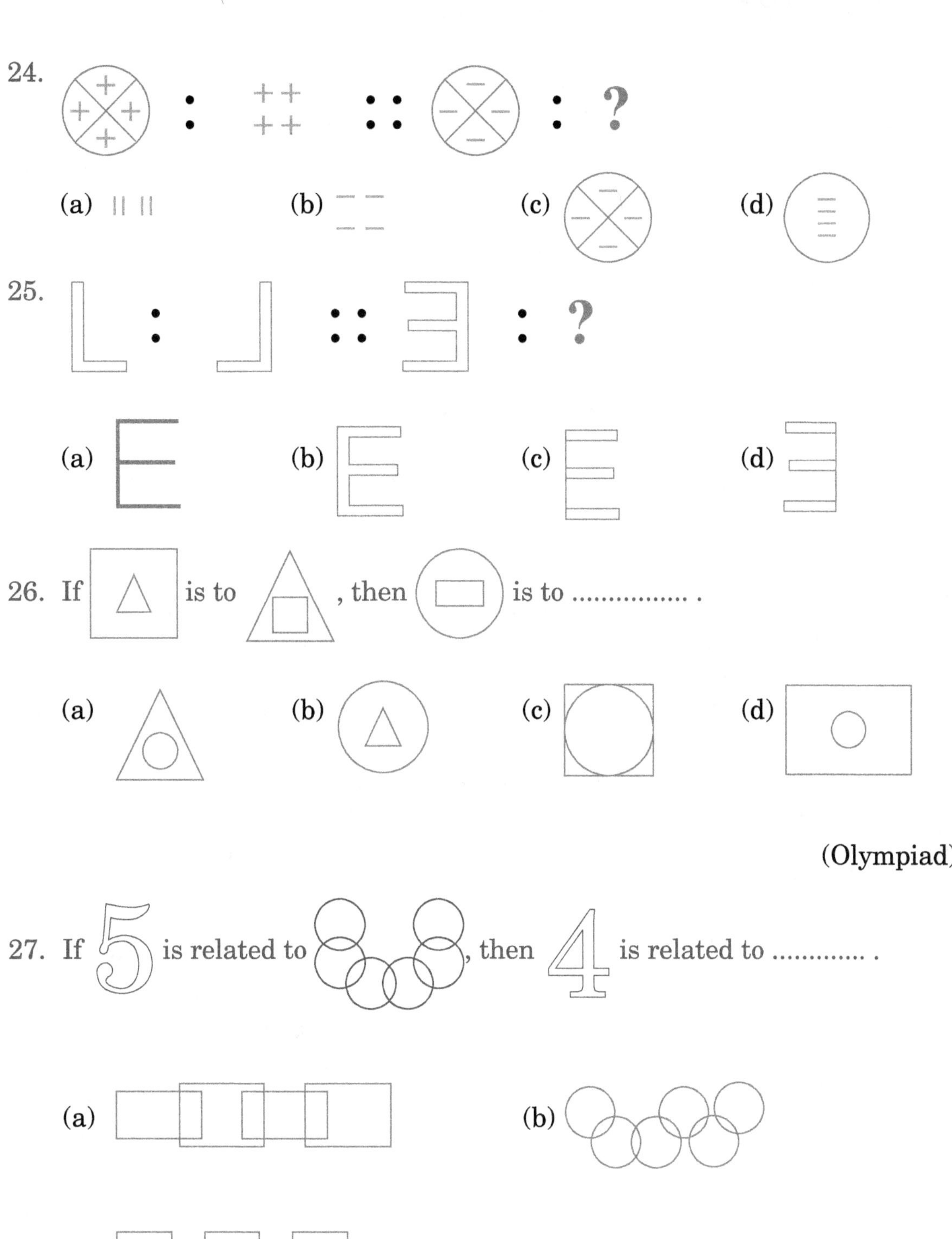

25.

26. If [△ in square] is to [△ with square inside], then [rectangle in circle] is to ....

(a)   (b)   (c)   (d)

(Olympiad)

27. If **5** is related to [circles figure], then **4** is related to ....

(a)   (b)

(c)   (d)   (Olympiad)

28. If ⬜ is related to ⭕ in some way, then in the same way △ is related to _____. **(2019)**

(a)   (b)   (c)   (d)

29. **If yesterday was Friday, then today is _______.** **(2022)**

(a) Saturday   (b) Sunday   (c) Thursday   (d) Monday

Answers and Explanations

Level-1

1. **(b)** Goggles are used to protect eyes from sun rays. Similarly, umbrella is used to protect body against rain.
2. **(d)** A bird uses its feathers to fly. Similarly, a fish uses fins to swim.
3. **(a)** A teacher teaches in a school. Similarly, a doctor diagnoses diseases in a hospital.
4. **(c)** As, $3 + 2 = 5$
   Similarly, $5 + 2 = 7$
   So, correct answer is (c).
5. **(b)** As, Ten is written as '10'. Similarly, Nine is written as '9'
6. **(c)** 6 is written as 600. Similarly, 8 is written as 800.
7. **(c)** The 2nd figure is the mirror image of the first.
8. **(a)** The 2nd figure is the same as the first figure with upper half shaded.
9. **(c)** The 2nd figure rotates anticlockwise.
10. **(d)** The 2nd figure is divided into four equal parts.
11. **(b)** First term is reversed to get the second term. So, correct answer is (b).
12. **(c)** First term is reversed to get the second term. So, correct answer is (c).
13. **(c)** Third letter is removed from the first term to get the second term. So, correct answer is (c).
14. **(b)** Upper case has been changed to lower case and lower case has been changed to upper case. So, correct answer is (b).
15. **(c)** Vertical lines become horizontal.
16. **(b)** Flowerpot is used to put the flowers. Similarly, pen stand is used to put the pen.
17. **(d)** First is used to cut the second.
18. **(d)** First figure is divided into two parts.

19. **(c)** Up and down are antonyms. Similarly, left and right are antonyms.

20. **(a)** We write with pen. Similarly, we paint with brush.

21. **(a)** As cow gives milk. Similarly, sheep gives wool.

Level-2

1. **(a)** As, $9 - 1 = 8$
Similarly, $4 - 1 = 3$
So, correct answer is (a).

2. **(b)** Number repeats itself after a number.

3. **(c)** As, $8 - 4 = 4$
Similarly, $6 - 4 = 2$
So, correct answer is (c).

4. **(a)** As, $1\ 3 \longrightarrow 31$
Similarly, $1\ 2 \longrightarrow 21$
So, correct answer is (a).

5. **(c)** Hairbrush is used to comb hair. Similarly, toothbrush is used to brush teeth.

6. **(c)** Birds are kept in cage. Similarly, dogs are kept in kennel.

7. **(a)** A kitchen is used for cooking. Similarly, a bedroom is used for sleeping.

8. **(b)** Bat and ball are complementary to each other.
Similarly, bread and butter are complementary to each other.

9. **(b)** D is moved one step backward to get C.
$$D \xrightarrow{-1} C$$
$$G \xrightarrow{-1} F$$
So, correct answer is (b).

10. **(b)** A is moved two steps forward to get C.
$$A \xrightarrow{+2} C$$
$$D \xrightarrow{+2} F$$
So, correct answer is (b).

11. **(c)** First term is repeated to get the second one. So, correct answer is (c).

12. **(a)** First term is reversed to get the second term. So, correct answer is (a).

13. **(c)** The same shape, reduced in size is fitted in larger one.

14. **(b)** In the 2nd figure, the one fourth part of the first figure has been shaded.

15. **(c)** Four lines have been added.

16. **(c)** The 4th figure is the same as the third figure with dotted outline.

17. **(a)** Shaded portion becomes unshaded.

18. **(b)** Rose is a flower. Similarly, apple is a fruit.

19. **(c)** A tub is kept in the bathroom. Similarly, a stove is kept in the kitchen.

20. **(a)** The colour of banana is yellow. Similarly, apple is red in colour.

21. **(a)** November comes after October. Similarly, April comes after March.

22. **(c)** We see with our eyes Similarly, we hear our ears.

23. **(c)** In the first pair, ▲ becomes ● and ● becomes ▲. Similarly, in second pair, ● becomes ★ and ★ becomes ●.

24. **(b)** Large element in first figure will disappear in second figure.

25. **(b)** Second figure is mirror image of first figure.

26. **(d)** Inner element and outer element interchanges.

27. **(c)** As, 5 is related to 6 circles. Similarly, 4 is related to 5 squares.

28. **(b)** 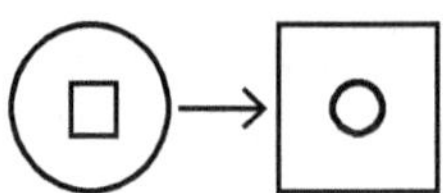

In this inner shape becomes outter shape and outter shape becomes inner shape. So, 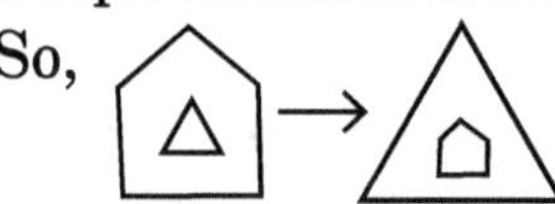

29. **(a)**

Monday	
Tuesday	
Wednesday	
Thursday	
Friday	Yesterday
Saturady	Today

Grouping

THEORY

Grouping is a set or arrangement of pictures, things or objects in a group.

Type I: In this type of questions, the student is required to analyse the given set of things, pictures, numbers and put them into groups of 2's, 3's...

Type II: Finding the number of groups of 2's, 3's, ... that could be formed from the given things/objects.

Examples:

1. There are 4 equal groups of ___________ cookies.

(a) 3　　　　　(b) 4　　　　　(c) 2　　　　　(d) 1

Ans. (c)

There are 4 equal groups of 2 cookies.

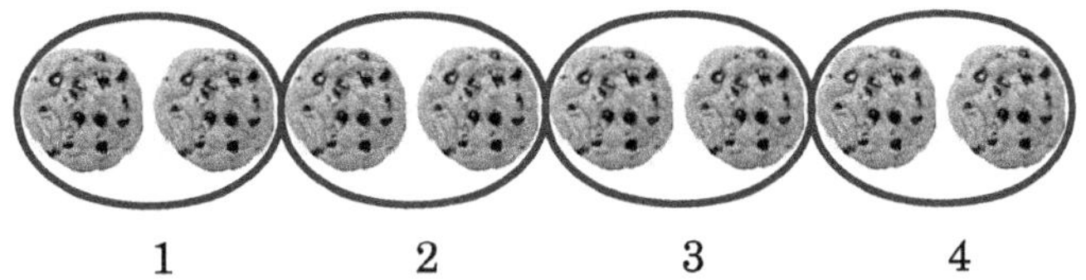

2. The shape ◯ can be placed in which group?

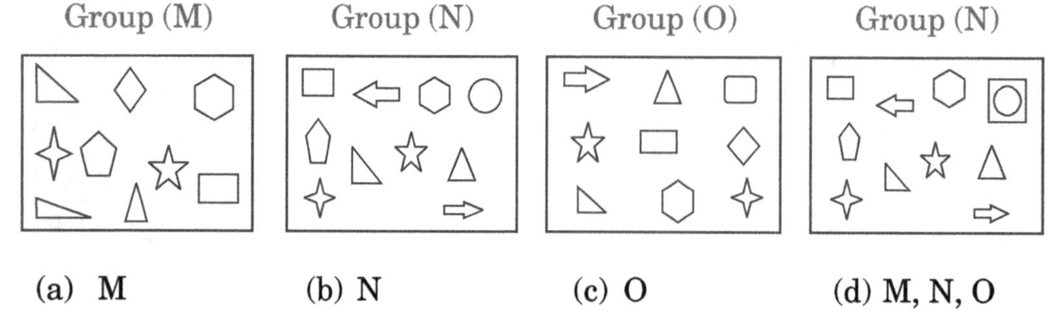

(a) M   (b) N   (c) O   (d) M, N, O

Ans. (b)

The shape ◯ can be placed in group N.

3.   There are __________ groups of 6 toys.

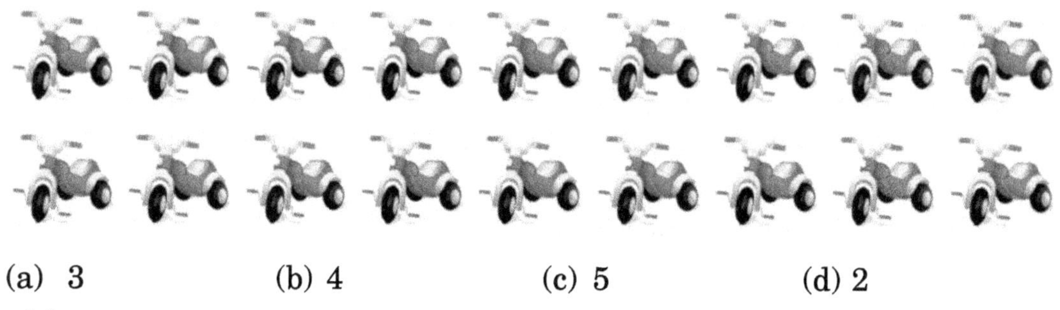

(a) 3   (b) 4   (c) 5   (d) 2

Ans. (a)

There are 3 groups of 6 toys.

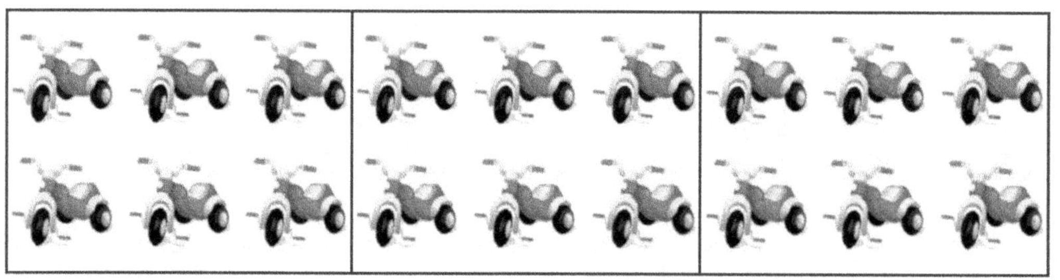

4.   Arrange the transports according to their weight (Light to Heavy).

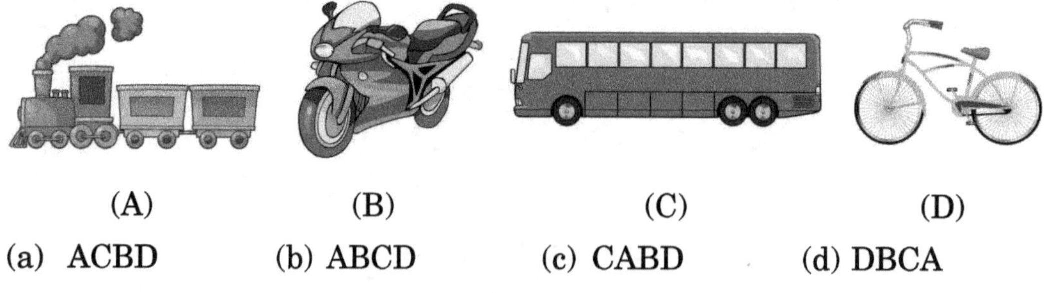

(a) ACBD   (b) ABCD   (c) CABD   (d) DBCA

Ans. (d)

The arrangement of transports according to their weight (light to heavy) is as following:

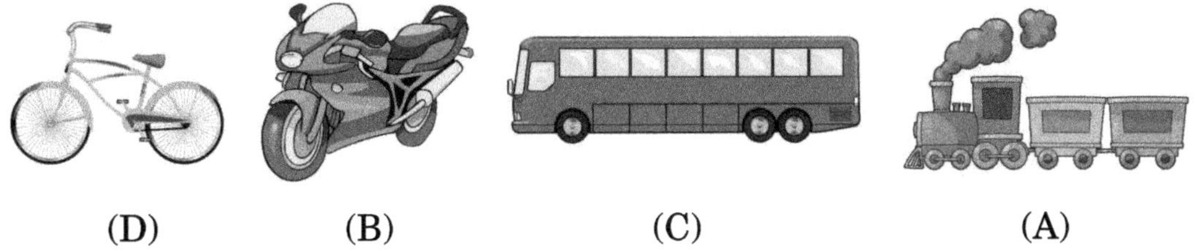

(D)   (B)   (C)   (A)

5. Identify the number of sad faces in the given diagram.

(a) 3   (b) 4   (c) 5   (d) 6

Ans. (b)

There are 4 sad faces in the diagram.

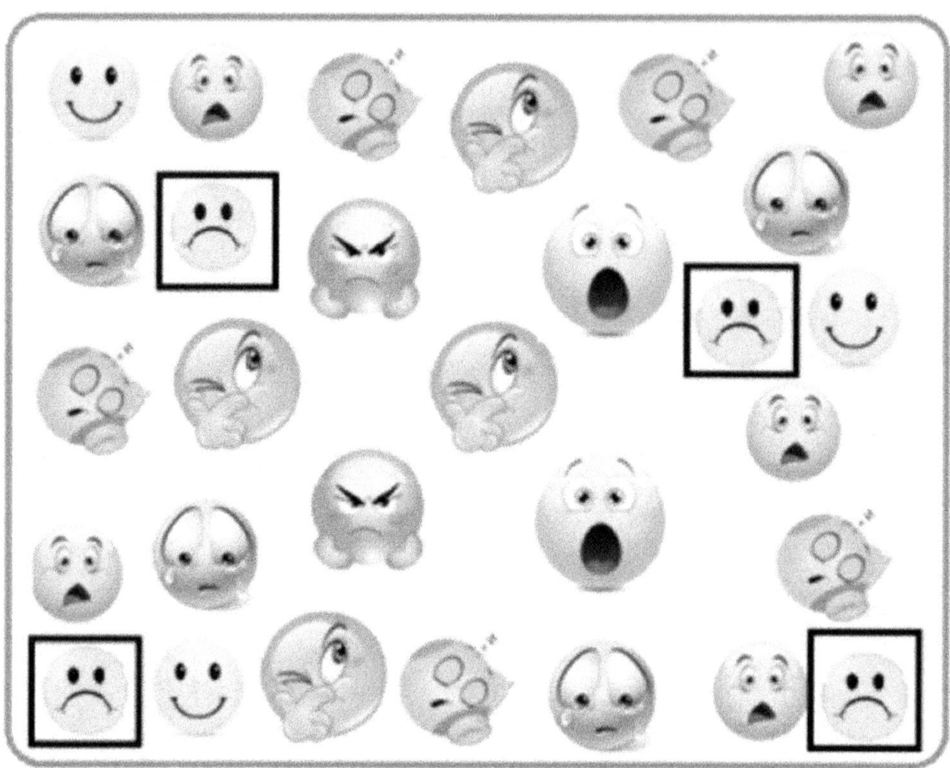

1. How many groups of 2's can be formed from the flowers given below?

   (a) 8   (b) 9   (c) 10   (d) 12

2. The given figure 'Δ' belongs to group _______.

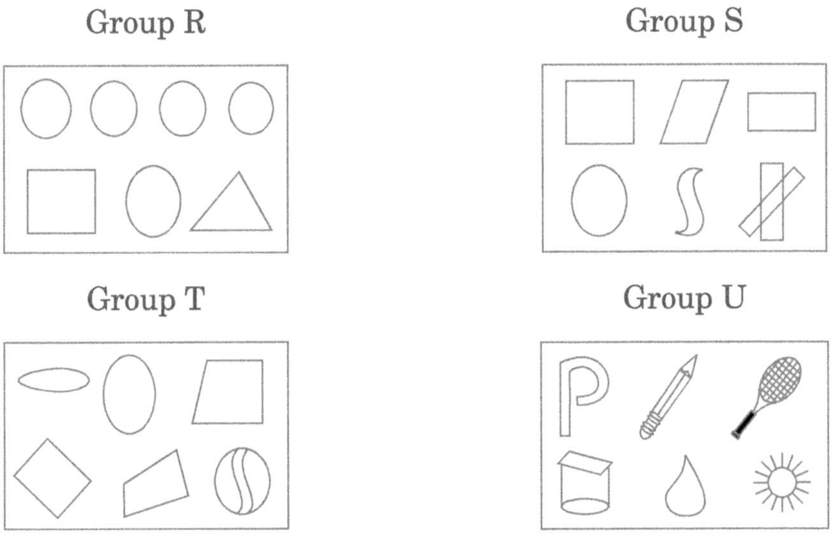

   Group R

   Group S

   Group T

   Group U

   (a) S   (b) T   (c) R   (d) U

3. There are _______ groups of 9 triangles.

   (a) 3   (b) 4   (c) 3   (d) 2

4. There are _______ groups of 3 ice-creams.

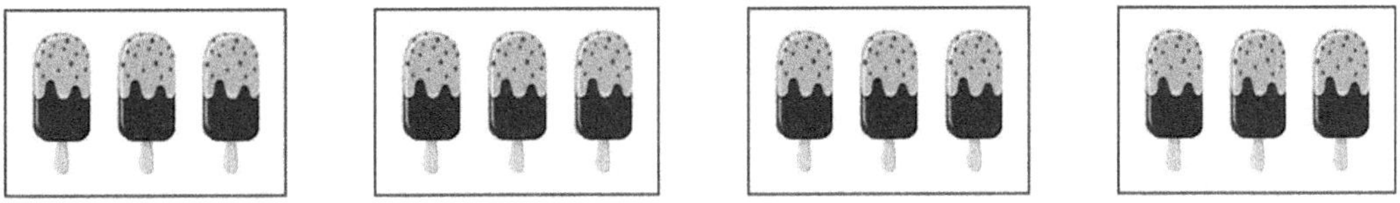

   (a) 5   (b) 4   (c) 6   (d) 8

5. Given below are the _______ groups of 3 butterflies.

(a) 5   (b) 9   (c) 4   (d) 2

6. There are _______ apples in each group.

(a) 8   (b) 9   (c) 5   (d) 6

7. There are _______ carrots altogether.

(a) 8   (b) 10   (c) 6   (d) 5

8. Arrange the animals according to their sizes, from big to small.

(P)   (Q)   (R)   (S)

(a) SPRQ   (b) PQRS   (c) SQRP   (d) QRSP

9. Arrange the animals by their speed, from fast to slow.

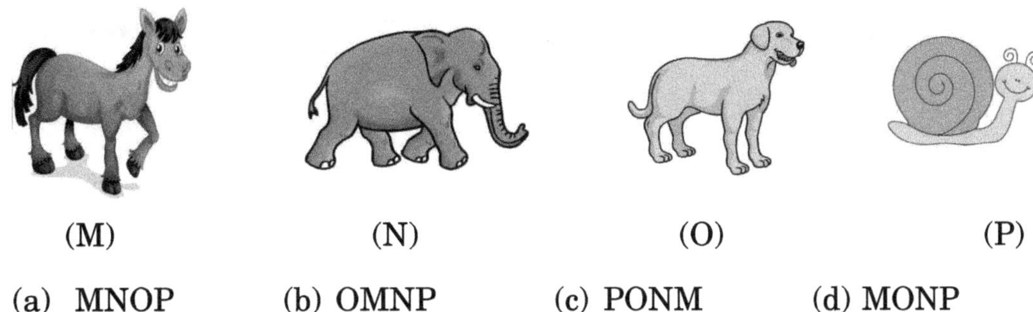

| (M) | (N) | (O) | (P) |

(a) MNOP   (b) OMNP   (c) PONM   (d) MONP

10. Arrange the following parts of your body as they are from bottom to top.

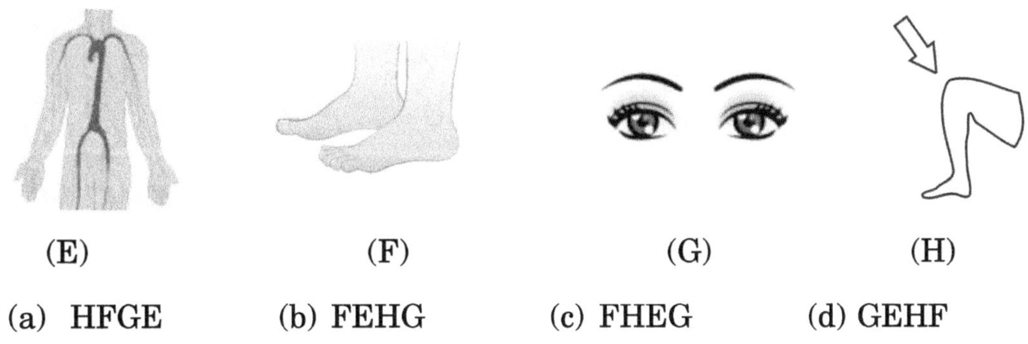

| (E) | (F) | (G) | (H) |

(a) HFGE   (b) FEHG   (c) FHEG   (d) GEHF

11. Sort the living things.

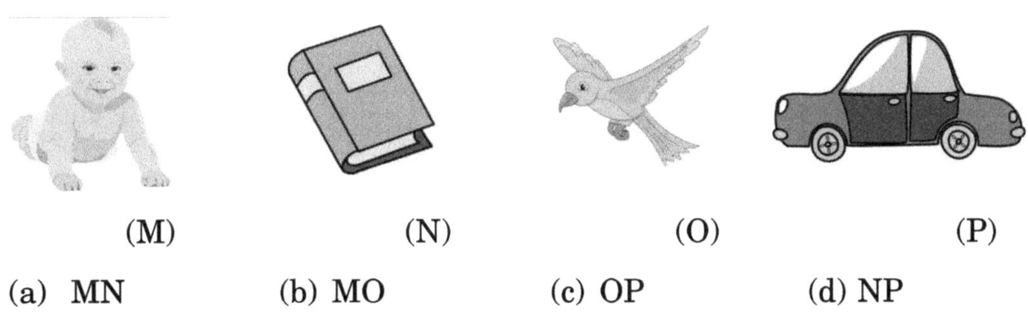

| (M) | (N) | (O) | (P) |

(a) MN   (b) MO   (c) OP   (d) NP

12. Arrange the items according to their weight (Heavy to light).

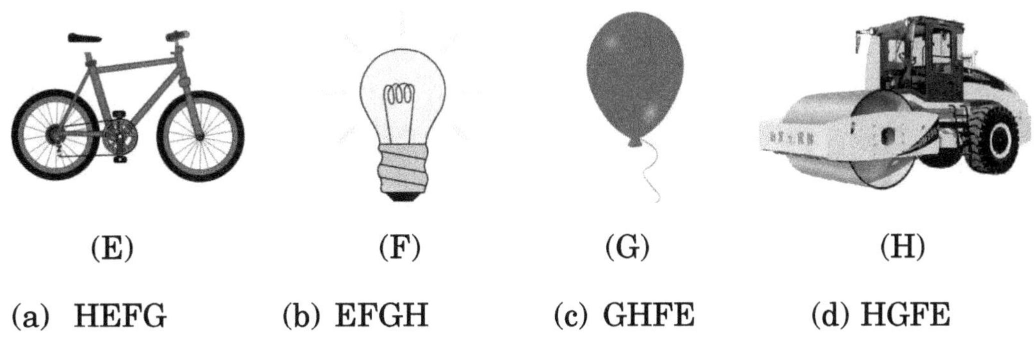

| (E) | (F) | (G) | (H) |

(a) HEFG   (b) EFGH   (c) GHFE   (d) HGFE

13. Sort the shapes which are solids.

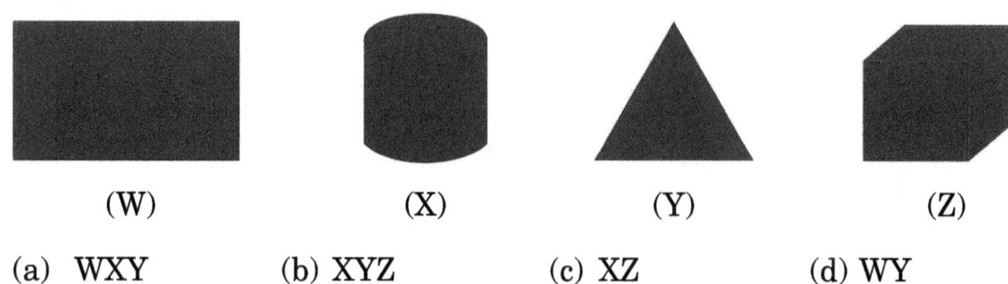

(W)   (X)   (Y)   (Z)

(a) WXY   (b) XYZ   (c) XZ   (d) WY

14. Sort the birds which cannot fly.

(I)   (J)   (K)   (L)

(a) IJK   (b) IL   (c) IKL   (d) IJKL

15. Select the thing that are used by men.

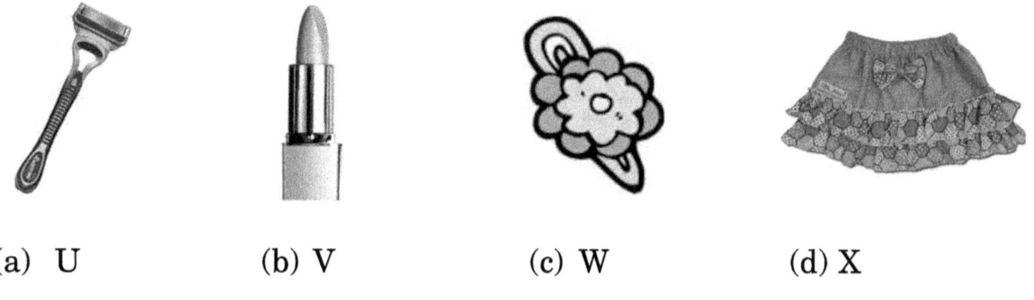

(a) U   (b) V   (c) W   (d) X

16. Sort out the external part of the body.

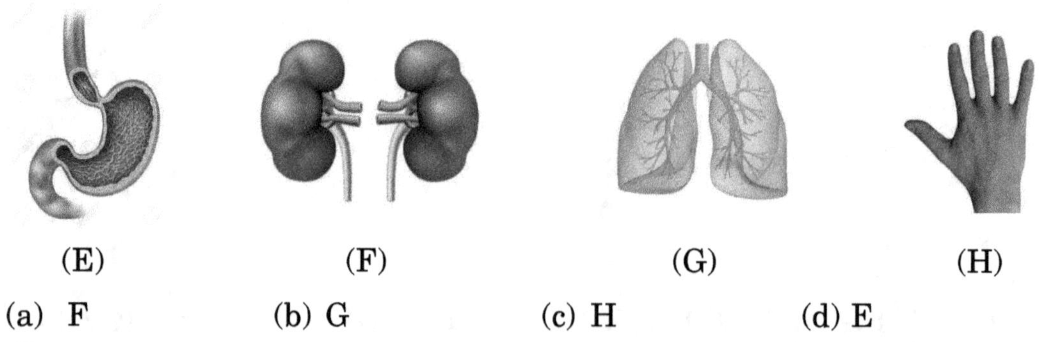

(E)   (F)   (G)   (H)

(a) F   (b) G   (c) H   (d) E

17. Identify the number of triangles in the given diagram.

(a) 7   (b) 6   (c) 8   (d) 10

18. How many blue colour shapes are there in the given figure?

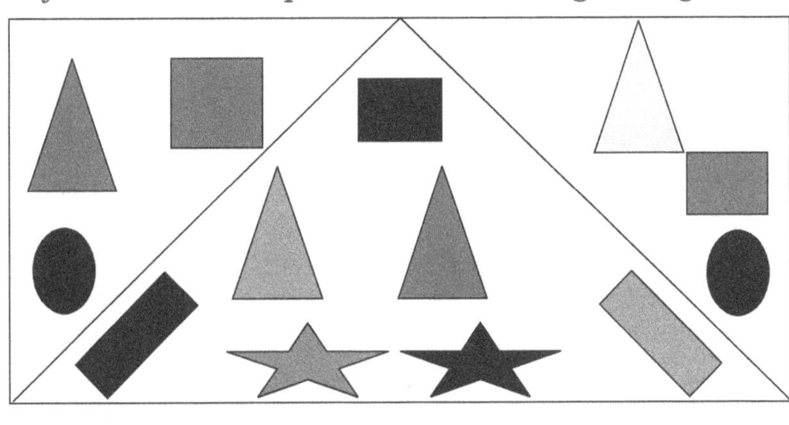

(a) 3   (b) 5   (c) 4   (d) 2

19. How many stationery items are there in the given picture?

(a) 9   (b) 8   (c) 6   (d) 4

20. How many red fruits and vegetables are there in the given picture?

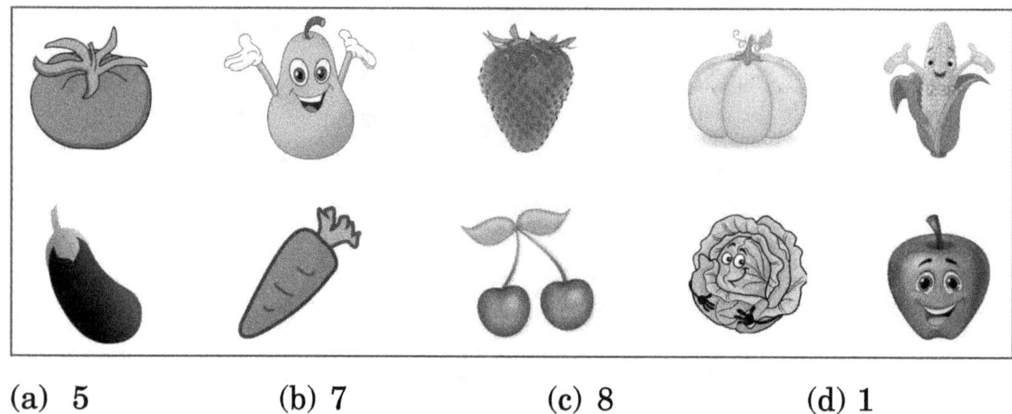

(a) 5　　　　(b) 7　　　　(c) 8　　　　(d) 1

21. How many items are there in the picture that are used by Teacher?

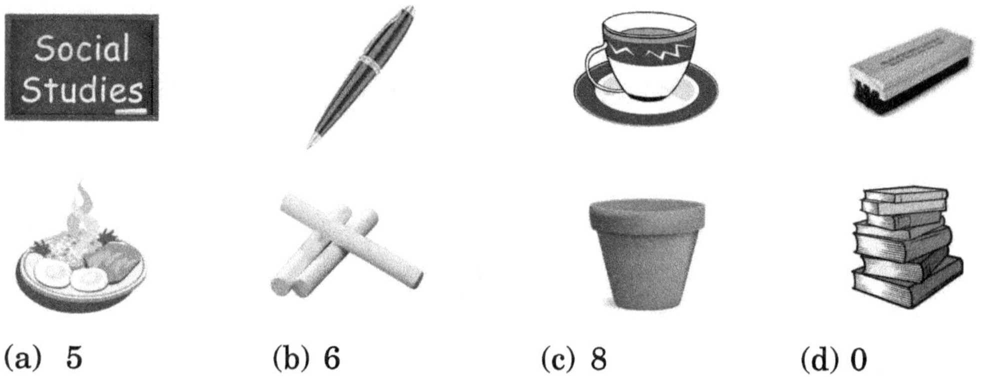

(a) 5　　　　(b) 6　　　　(c) 8　　　　(d) 0

22. Classify the number of Tomatoes and Brinjals in the given box.

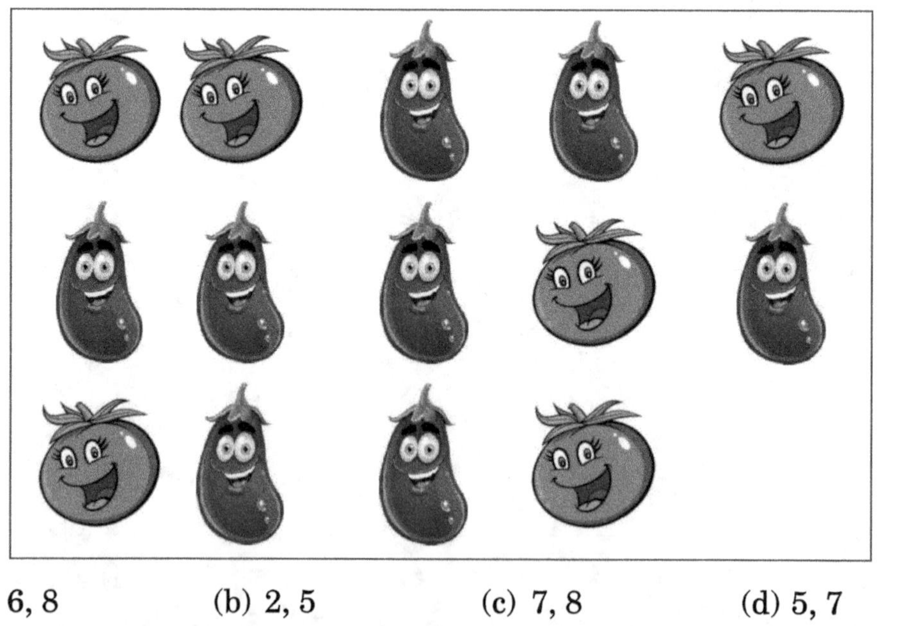

(a) 6, 8　　　　(b) 2, 5　　　　(c) 7, 8　　　　(d) 5, 7

23. Classify the number of cold and hot things that are given below.

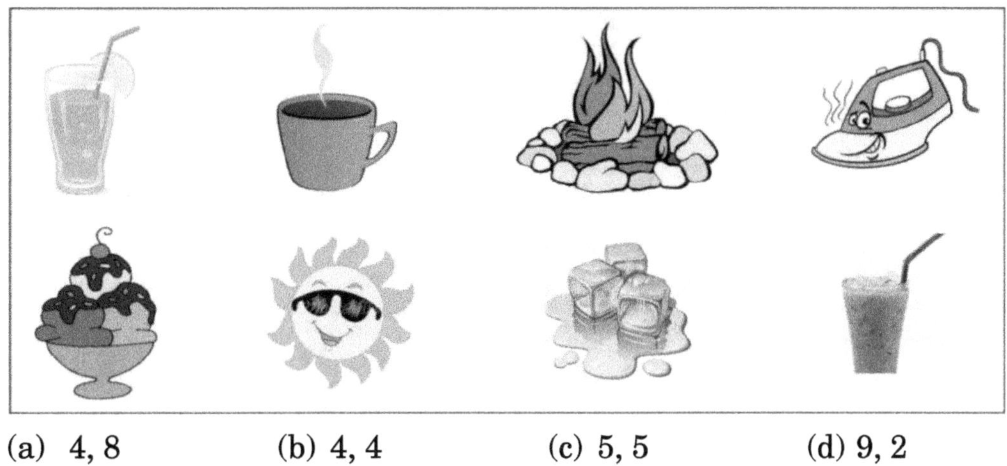

(a) 4, 8   (b) 4, 4   (c) 5, 5   (d) 9, 2

24. Classify the number of ribbons, candles and ropes in the given picture.

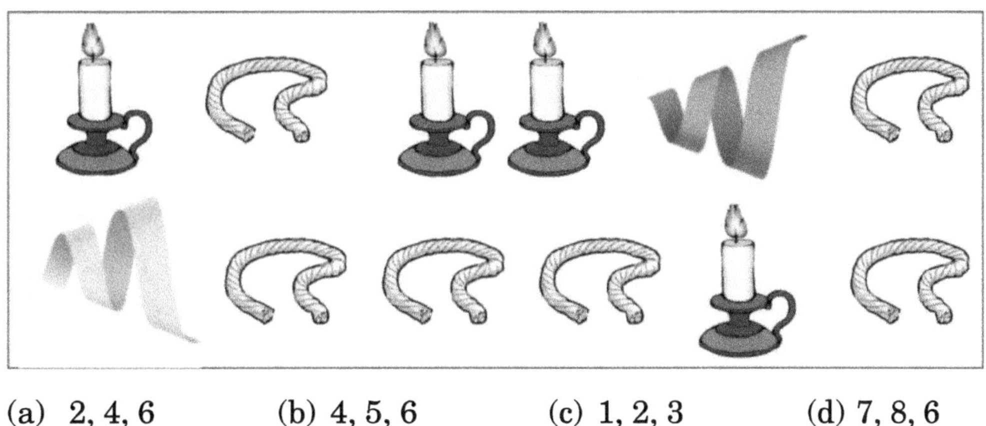

(a) 2, 4, 6   (b) 4, 5, 6   (c) 1, 2, 3   (d) 7, 8, 6

25. How many circles are there in the diagram?

(a) 20   (b) 15   (c) 10   (d) 25

26. There are _______ equal groups of 4 balls each. (2018)

(a) 5   (b) 4   (c) 10   (d) 7

27. _______ groups of 4 squares each can be formed from the given shapes. (2019)

(a) 4   (b) 1   (c) 3   (d) 2

28. _______ groups of 3 deer each can be formed from the given deer. **(2020)**

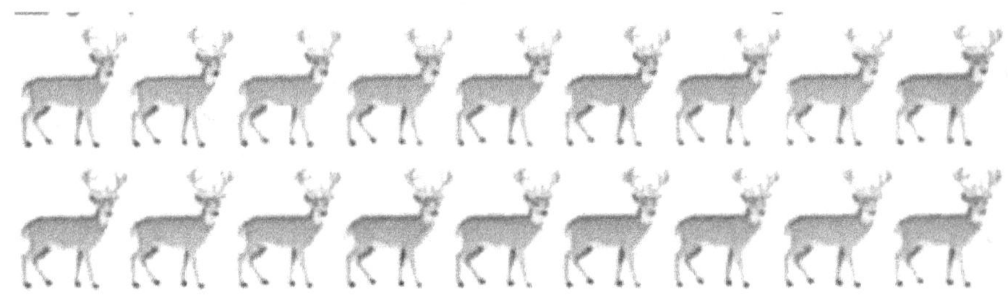

(a) 3   (b) 6   (c) 4   (d) 8

29. Tree _______ is the tallest. **(2021)**

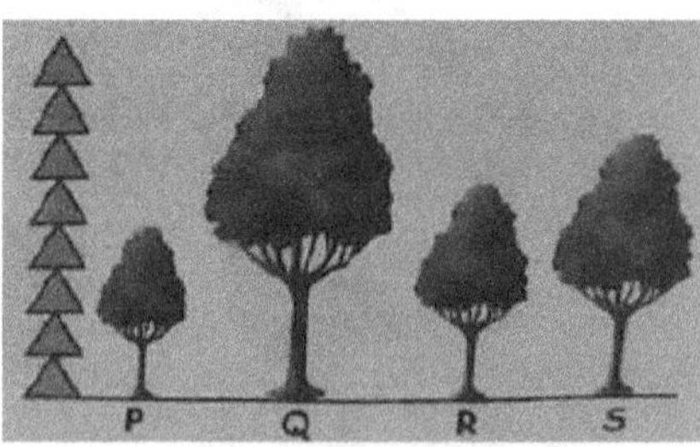

(a) P   (b) Q   (c) R   (d) S

30. _______ groups of 5 helmets each can be formed from the given helmets.

(2022)

(a) 3   (b) 5   (c) 4   (d) 2

LEVEL-2

1. Find out the total number of black and white dolls.

(a) 5, 6   (b) 8, 5   (c) 9, 6   (d) 5, 5

2. Classify the number of rings attached in the circle.

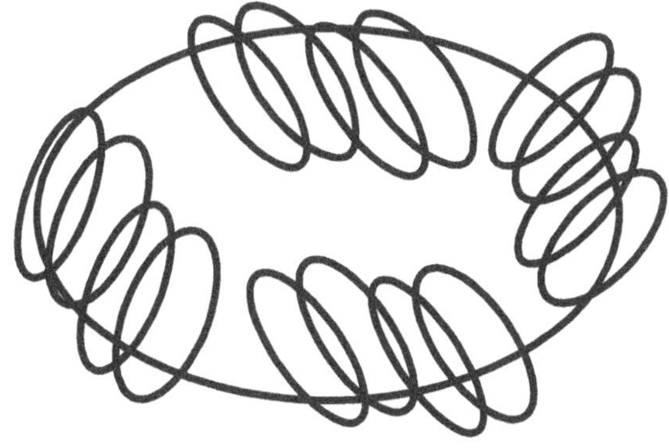

(a) 20   (b) 25   (c) 16   (d) 30

3. Classify the number of super heroes and famous cartoon characters.

(a) 5, 3   (b) 8, 0   (c) 5, 5   (d) 4, 2

4. Find out the number of uncolored butterflies from the colored ones.

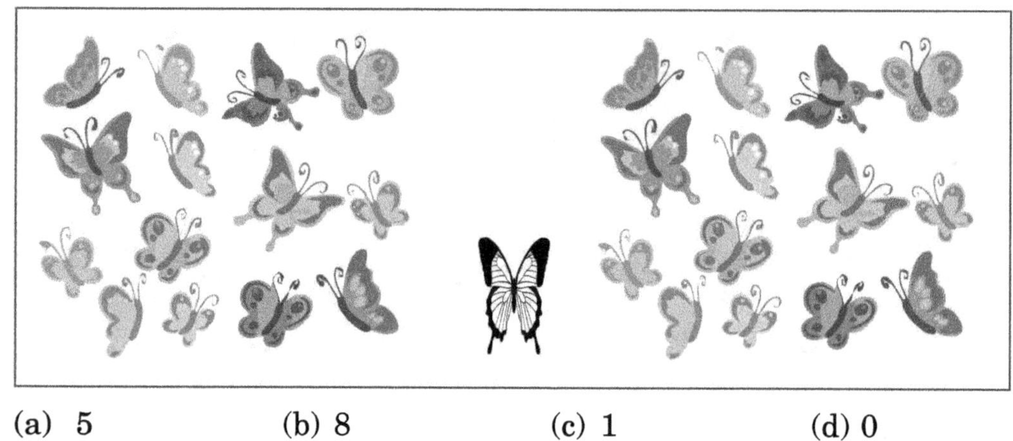

(a) 5   (b) 8   (c) 1   (d) 0

5. Shape (X) belongs to group _______.

(X)

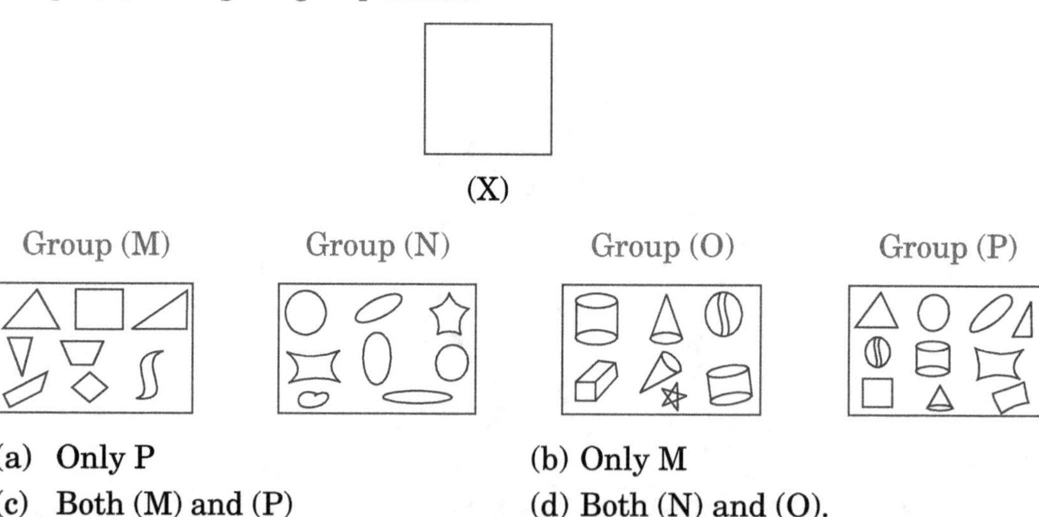

Group (M)   Group (N)   Group (O)   Group (P)

(a) Only P   (b) Only M

(c) Both (M) and (P)   (d) Both (N) and (O).

6. Number 4 belongs to group ______.

Group (Q)	Group (R)	Group (S)	Group (T)
3, 9, 11, 15 17, 13, 31 33, 35, 37	2, 3, 5, 6, 7 8, 9, 10, 11 12, 13, 14	1, 4, 8, 12 16, 20, 2, 4 28, 32, 36	7, 21, 29 35, 49, 47 43, 51, 91

(a) Q   (b) S   (c) R   (d) T

7. How many balls are there in each group, if 3 groups of equal number of balls are formed from given balls?

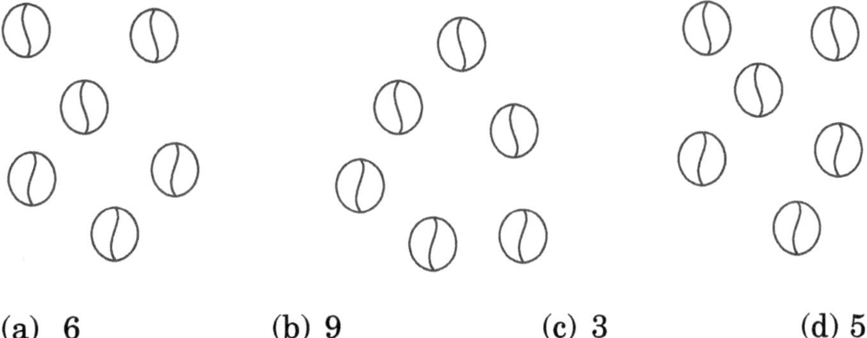

(a) 6   (b) 9   (c) 3   (d) 5

8. Reeta has some cherries as shown below. How many cherries are there in each group, if 4 groups having the same number of cherries are formed?

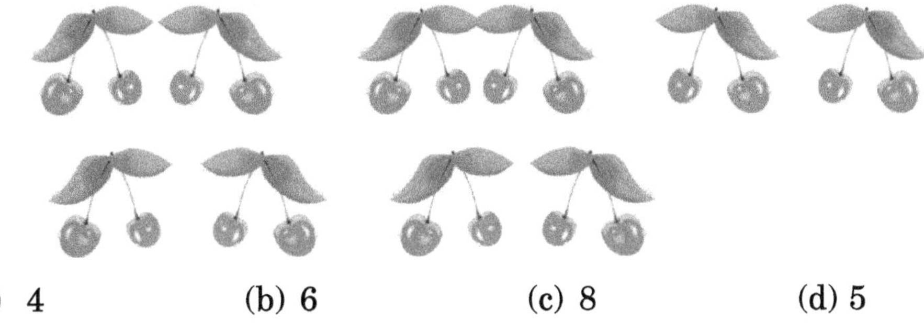

(a) 4   (b) 6   (c) 8   (d) 5

9. There are __________ eyes in the given picture.

(a) 16   (b) 14   (c) 18   (d) 20

(Olympiad)

10. There are _________ equal groups of 4 butterflies.

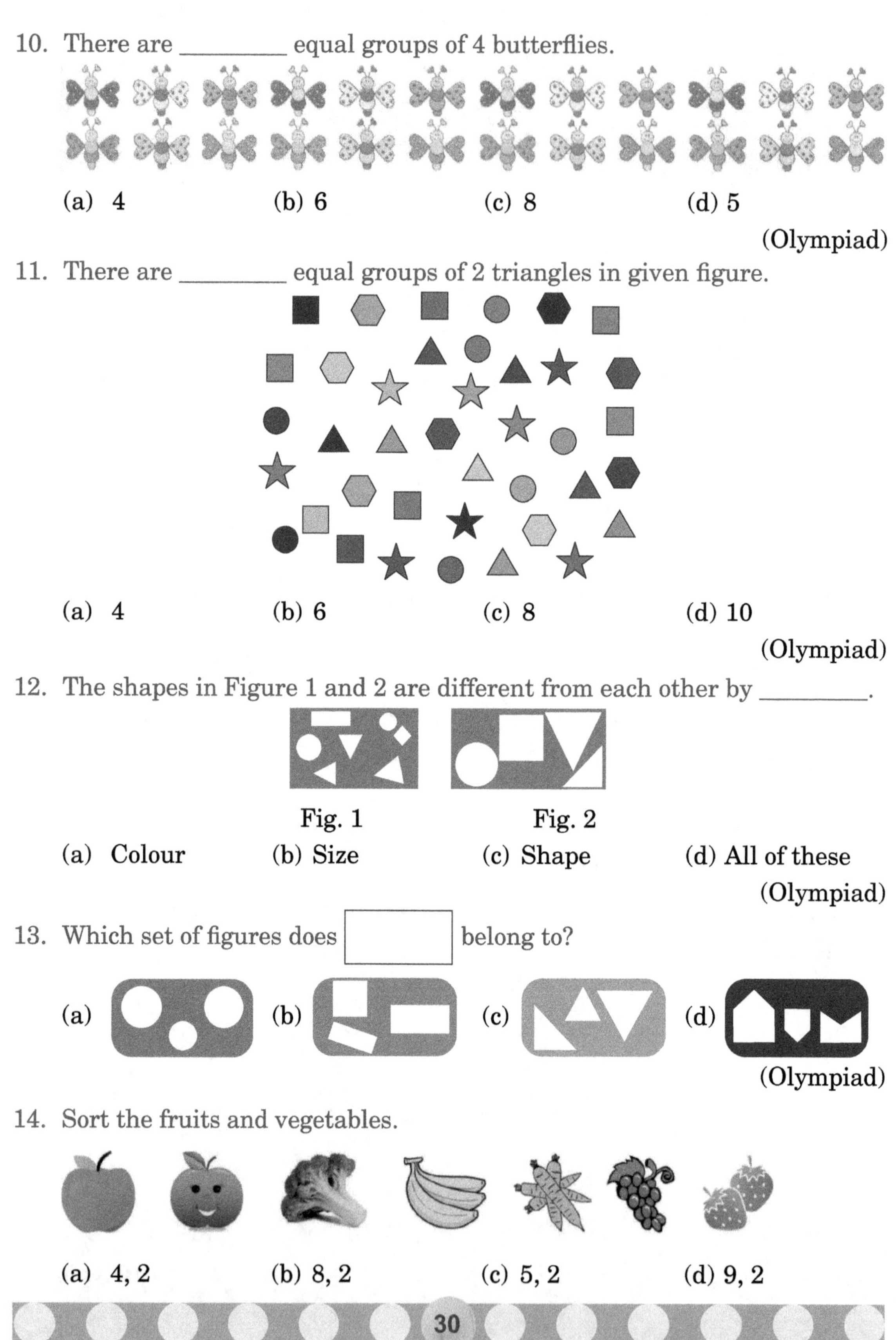

(a) 4   (b) 6   (c) 8   (d) 5

(Olympiad)

11. There are _________ equal groups of 2 triangles in given figure.

(a) 4   (b) 6   (c) 8   (d) 10

(Olympiad)

12. The shapes in Figure 1 and 2 are different from each other by _________.

Fig. 1   Fig. 2

(a) Colour   (b) Size   (c) Shape   (d) All of these

(Olympiad)

13. Which set of figures does [ ] belong to?

(a)   (b)   (c)   (d)

(Olympiad)

14. Sort the fruits and vegetables.

(a) 4, 2   (b) 8, 2   (c) 5, 2   (d) 9, 2

15. Sort the means of transport which are not used in water.

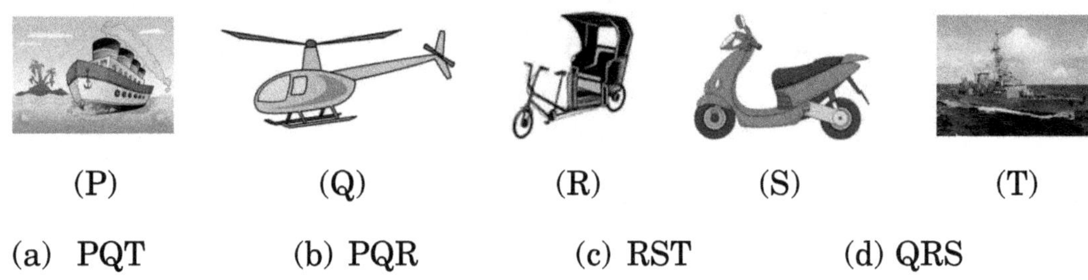

    (P)   (Q)   (R)   (S)   (T)

(a) PQT   (b) PQR   (c) RST   (d) QRS

16. Sort the name of this shape 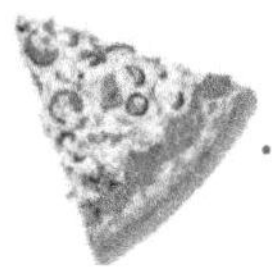 .

(a) Square   (b) Circle   (c) Triangle   (d) Rectangle

17. Sort the plants from the given pictures by counting the total number of plants.

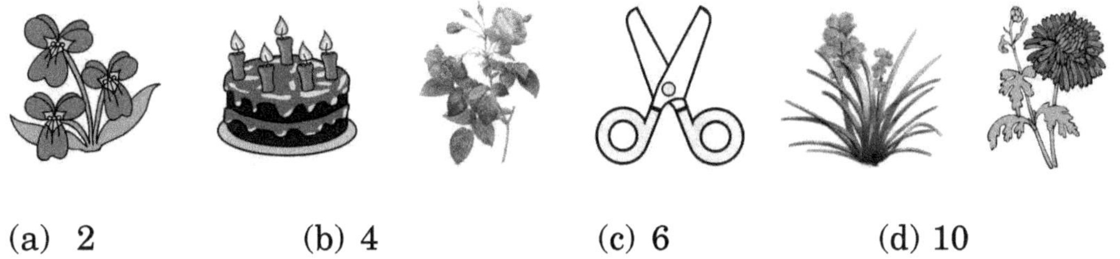

(a) 2   (b) 4   (c) 6   (d) 10

18. Sort the shapes of circles and stars.

(a) 5, 7   (b) 8, 9   (c) 4, 7   (d) 10, 15

19. Sort the kitchen items by counting them.

(a) 6   (b) 5   (c) 7   (d) 8

20. Sort the soft objects by counting them.

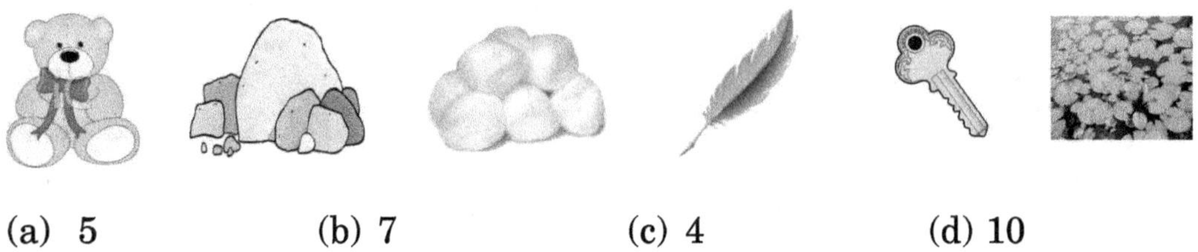

   (a) 5   (b) 7   (c) 4   (d) 10

21. Sort the eatable things in the given pictures.

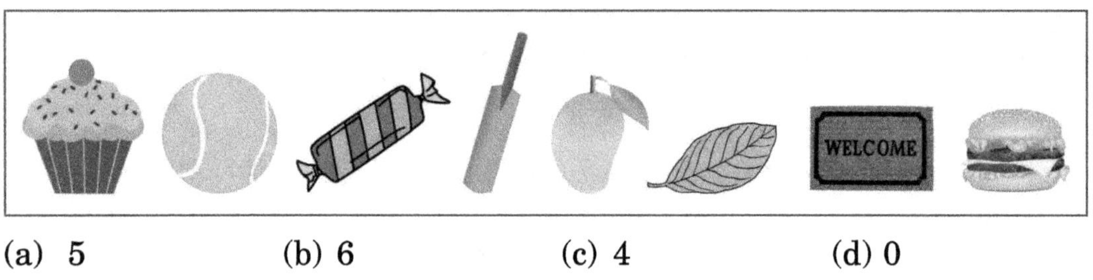

   (a) 5   (b) 6   (c) 4   (d) 0

22. Classify the number of triangles in the given figure.

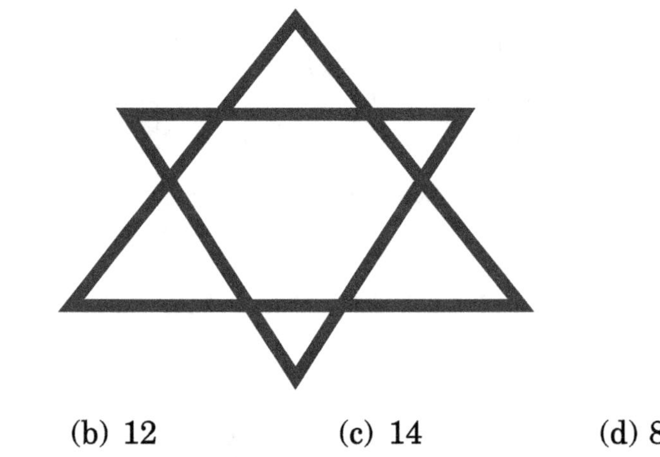

   (a) 10   (b) 12   (c) 14   (d) 8

23. Classify the number of circles in the given figure.

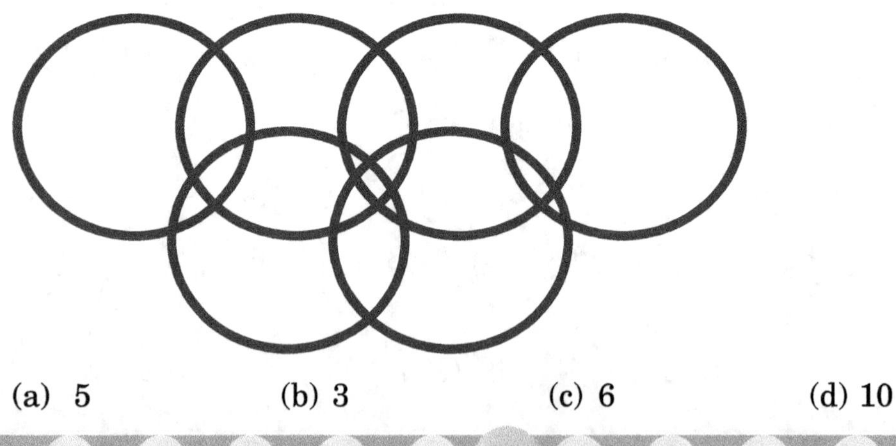

   (a) 5   (b) 3   (c) 6   (d) 10

24. Classify the number of domestic animals in the given pictures.

(a) 6   (b) 8   (c) 4   (d) 15

25. Classify the directions in which the sun rise and sun sets.

    (a) East and West   (b) North and South

    (c) East and South   (d) North and West

26. Classify the number of visible cubes in the given figure.

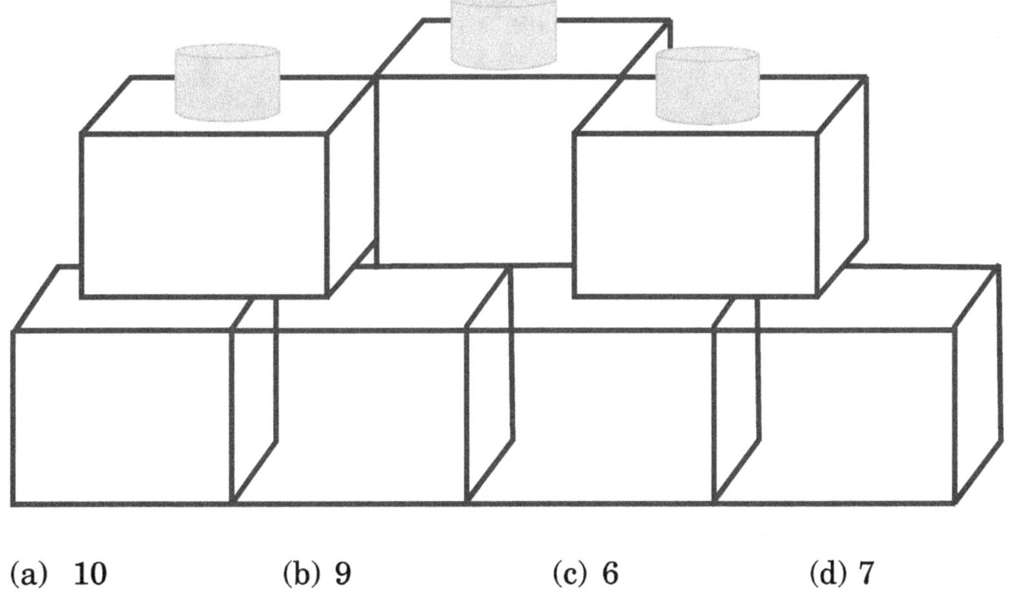

(a) 10   (b) 9   (c) 6   (d) 7

27. Classify the number of stars and hearts from the given figure.

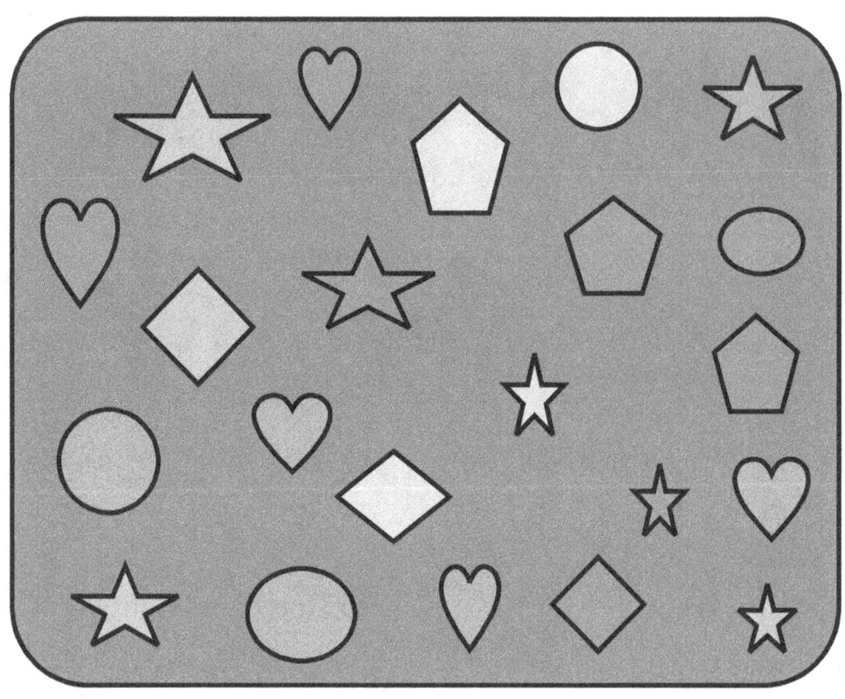

    (a) 6, 8   (b) 7, 5   (c) 5, 8   (d) 5, 9

28. There are _______ groups of 4 bags each can be formed from the given bags. **(2020)**

    (a) 1   (b) 2   (c) 3   (d) 4

29. 6 groups of ______ cubes each can be formed from the given cubes.

(2022)

    (a) 4   (b) 3   (c) 2   (d) 5

30. _______ groups of 6 diamonds each can be formed from the given diamonds.

(2022)

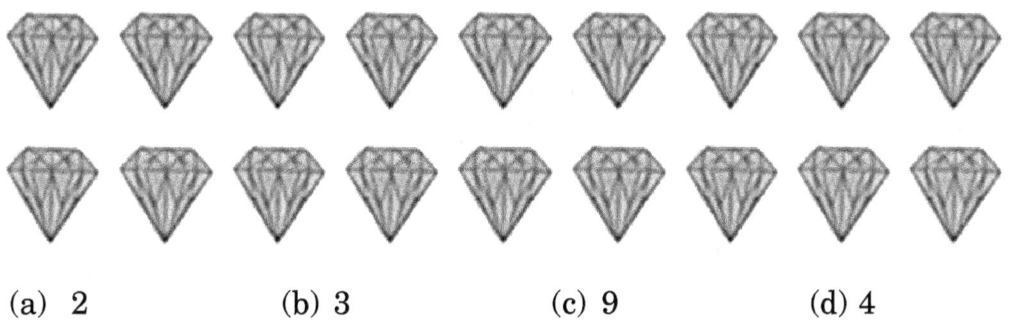

(a) 2 (b) 3 (c) 9 (d) 4

Answers and Explanations

Level-1

1. **(b)** 9 groups of 2's can be formed from the flowers.

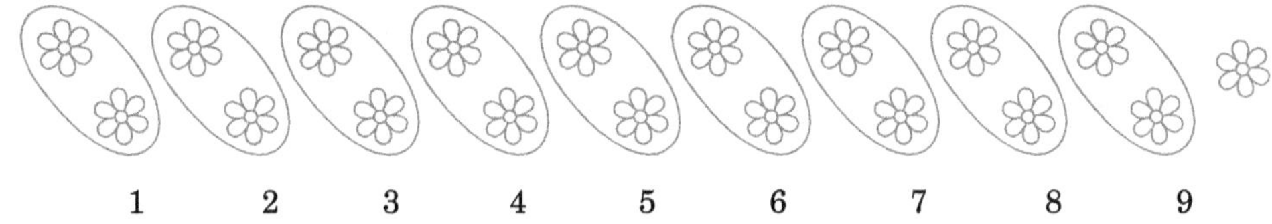

2. **(c)** The figure 'Δ' belongs to group R.

Group R

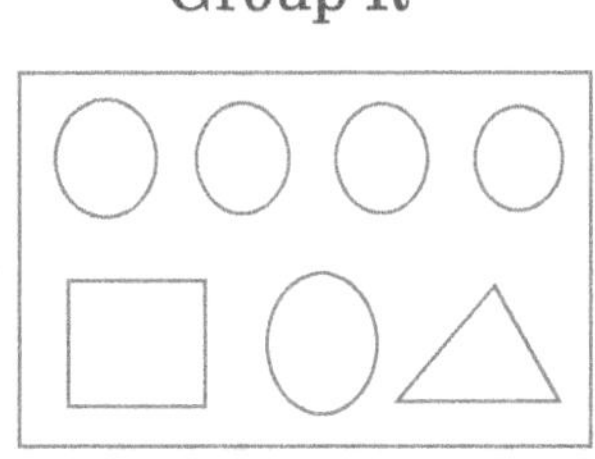

3. **(b)** There are four groups of 9 triangles.

$\triangle\triangle\triangle\triangle\triangle$ = 1 $\triangle\triangle\triangle\triangle\triangle$ = 2

$\triangle\triangle\triangle\triangle\triangle$ = 3 $\triangle\triangle\triangle\triangle\triangle$ = 4

4. **(b)** Each group has 3 ice-creams. So, there are 4 groups of 3 ice-creams.

5. **(c)** There are 4 groups of 3 butterflies.

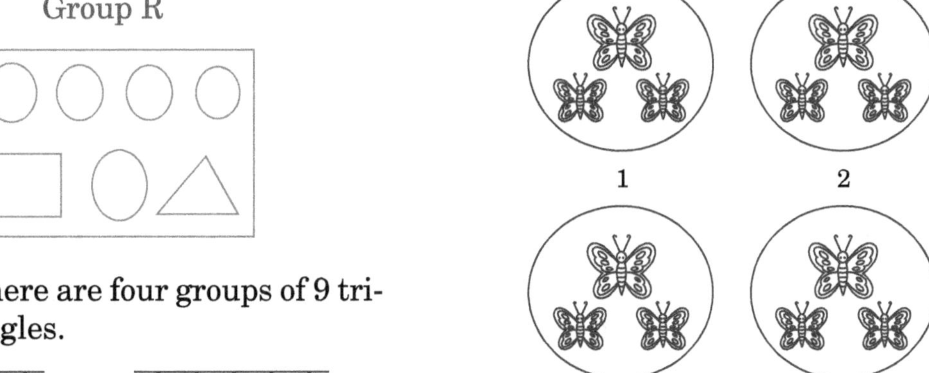

6. **(d)** There are 6 apples in each group.

7. **(b)** There are 10 carrots altogether.

8. **(a)** Arrangement from big to small as shown below:

S   P   R   Q

9. **(d)** Arrangement from fast to slow as shown below:

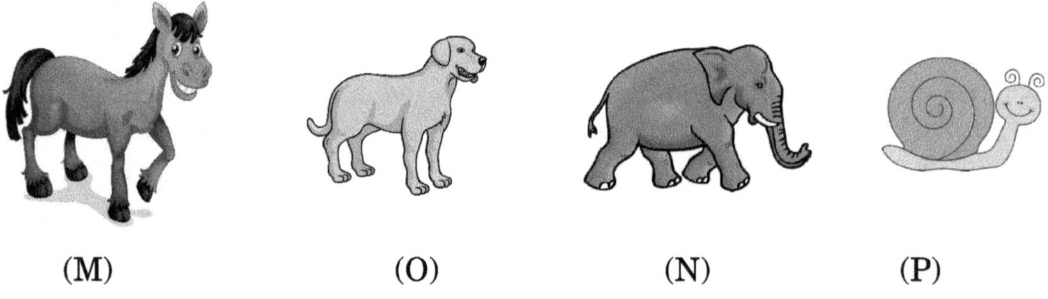

(M)   (O)   (N)   (P)

10. **(c)** Arrangement according to body parts from bottom to top

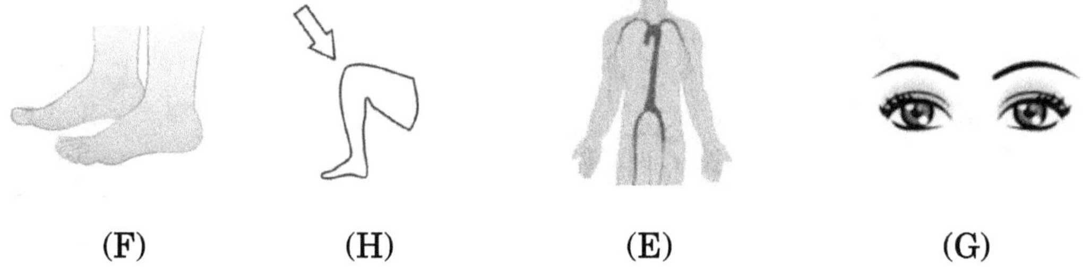

(F)   (H)   (E)   (G)

11. **(b)** M = Baby (Living)

    O = Bird (Living)

    So, MO are the living things.

12. **(a)** Arrangement according to weight (Heavy to Light).

    H = Bulldozer → E = Cycle →

    → F = Bulb (light) → G = Balloon

13. **(c)** W = Rectangle (Flat shape)

    Y = Triangle (Flat shape)

    X = Cylinder (Solid Shape)

    Z = Cuboid (Solid Shape)

    So, XZ are solid shapes.

14. **(b)** I = Dodo and L = Penguine

    So, IL cannot fly.

15. **(a)** U = Razor (used by men)

16. **(c)** E = Stomach (Internal Part)

    F = Kidney (Internal Part)

    G = Lungs (Internal Part)

    H = Hand (External Part)

    So, H is the external part of the body.

17. **(b)** There are 6 triangles in the given diagram

18. **(b)** There are total 5 blue colour shapes in the given figure.

19. **(d)** There are 4 stationery items in the given picture.

    1. Eraser   2. Book

    3. Pencil   4. Crayons

20. **(a)** Total number of red colour fruits and vegetables in the given picture are 5.

    1. Apple   2. Carrot

    3. Tomato   4. Cherry

    5. Strawberry

21. **(a)** There are total 5 things in the given picture that are used by the teacher.

    1. Chalk   2. Blackboard

    3. Duster   4. Pen

    5. Book

22. **(a)** There are 6 Tomatoes and 8 Brinjals in the box.

23. **(b)** There are 4 cold and 4 hot things.

Cold	Hot
1. Juice	1. Tea
2. Ice - cream	2. Fire
3. Ice Cubes	3. Sun
4. Cold Coffee	4. Iron

24. **(a)** There are 2 ribbons, 4 candles and 6 ropes in the picture.

25. **(c)** There are 10 circles in the given diagram.

26. **(a)** There are total 20 balls.

    So, $20 \div 4 = 5$ equal groups of 4 balls each.

27. **(d)** There are 8 squres in the given figure.

    So, $8 \div 4 = 2$ group of 4 squares each can be formed.

28. **(b)** There are total 18 deer.

    So, $\dfrac{18}{3} = 6$ group of 3 deer each can be formed

29. **(b)**

30. **(a)** There are total 3 sets of 5 helmets.

1. **(d)** Total number of black and white dolls in the picture is 5, 5.

2. **(c)** Each group of ring has 4 rings in it. Therefore, 4 × 4 = 16. So, the total number of rings attached in circle are 16.

3. **(a)** There are 5 super heroes:

   Superman, Batman, Spiderman, Hulk and Wonder women and 3 famous cartoon characters are:

   Mickey mouse, Donald Duck and Doraemon.

4. **(c)** In the given picture all butterflies are coloured except 1.

5. **(a)** Only P has Shape (X) in it.

6. **(b)** Number 4 belongs to group S.

7. **(a)** There are 6 balls in each group.

8. **(d)** 5 cherries are there in each group.

9. **(a)** There are 16 eyes in the given picture.

10. **(b)** There are 6 equal groups of 4 butterflies.

11. **(a)** There are 4 equal groups of 2 triangles in given picture.

12. **(d)** All of these.

13. **(b)** ☐ belongs to the set of figures (b).

14. **(c)** There are 5 fruits and 2 vegetables.

15. **(d)** P and T are means of water transport.

16. **(c)** The name of the given shape is triangle.

17. **(b)** There are total 4 number of plants.

18. **(c)** There are 4 circles and 7 stars in total.

19. **(b)** There are 5 kitchen items.

20. **(c)** There are 4 soft objects.

21. **(c)** There are 4 eatable things in the figure.

22. **(d)** There are 8 number of triangles in the figure.

23. **(c)** There are 6 circles in the figure.

24. **(a)** There are 6 domestic animals in the given picture.

25. **(a)** The sun rises in the East and sets in the west.

26. **(d)** There are 7 number of cubes in the given figure.

27. (b) There are 7 stars and 5 hearts in the given figure.

28. (b) Total bags = 8

One group consists = 4 bags

Total groups = $\dfrac{8}{4}$ = 2 groups

There are 2 groups of 4 bags each can be formed from the given bags

29. (c) Total cubes = 12

So, $\dfrac{12}{6}$ = 2 cubes each can be formed 6 groups.

30. (b) There are total 18 diamonds.

So, $\dfrac{18}{6}$ = 3 groups of 6 diamonds each can be formed.

Patterns

OBJECTIVES

- Students will identify patterns in pictures/shapes, numbers and letters.
- They will develop to extend given patterns.
- They help students to be aware of patterns in their daily surroundings.
- They will help them to sort and group objects.
- Patterns serve as the foundation of algebraic thinking.

INTRODUCTION

A pattern is a repeated design or recurring sequence. It is a set of pictures/shapes, letters or numbers arranged according to a certain rule.

Type I

Find the missing term or next term in (number or letter) series to continue the given series.

- Identify the order of series (descending or ascending order). Observe the pattern using operations: addition, subtraction, skip counting and reverse counting.
- Identify the order of alphabetical series either A to Z or Z to A.
- Numbering of alphabets series either A to Z or Z to A.
- Skipping letters/numbers.

Type II

Find the missing term in the pattern?

- Identify the missing term in the pattern by observing the rule followed in rest of the given terms.

Type III

Find the missing part in the figure pattern.

- Complete the figure pattern by drawing its incomplete part in the pattern.

Examples:

(i) Picture / Shape-based Pattern

1. What comes next in the pattern given?

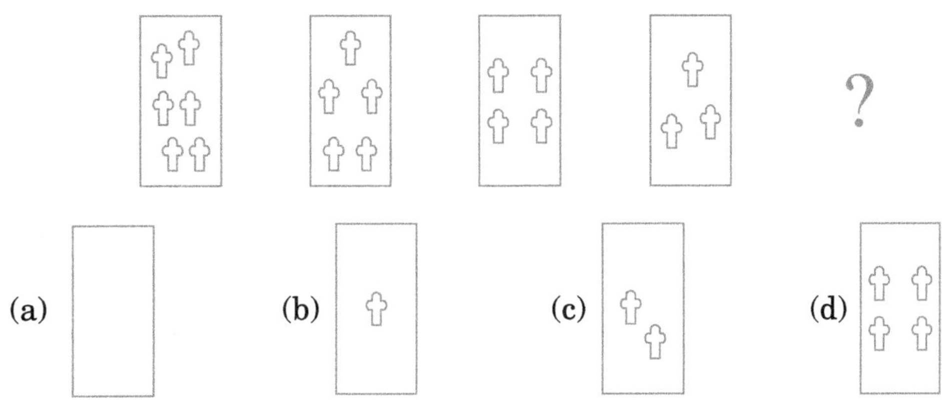

Ans. (c)

The elements are decreasing by one in each step. So, the correct answer is (c).

2. Find the rule followed in the figure pattern and the missing figure.

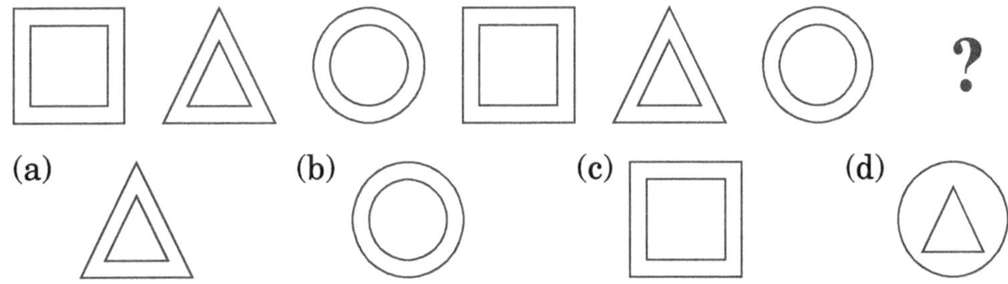

Ans. (c)

Each figure in the row repeats itself after two figures. So, the missing figure is (c).

(ii) Number-based Pattern

3. What comes next in the given pattern?

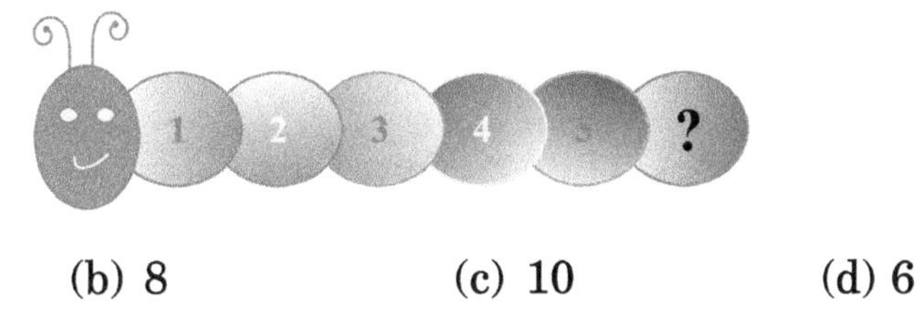

(a) 7   (b) 8   (c) 10   (d) 6

Ans. (d)

Numbers are given in ascending order. So, the correct answer is (d).

4. Complete the number pattern.

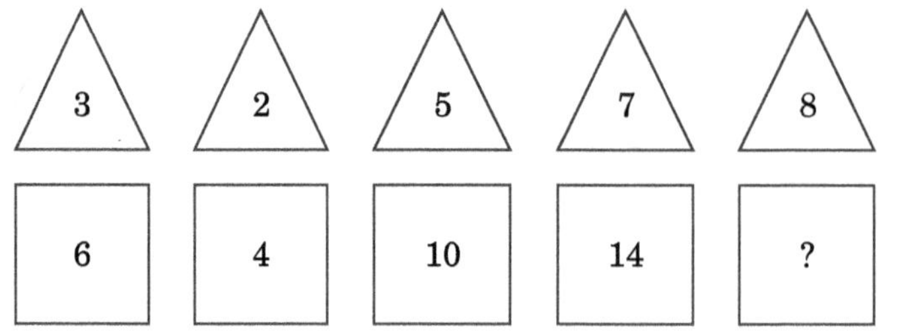

 (a) 15   (b) 8   (c) 16   (d) 14

Ans. (c) The pattern is as follows:

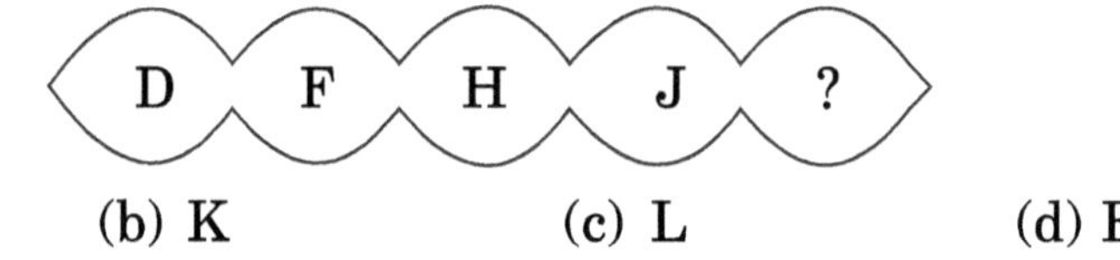

(iii) Alphabet-based Pattern

5. What comes next in the alphabet-pattern given.

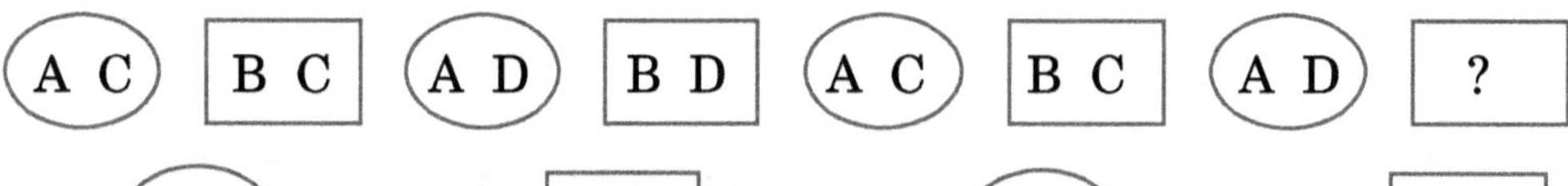

 (a) M   (b) K   (c) L   (d) E

Ans. (c)

Alphabets are moved on two steps forward.

$$D \xrightarrow{+2} F \xrightarrow{+2} H \xrightarrow{+2} J \xrightarrow{+2} L$$

So, the correct answer is (c).

6. Which is the next letter?

A C   B C   A D   B D   A C   B C   A D   ?

 (a) AC   (b) BC   (c) AC   (d) BD

Ans. (d) The pattern of letters is as follows:

A C   B C   A D   B D   A C   B C   A D   B D

Direction (Qs. 1-14): What comes next in the given series ?

1.

   ?

(a)    (b)    (c)    (d) 

2.

  ?

(a) 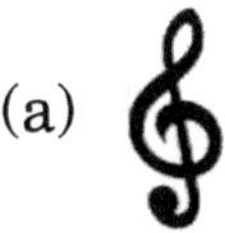   (b)   (c)   (d)

3.

   ?

(a)    (b)    (c)    (d) 

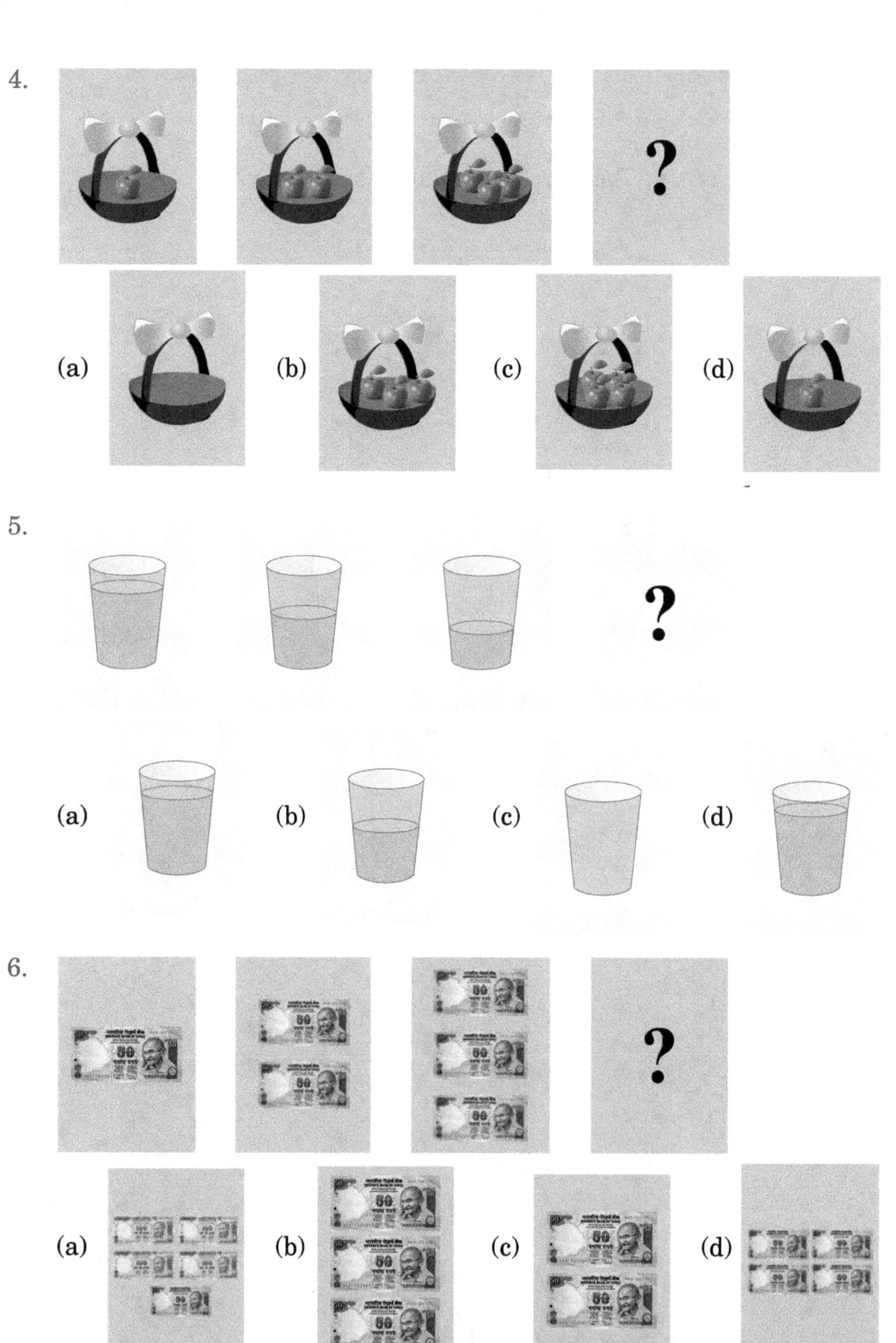

4.
?
(a)
(b)
(c)
(d)
5.
?
(a)
(b)
(c)
(d)
6.
?
(a)
(b)
(c)
(d)

7.

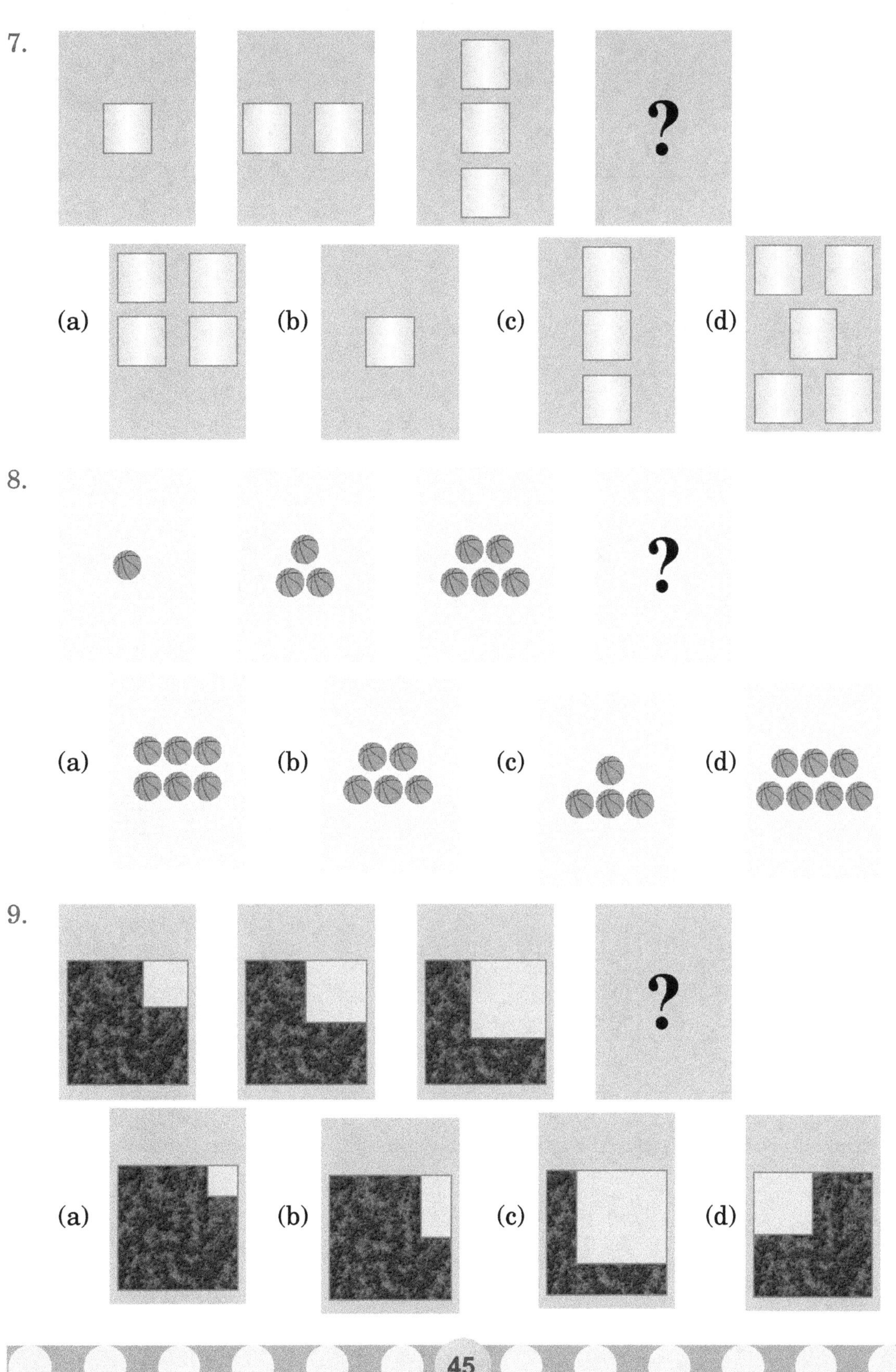

8.

9.

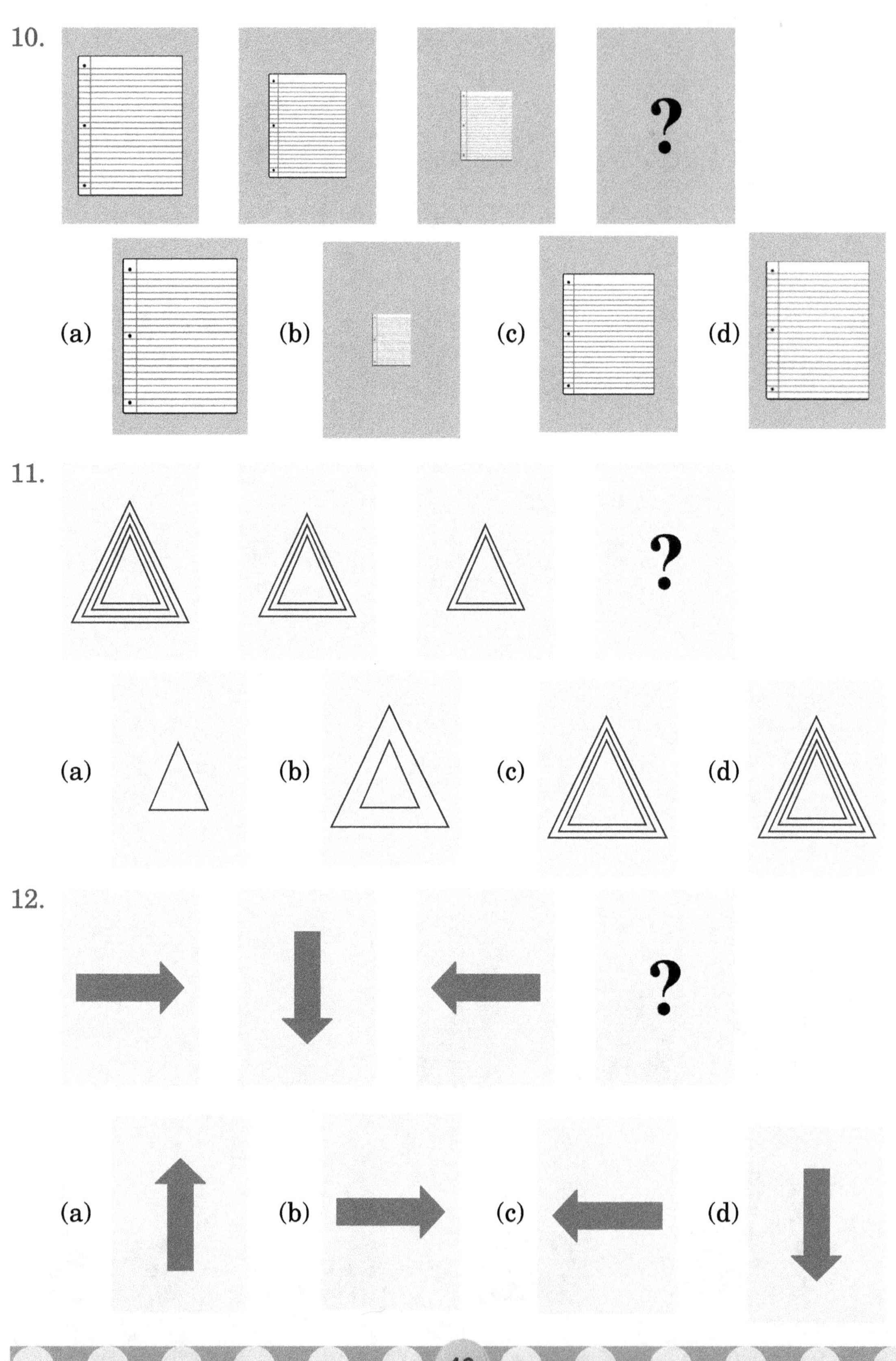

10.
(a) (b) (c) (d)
11.
(a) (b) (c) (d)
12.
(a) (b) (c) (d)

13.

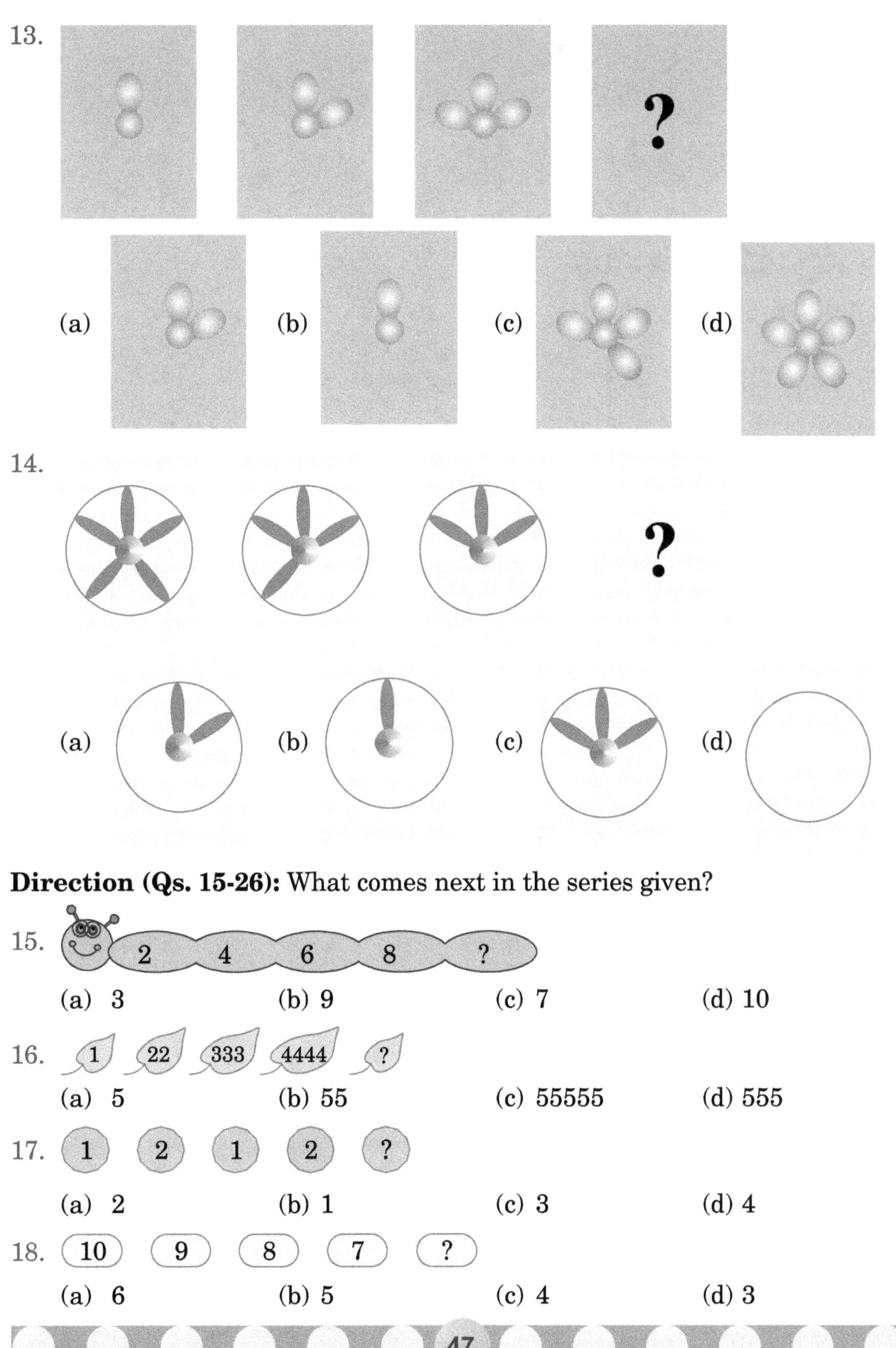

14.

Direction (Qs. 15-26): What comes next in the series given?

15.
2 4 6 8 ?

(a) 3   (b) 9   (c) 7   (d) 10

16.
1 22 333 4444 ?

(a) 5   (b) 55   (c) 55555   (d) 555

17.
1 2 1 2 ?

(a) 2   (b) 1   (c) 3   (d) 4

18.
10 9 8 7 ?

(a) 6   (b) 5   (c) 4   (d) 3

19. 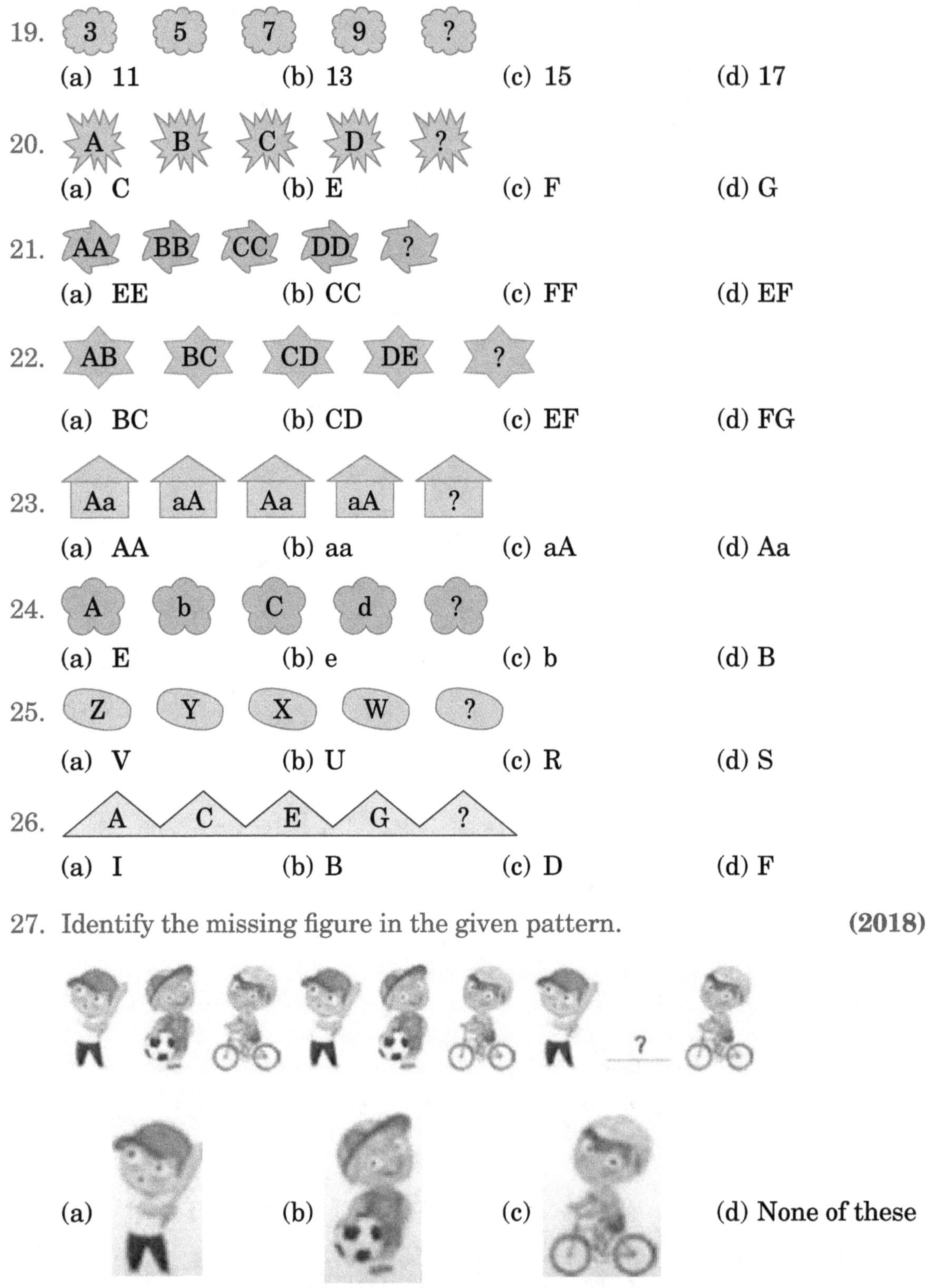

19. 3 5 7 9 ?

(a) 11   (b) 13   (c) 15   (d) 17

20. A B C D ?

(a) C   (b) E   (c) F   (d) G

21. AA BB CC DD ?

(a) EE   (b) CC   (c) FF   (d) EF

22. AB BC CD DE ?

(a) BC   (b) CD   (c) EF   (d) FG

23. Aa aA Aa aA ?

(a) AA   (b) aa   (c) aA   (d) Aa

24. A b C d ?

(a) E   (b) e   (c) b   (d) B

25. Z Y X W ?

(a) V   (b) U   (c) R   (d) S

26. A C E G ?

(a) I   (b) B   (c) D   (d) F

27. Identify the missing figure in the given pattern.   **(2018)**

(a)   (b)   (c)   (d) None of these

28. Find the missing number in the given number pattern. **(2019)**

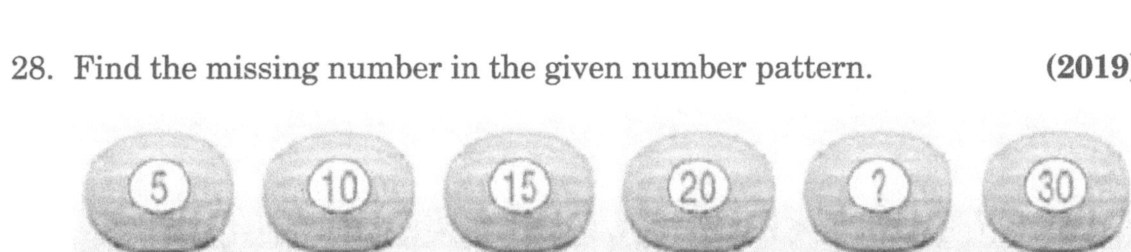

(a) 25   (b) 28   (c) 22   (d) 32

29. Select a figure from the options which will complete the pattern in the given figure. **(2019)**

(a)    (b)    (c)    (d) 

30. Which of the following will complete the given number pattern? **(2020)**

(a) 13   (b) 15   (c) 21   (d) 24

31. Which of the following options will complete the given pattern? **(2021)**

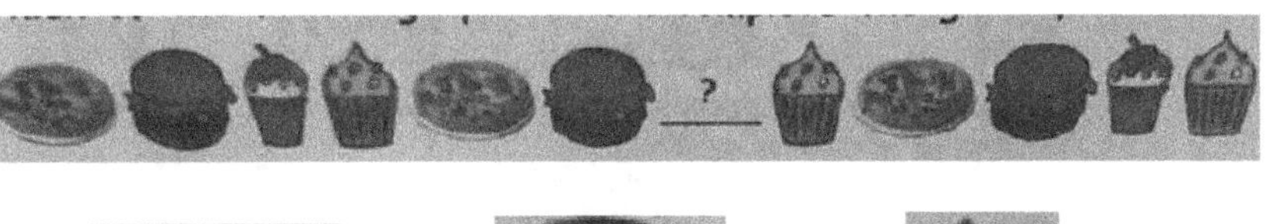

(a) 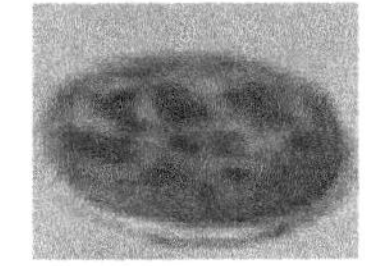   (b) 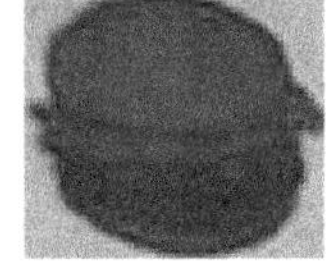   (c)    (d) 

32. Find the missing number in the given number pattern. **(2021)**

(a) 19   (b) 20   (c) 23   (d) 21

1. Which one is the missing number in the following number pattern?

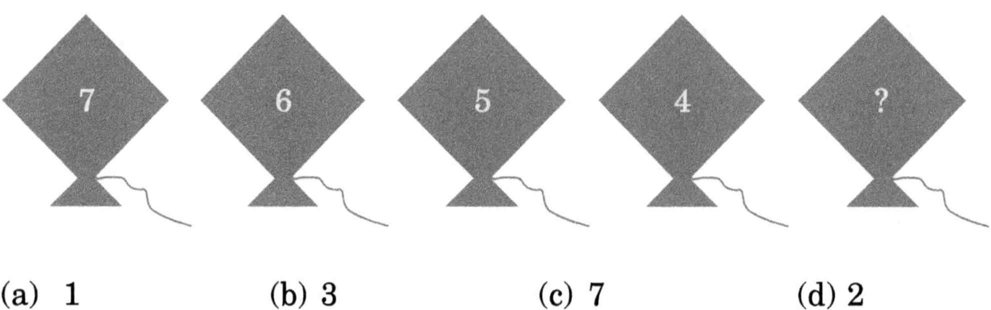

    (a) 1   (b) 3   (c) 7   (d) 2

2. Identify the missing alphabet in given below series.

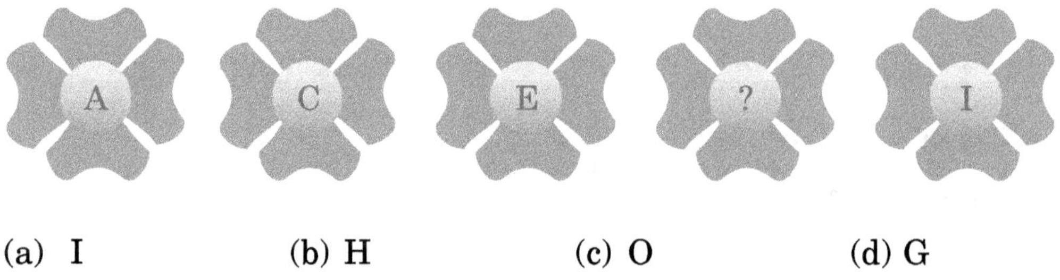

    (a) I   (b) H   (c) O   (d) G

3. Find out the pattern and missing figure.

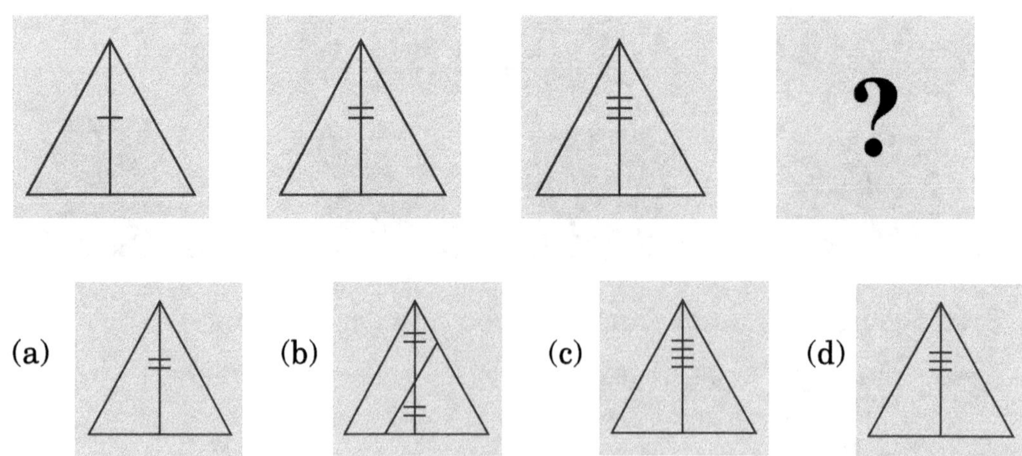

4. Study the numbers that are given in the box and fill the missing numbers in the empty box.

8	7	6	5
	?		
6	5	4	3
5	4	3	2

(a) 8765   (b) 7654   (c) 6578   (d) 5678

5. Which will be the next figure in the given series?

(a)    (b)    (c)    (d) 

6. Which one comes next from the given alternatives?

 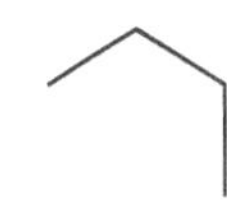 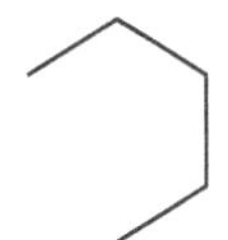 

(a) 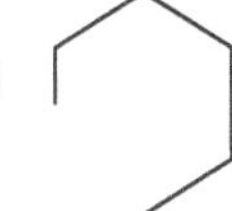   (b) 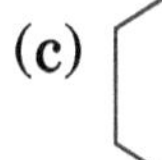   (c)   (d)

7. Which one comes next from the given alternatives?

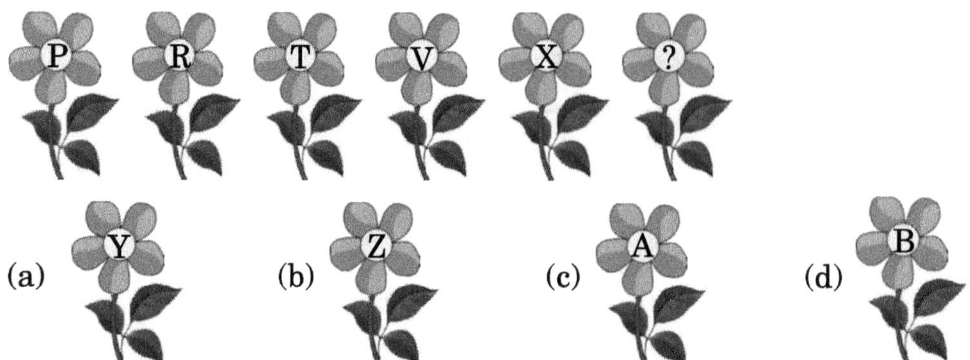

(a)   (b)   (c)   (d)

8. Complete the figure pattern shown below.

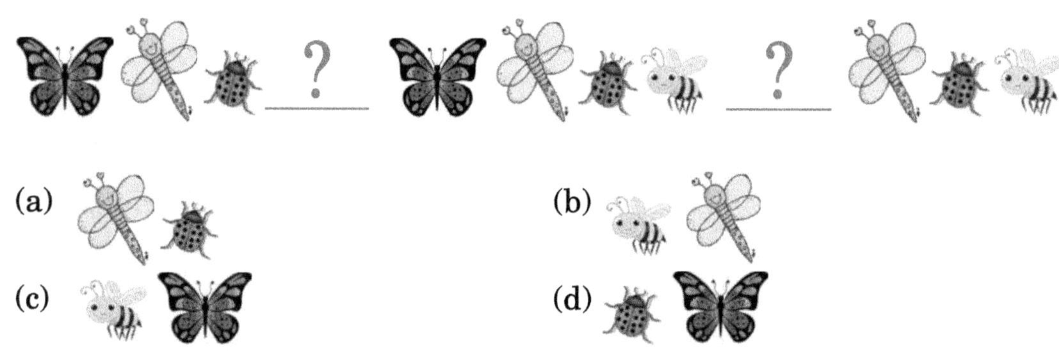

(a)   (b)

(c)   (d)

9. Which number will come next to complete the series?

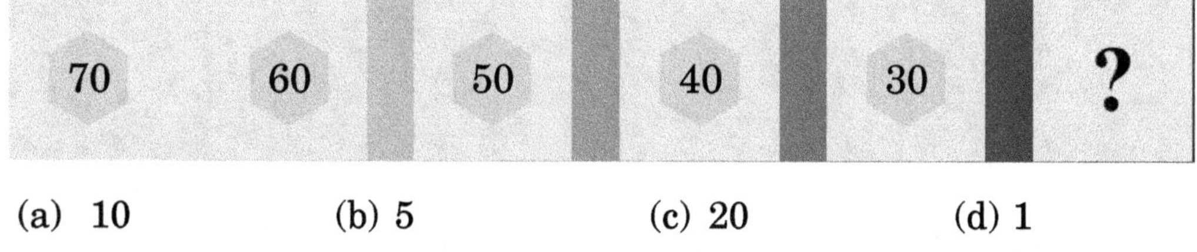

(a) 10   (b) 5   (c) 20   (d) 1

10. Which figure comes next?

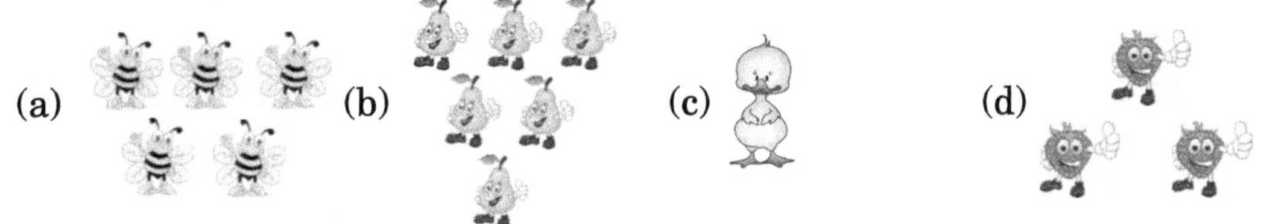

(a)   (b)   (c)   (d)

11. Analyse the alphabets in the given figure. Fill the missing letters.

X	U	R	O
U	X	U	R
R	U	X	U
	?		

(a) ORUX   (b) ORRR   (c) RUXU   (d) XXXX

12. Choose the correct option to replace the (?) mark.

22   ?   44   55   66

(a) 44   (b) 24   (c) 33   (d) 77

13. How many flowers will be there in Pattern 4?

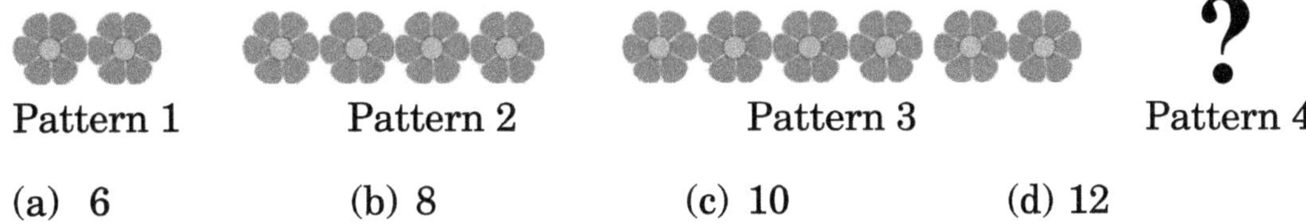

Pattern 1   Pattern 2   Pattern 3   Pattern 4

(a) 6   (b) 8   (c) 10   (d) 12

14. Which is the missing number in the number pattern?

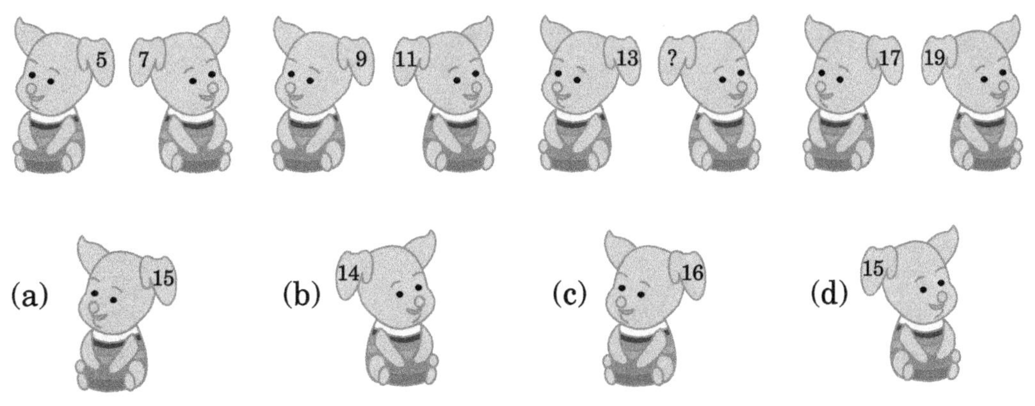

(a)   (b)   (c)   (d)

15. Identify the missing shape which will complete the series.

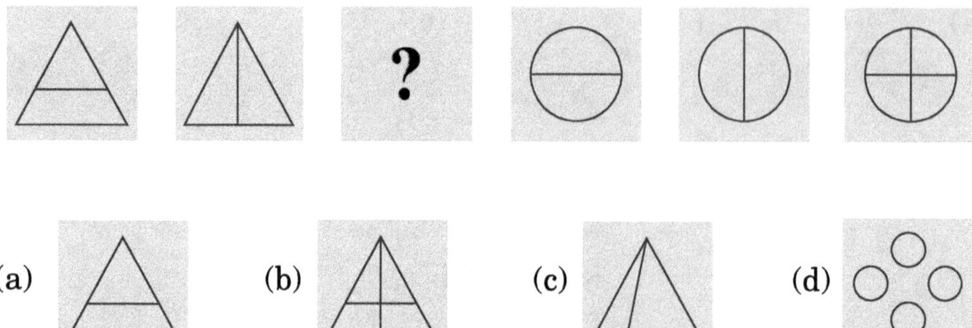

(a)   (b)   (c)   (d)

16. Identify the missing figure.

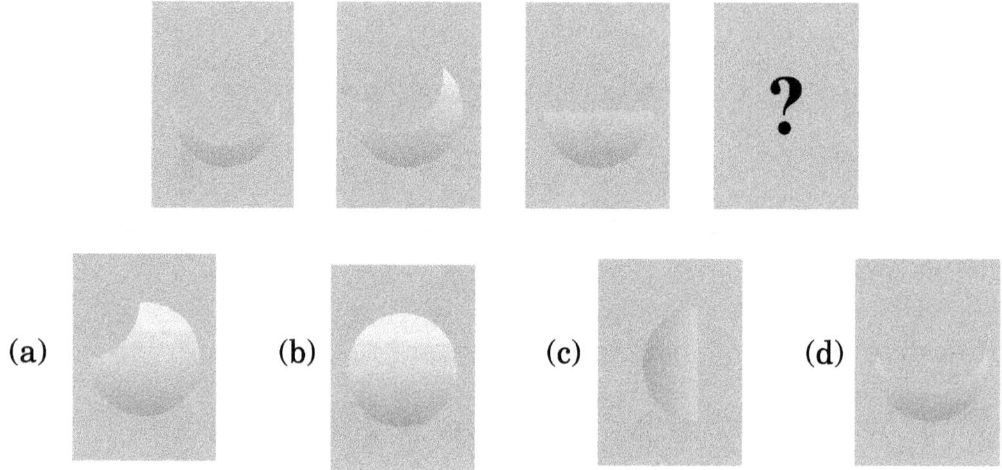

(a)   (b)   (c)   (d)

17. Identify the missing figure.

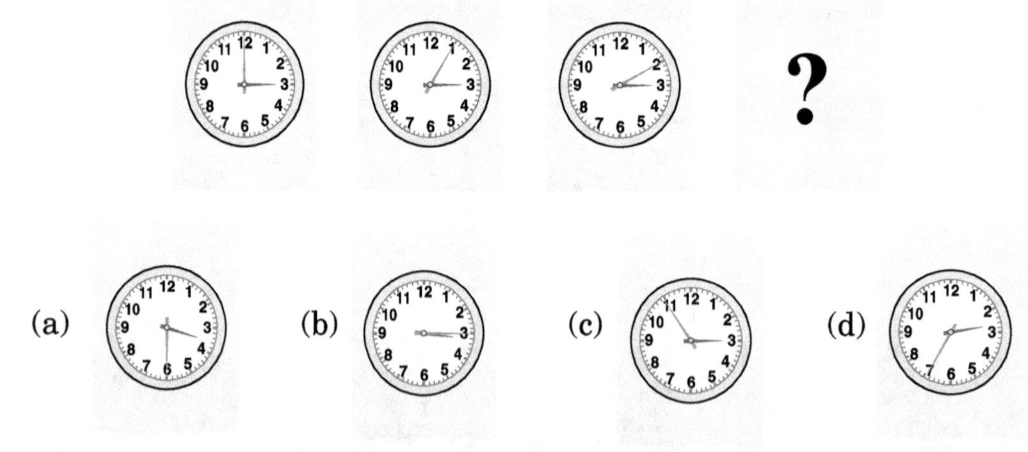

(a)   (b)   (c)   (d)

18. Identify the missing figure.

(a)　　　(b)　　　(c)　　　(d)

Direction (Qs. 19-21): Identify the next sequence from the given alternatives.

19.　10　20　30　40　?

(a) 50　　　(b) 60　　　(c) 70　　　(d) 80

20.　CLASS　CLAS　CLA　CL　?

(a) CLA　　　(b) CLAS　　　(c) C　　　(d) CC

21.　ABC　BCD　CDE　DEF　?

(a) EFD　　　(b) CDE　　　(c) EFG　　　(d) ABC

22. Next figure in the given pattern is __________.

(a)　　　(b)　　　(c)　　　(d)

(Olympiad)

23. Next figure in the given below figure pattern is __________.

(a)   (b)   (c)   (d)

(Olympiad)

24. Which figure will complete the figure (X)?

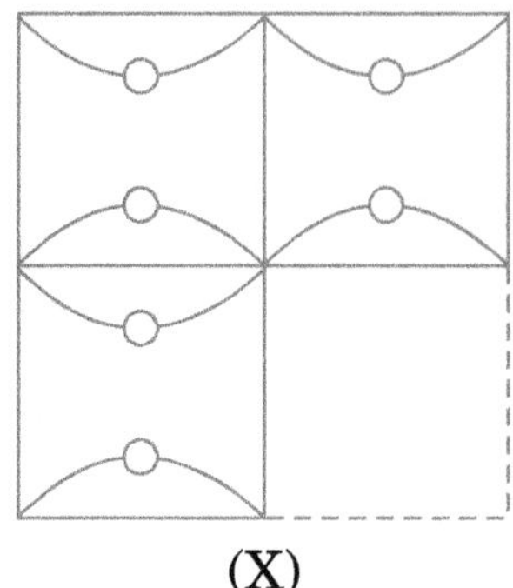

(X)

(a) (b) (c) (d)

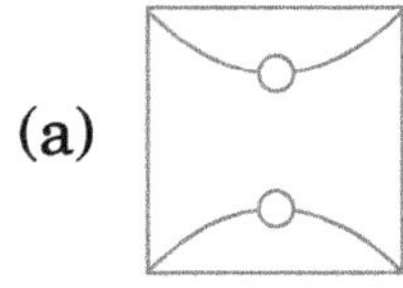 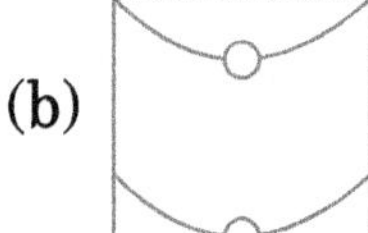 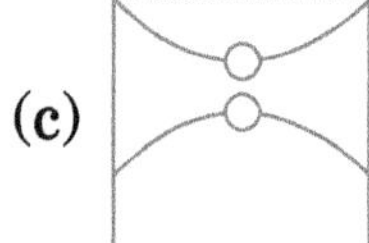 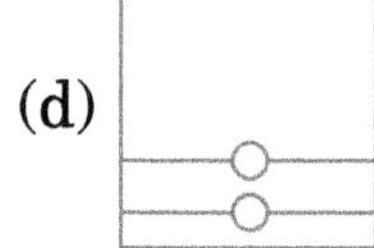

(Olympiad)

25. Complete the figure pattern shown below.

(a) (b) (c) (d)

(Olympiad)

26. __________ replaces the question mark (?) in the given number pattern.

(a) 40 (b) 30 (c) 25 (d) 35

(Olympiad)

27. ___________ is the next figure in the given figure pattern.

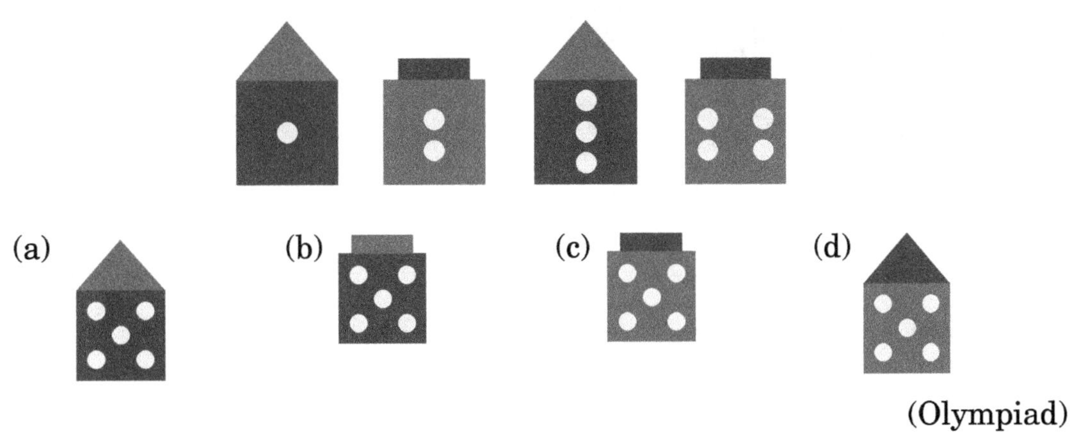

(a)   (b)   (c)   (d)

(Olympiad)

28. Identify the missing number in the given number pattern.

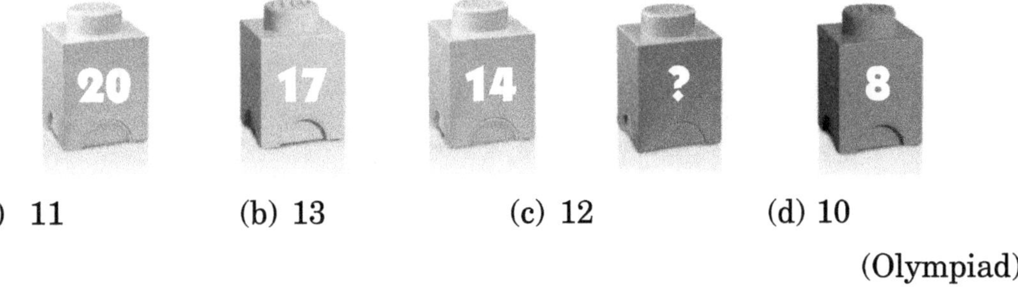

(a) 11   (b) 13   (c) 12   (d) 10

(Olympiad)

29. Find the value of P and Q in the number pattern.

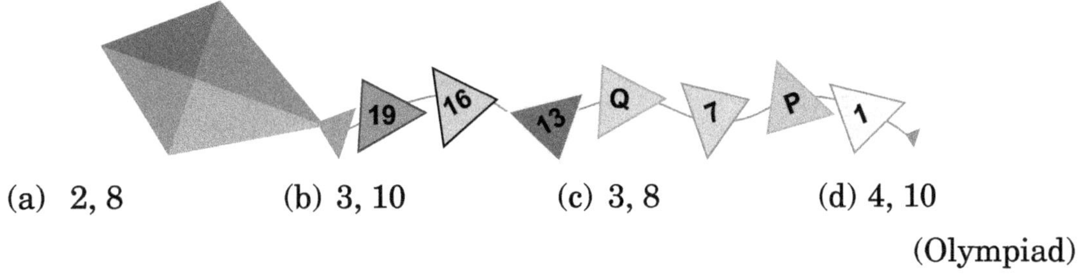

(a) 2, 8   (b) 3, 10   (c) 3, 8   (d) 4, 10

(Olympiad)

30. If the same rule is followed in P, Q and R, then find the missing number.

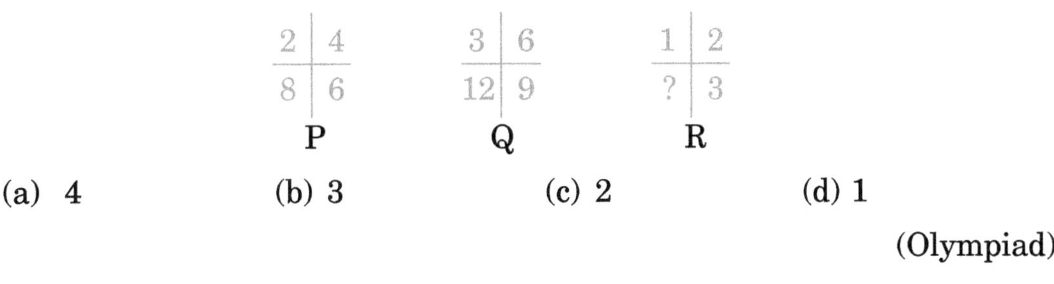

(a) 4   (b) 3   (c) 2   (d) 1

(Olympiad)

31. Which figure completes the given series?

(a)   (b)   (c)   (d)

32. Find the missing number in the given number pattern.   **(2022)**

(a) 20   (b) 22   (c) 24   (d) 25

33. Find the missing number in given number pattern.   **(2022)**

(a) 6   (b) 7   (c) 8   (d) 10

34. Complete the pattern given below: **(2022)**

A 1 2 , B 3 4 , C 5 6 , D 7 8 , E 9 10 , ?

(a) F 11 12   (b) F 10 11   (c) F 9 10   (d) F 9 11

Level-1

1. **(b)** The growth of the plant is shown in each step.

2. **(c)** The pattern repeats itself after four figures.

3. **(c)** In each step, one ball is increasing.

4. **(c)** In each step, one apple is added.

5. **(c)** In each step, water is decreasing.

6. **(d)** In each step, a 50 rupee note is increasing in numbers.

7. **(a)** One square box is added in each step.

8. **(d)** Two balls are increasing in each step.

9. **(c)** The orange square increases in size in every step.

10. **(b)** In each step, the size of the sheet is decreasing.

11. **(a)** In each step, a triangle is removing.

12. **(a)** Arrow is rotating clockwise.

13. **(c)** In each step, one petal is increasing.

14. **(a)** In each step, one leaf is decreasing.

15. **(d)** The pattern is + 2.
So, next term is 8 + 2 = 10.

16. **(c)** Consecutive numbers are increasing by one at each step.
So, next term is 55555.

17. **(b)** The pattern is + 1, –1.
So, next term is 1.

18. **(a)** Numbers are decreasing by one at each step.
So, next term is 6.

19. **(a)** The pattern is + 2.
So, next term is 11.

20. **(b)** The pattern is
$$A \xrightarrow{+1} B \xrightarrow{+1} C \xrightarrow{+1} D \xrightarrow{+1} E$$

21. **(a)** The same alphabet is repeated and each alphabet is moved on one step forward.

22. **(c)** Each pair has consecutive letter. Second letter of the first term is the first letter of the next term.

23. **(d)** Letter repeats itself after two steps.

24. **(a)**
$$A \xrightarrow{+1} b \xrightarrow{+1} C \xrightarrow{+1} d \xrightarrow{+1} E$$
lowercase uppercase lowercase uppercase

25. **(a)** Letters are in reverse order.
$$Z \xrightarrow{-1} Y \xrightarrow{-1} X \xrightarrow{-1} W \xrightarrow{-1} V$$

26. (a) Letters are moved two steps forwards.

$$A \xrightarrow{+2} C \xrightarrow{+2} E \xrightarrow{+2} G \xrightarrow{+2} \text{(I)}$$

27. (b) There are three activities given in a sequence.

Cricket, Football and Cycling

So, missing figure is of a boy with football.

28. (a) Every number is 5 more than the previous number.

5+5=10

10+5=15

15+5=20

20+5=25

29. (b)

30. (b) There is a difference of '3' between all the numbers or (table of 3).

So, 3 + 3 = 6

6 + 3 = 9

9 + 3 = 12

12 + 3 = (15)

15 + 3 = 18

18 + 3 = 21

31. (c)

32. (d) 12 + 3 = 15

15 + 3 = 18

18 + 3 = (21)

21 + 3 = 24

24 + 3 = 27

Level-2

1. (b) Rule followed in the number is the reverse counting:

2. (d) Rule followed: Skip letters.

A   B   C   D   E   F   (G)   H   I

3. (c) Each figure is formed by adding 1 short line on the middle line. So, the missing figure is (c).

4. (b)

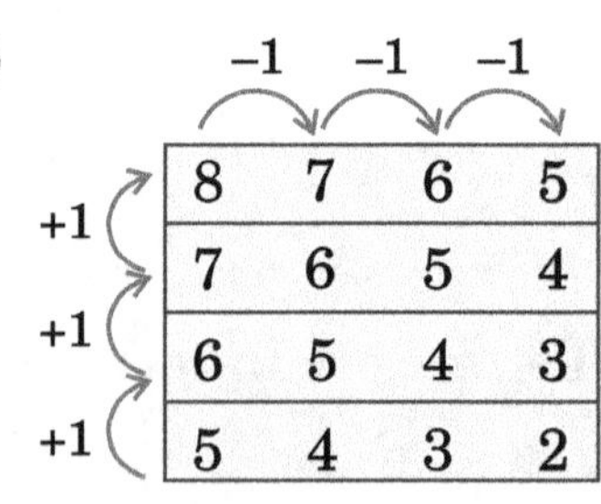

So, the missing numbers in the second row would be 7, 6, 5, 4.

7, 6, 5, 4.

5. **(c)** Each figure repeats itself after a figure.

6. **(d)** In every new figure, one new line appears.

7. **(b)** The pattern is

$$P \xrightarrow{+2} R \xrightarrow{+2} T \xrightarrow{+2} V \xrightarrow{+2} X \xrightarrow{+2} Ⓩ$$

8. **(c)** Option (c) is correct answer.

9. **(c)** Rule followed in the numbers is subtracting 10 from each number. So, last number in the series will be = 20.

10. **(c)** Number of cartoons decreased by 2 in every next figure.

11. **(a)** ORUX are the missing letters in the row.

So, 3rd row is the reverse of second row similarly, 4th row is the reverse of first row.

12. **(c)** Rule followed: Adding of 11 in each number from starting till end. So,

22 + 11 = 33.

13. **(b)** There will be 8 flowers in Pattern 4.

 = 2

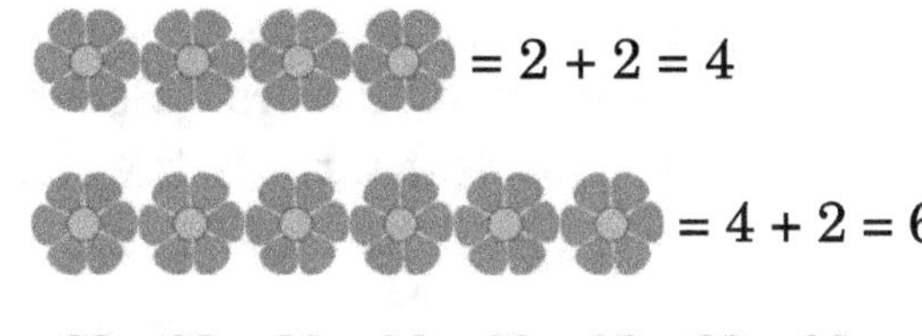

= 2 + 2 = 4

= 4 + 2 = 6

= 6 + 2 = 8

14. **(d)** The pattern is + 2. So, the missing number will be 15.

15. **(b)** When we see the circle pattern the last circle is divided into 4 parts. Similarly, when we come to triangle pattern the last triangle should be divided into four parts as well to complete the series properly.

16. **(a)** Moon is waxing in each step.

17. **(b)** Minute hand is moving five minute ahead in each step.

18. **(c)** The same figure has been added after increasing size.

19. **(a)** The pattern is + 10.

So, next term is 50.

20. **(c)** One letter has been removed in the next step.

CLASS

CLAS

CLA

CL

C

21. (c) Each term has three consecutive letters. Second letter of first term is the first letter of the second term.

22. (c) Figure repeats itself after four figures.

23. (b) Figure repeats itself after four figures.

24. (a) Option (a) will complete the figure (X).

25. (b) Figure repeats itself after four figures.

26. (c) The pattern is + 5. So, the next term is 25.

27. (a) The number of dots is increasing in every step and figure repeats itself after a figure.

28. (a) The pattern is − 3. So, the missing number is 11.

29. (d) The pattern is + 3. So, the value of P and Q is 4 and 10 respectively.

30. (a) In 1st figure- The pattern is, +2.

   In 2nd figure- The pattern is, +3.

   and

   In 3rd figure- The pattern is, +1.

   So, the missing number is 4.

31. (c) Option (c) will complete the given series.

32. (b) Pattern of series–

   $2 + 4 = 6$

   $6 + 4 = 10$

   $10 + 4 = 14$

   $14 + 4 = 18$

   $18 + 4 = ㉒$

   $22 + 4 = 26$

33. (b) There is a difference of two in every two consecutive numbers.

   $13-11=2$

   $11-2=9$

   $9-2=7$

34. (a) A, B, C, D, E in alphabetic series, so next alphabet is Ⓕ

   1 2, 3 4, 5 6, 7 8, 9 10 in continues number, so next number are 1112

Odd One Out

OBJECTIVES

- To train the students to find things that are similar or different.
- To distinctly identify things on the basis of their shape, size, colour etc.
- To help students make connections between the words and to know the process involved in it etc.

INTRODUCTION

Odd one out is the only one different from all in some manner. The student is required to choose this one item which does not fit into the given group.

Steps to Solve

Step 1: Look carefully each of pictures, numbers, words and figures.

Step 2: Find the common feature among them.

Step 3: Choose the item which does not has common feature.

Types of Odd One Out

(i) **Picture or figure-based odd one out**

Directions: Examples (1 to 5): Select the odd one out.

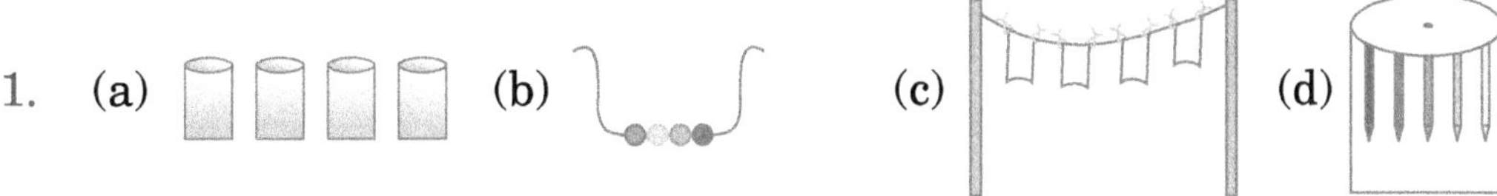

Ans. (d)

All others have four objects while option (d) has five objects. So, the correct answer is d.

2. (a) (b)  (c) 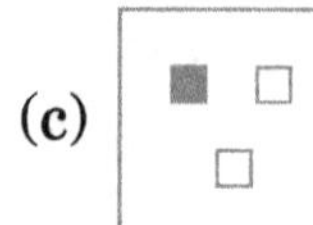 (d) 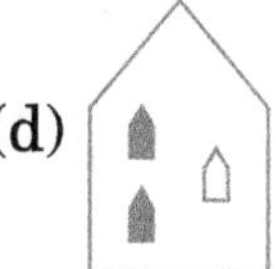

Ans. (d) Except (d), in all other figures there are one small shaded figure.

(ii) Number-based odd one out

3. (a) 5 (b) 10 (c) 12 (d) 20

Ans. (c)

All others except (c) are multiples of 5. So, the correct answer is (c).

(iii) Alphabet-based odd one out

4. (a) A (b) R (c) P (d) Q

Ans. (a)

All others except (a) are consonant, while A is a vowel. So, the correct answer is (a).

(iv) Word-based odd one out

5. (a) Mug (b) Bucket (c) Soap (d) Bed

Ans. (d)

All the objects except (d) belong to bathroom. So, the correct answer is (d).

Direction (Qs. 1-9): Find the odd one out.

1. (a)  (b)  (c)  (d) 

2. (a)  (b)  (c)  (d) 

3. (a)  (b)  (c)  (d) 

4. (a)  (b)  (c)  (d) 

5. (a)  (b)  (c) 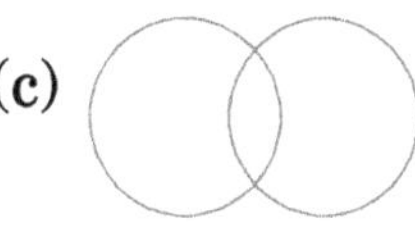 (d) 

6. (a)  (b) 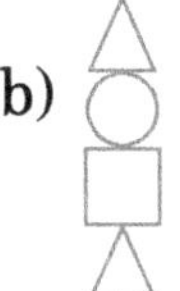 (c) 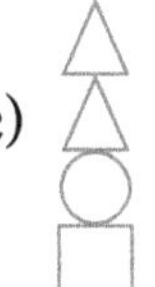 (d) 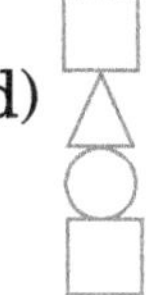

7. (a) 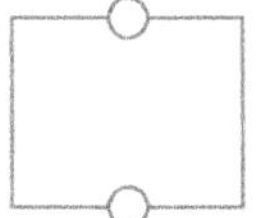 (b) 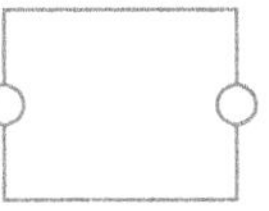 (c) 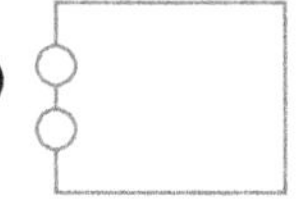 (d) 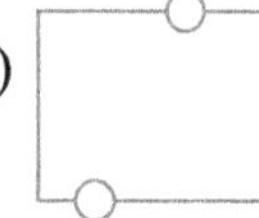

8. (a) 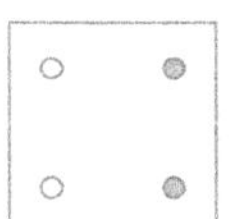 (b) 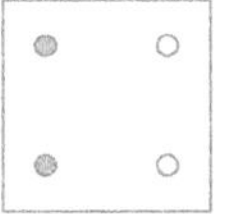 (c) 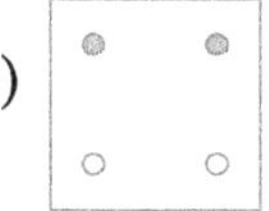 (d) 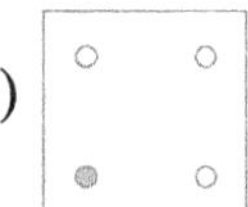

9. (a) 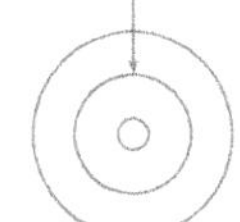 (b) 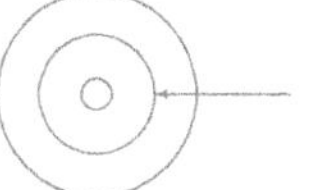 (c) 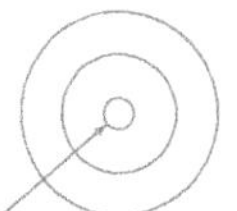 (d) 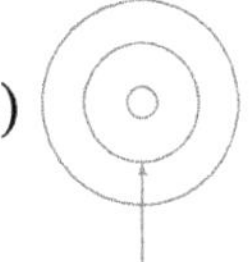

10. Find the odd one which is not related to the same group.

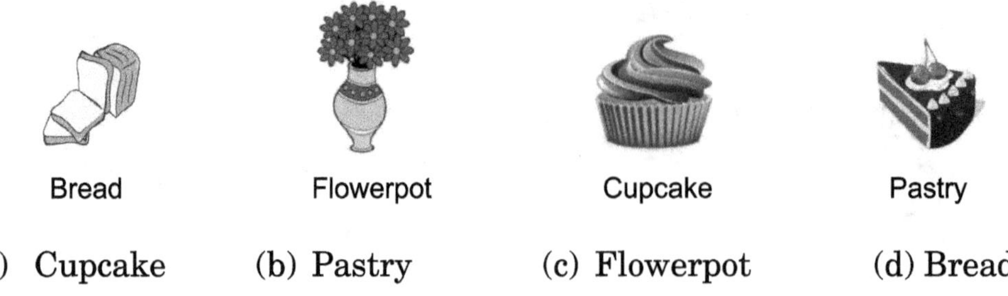

(a) Cupcake   (b) Pastry   (c) Flowerpot   (d) Bread

11. Find the one which is not related to the group.

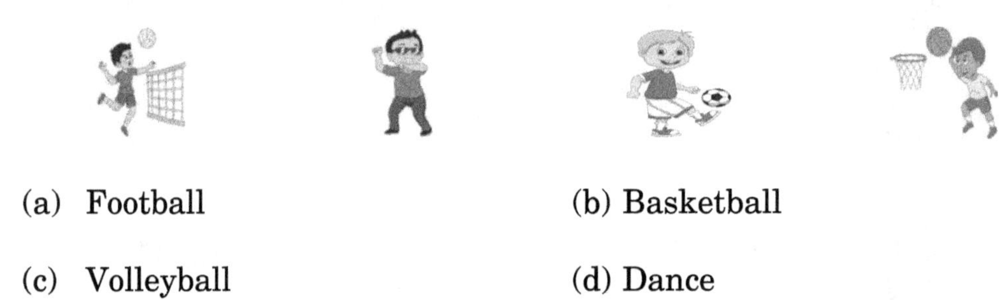

(a) Football   (b) Basketball

(c) Volleyball   (d) Dance

12. Pick the odd one which is not related to the group.

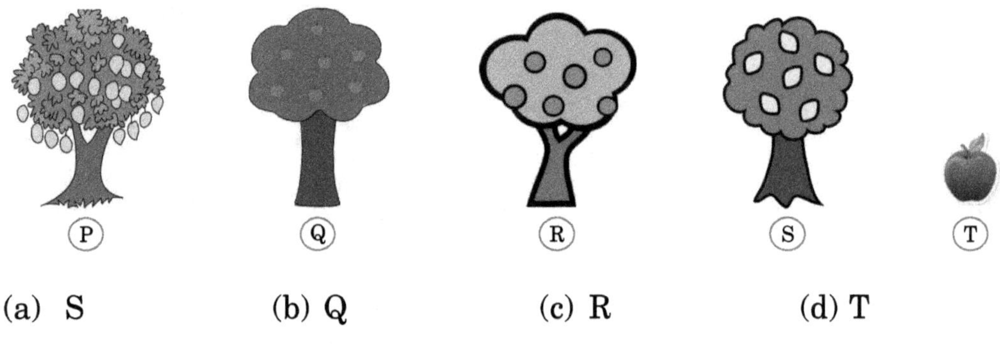

(a) S   (b) Q   (c) R   (d) T

13. Identify the odd one from the given words.

(a) Sun   (b) Cold drink   (c) Sweater   (d) Ice-cream

14. Find the odd one from the given pictures.

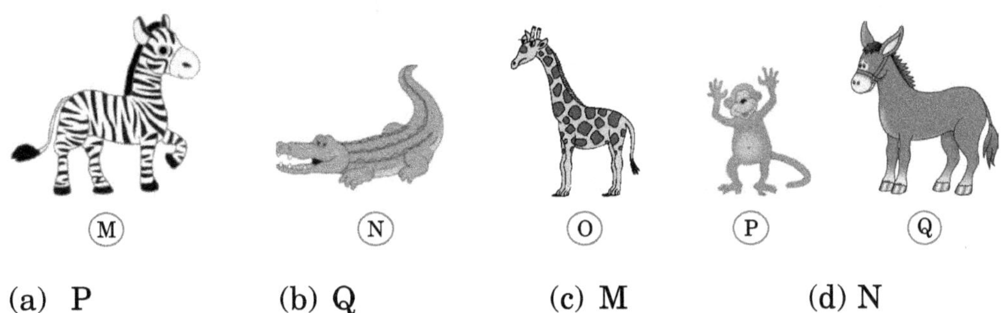

(a) P (b) Q (c) M (d) N

15. Identify the odd one from the given words.

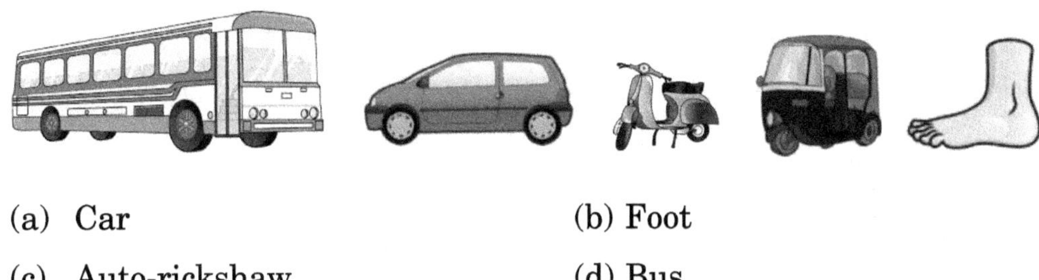

(a) Car (b) Foot

(c) Auto-rickshaw (d) Bus

Direction (Qs. 16-30): Find the odd one out.

16. (a) 2 (b) 4 (c) 5 (d) 8

17. (a) 10 (b) 20 (c) 200 (d) 30

18. (a) 01 (b) 02 (c) 30 (d) 04

19. (a) 13–31 (b) 12–21 (c) 14–41 (d) 15–16

20. (a) 8–7 (b) 5–4 (c) 2–1 (d) 9–10

21. (a) AB (b) JK (c) EF (d) SK

22. (a) DD (b) KK (c) LR (d) PP

23. (a) Pa (b) Pe (c) Pi (d) Pk

24. (a) NM (b) DC (c) ZY (d) AB

25. (a) A   (b) E   (c) I   (d) B

26. (a) January   (b) Monday   (c) May   (d) July

27. (a) Apple   (b) Grapes   (c) Potato   (d) Orange

28. (a) Parrot   (b) Tiger   (c) Owl   (d) Pigeon

29. (a) Cow   (b) Goat   (c) Zebra   (d) Sheep

30. (a) Temple   (b) Church   (c) Park   (d) Mosque

31. Select the odd one out.   **(2020)**

32. Select the odd one out.   **(2021)**

33. Select the odd one out.   **(2021)**

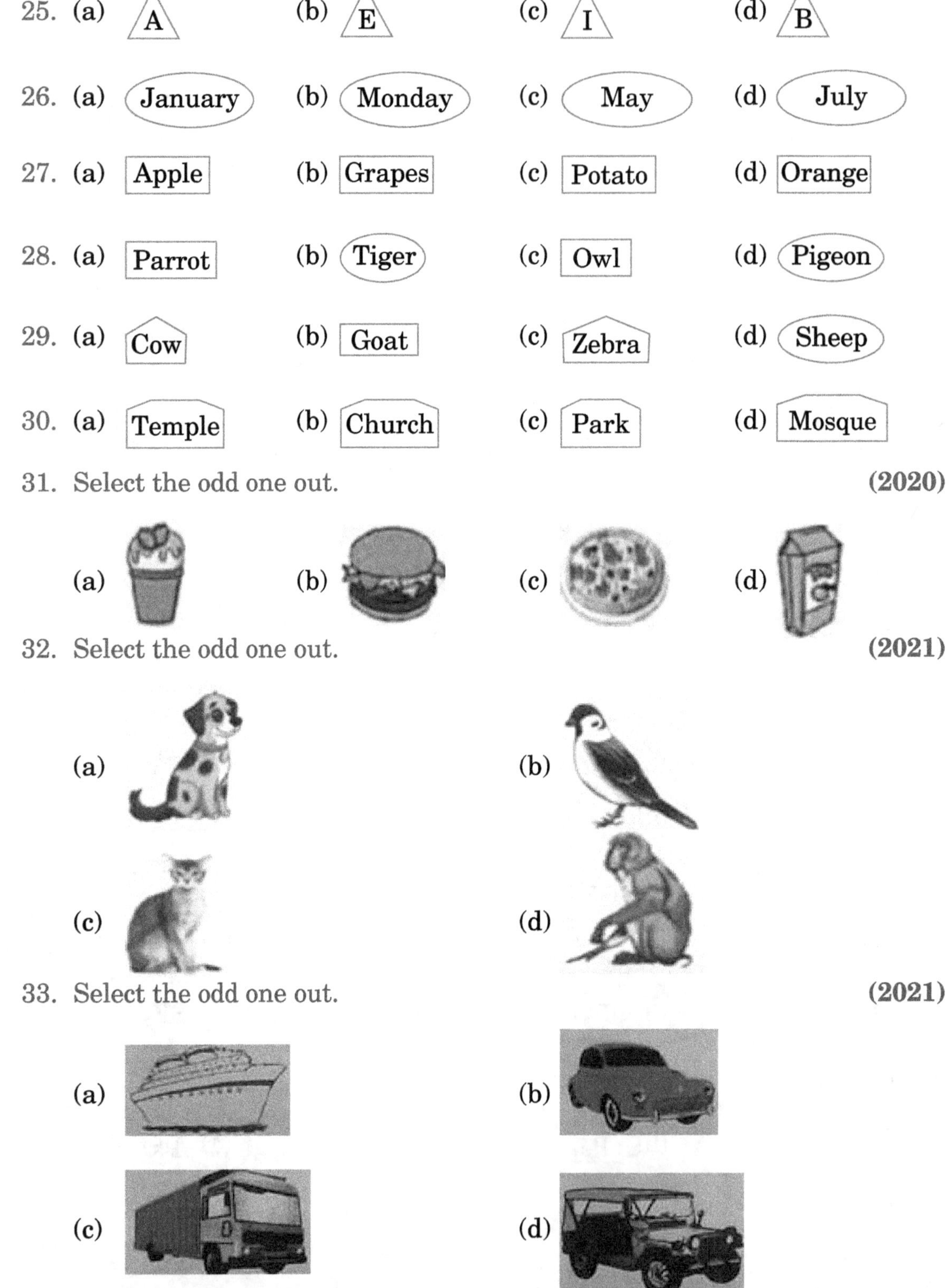

34. Select the odd one out. (2022)

(a)  (b)  (c)  (d) 

LEVEL-2

Direction (Qs. 1-14): Choose the one which is different from others in the group.

1. (a)  (b)  (c)  (d) 

2. (a)  (b)  (c)  (d) 

3. (a)  (b)  (c)  (d) 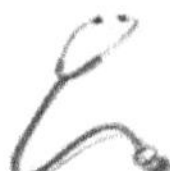

4. (a) 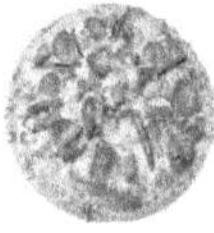 (b)  (c)  (d) 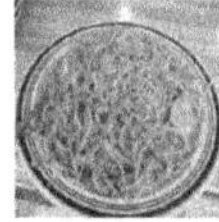

5. (a)  (b)  (c)  (d) 

6. (a)  (b)  (c)  (d) 

7. (a) 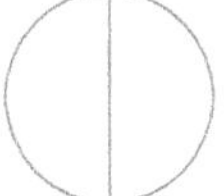 (b)  (c) 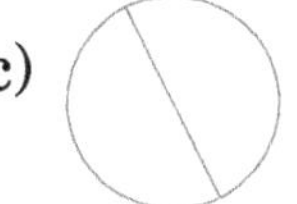 (d) 

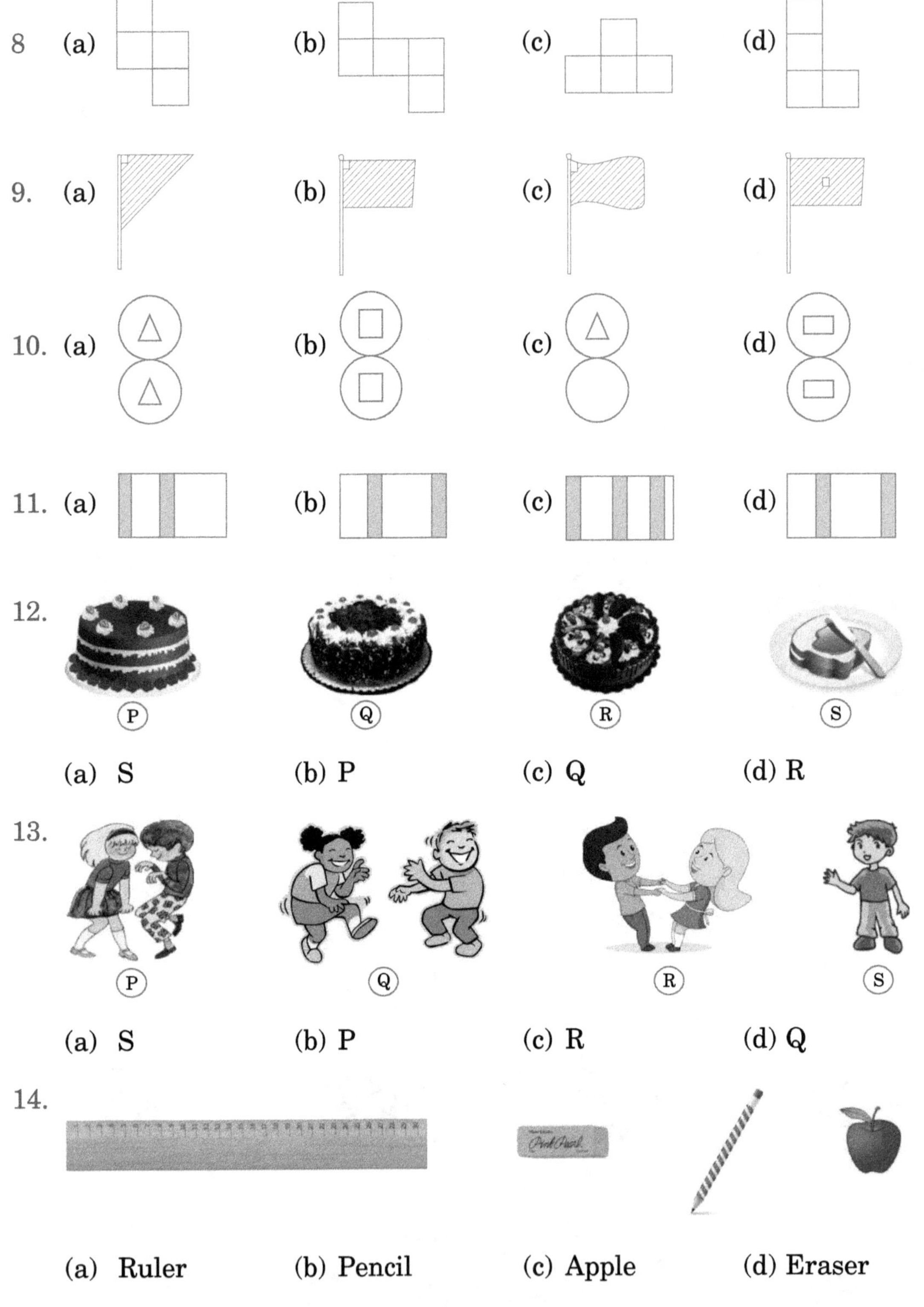

8 (a) (b) (c) (d)

9. (a) (b) (c) (d)

10. (a) (b) (c) (d)

11. (a) (b) (c) (d)

12.

(a) S (b) P (c) Q (d) R

13.

(a) S (b) P (c) R (d) Q

14.

(a) Ruler (b) Pencil (c) Apple (d) Eraser

Direction (Qs. 15-29): Find the odd one out.

15. (a) 11   (b) 50   (c) 22   (d) 33

16. (a) 3   (b) 4   (c) 9   (d) 5

17. (a) 101   (b) 202   (c) 330   (d) 404

18. (a) 4–5   (b) 6–7   (c) 9–10   (d) 13–12

19. (a) 3–5   (b) 5–3   (c) 7–3   (d) 6–2

20. (a) UBU   (b) RBR   (c) ABB   (d) LBL

21. (a) AbA   (b) CdC   (c) EfE   (d) LaL

22. (a) aa   (b) SS   (c) tt   (d) pp

23. (a) QQ   (b) UU   (c) kk   (d) ZZ

24. (a) GGg   (b) RrR   (c) BbB   (d) TtT

25. (a) Rose   (b) Lotus   (c) Marigold   (d) Mango

26. (a) Fish   (b) Crab   (c) Lizard   (d) Turtle

27. (a) Calf   (b) Cub   (c) Horse   (d) Puppy

28. (a) Car   (b) Scooter   (c) Bus   (d) Aeroplane

29. (a) Leaf   (b) Flower   (c) Tree   (d) Root

30. Find the odd one out.

(a)   (b)   (c)   (d)

(Olympiad)

31. Find the odd one out.

(a)  (b) (c) (d)

32. Select the odd one out.

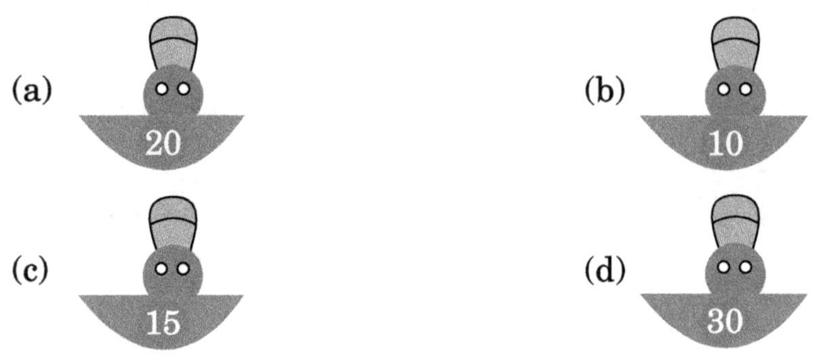

(a) 20 (b) 10

(c) 15 (d) 30

33. Select the figure which is the same as the given fig (X).

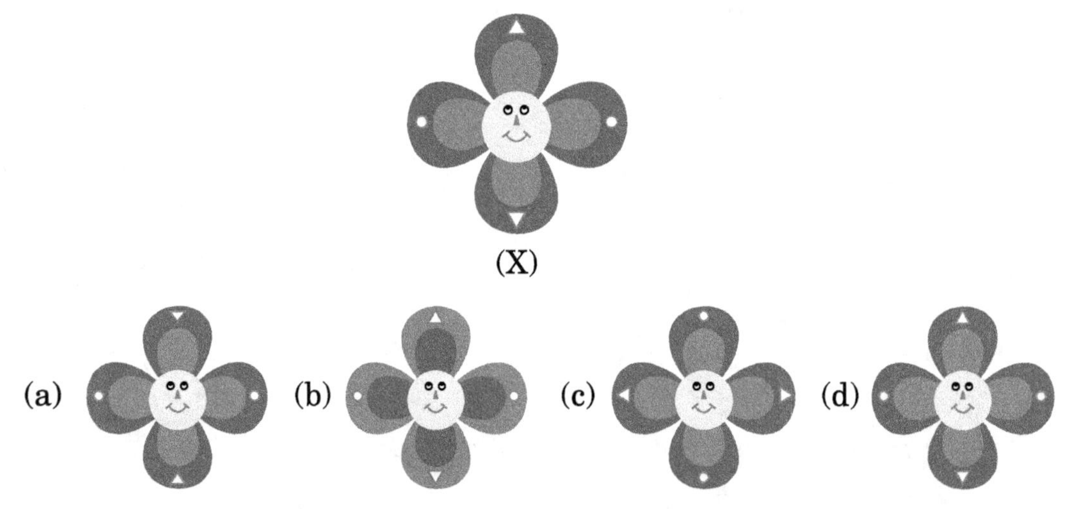

(X)

(a) (b) (c) (d)

1. **(d)** All except ball are stationery items.

2. **(d)** All except (d) are fruits, while potato is a vegetable.

3. **(d)** All except (d) are sense organs.

4. **(d)** All except (d) are electronic items.

5. **(d)** All except (d) cut each other at two points.

6. **(d)** Only (d) has 2 squares, and all others have two triangles other than a square and a circle.

7. **(c)** Only (c) has both the circles on the same side.

8. **(d)** All except (d) has equal number of white and blue dots.

9. **(c)** Except (c), all the others have darts on the middle circle.

10. **(c)** It is odd because all the things except flowerpot are eatable things. But flowerpot is a decorative item.

11. **(d)** All except dance are games.

12. **(d)** T is an apple. Rest are trees.

13. **(c)** Sweater is not related to the summer season.

14. **(d)** N (Crocodile) can live inside or outside the water but others are live only on land.

15. **(b)** Foot is the part of Human's body we use it for walking. Rest are vehicles.

16. **(c)** All others except (c), are multiples of 2.

17. **(c)** All others except (c), have only one zero, while option (c) has two zeroes. So, the correct answer is (c).

18. **(c)** Except (c), in all other numbers zero has tens place while in option (c) it has ones place.

19. **(d)** Except (d), in all other number digits are interchanged.

20. **(d)** Except (d), in all other pairs second number is less than the first.

21. **(d)** All other groups contain two consecutive letters.

22. **(c)** In all other groups, letters have been repeated.

23. **(d)** All other groups contain vowel after letter.

24. **(d)** All other groups contain two consecutive letters in reverse order.

25. **(d)** All other letters are vowels.

26. **(b)** All except Monday are months of a year.

27. (c) All except Potato are fruits.

28. (b) All except Tiger are birds.

29. (c) All except Zebra are domestic animals..

30. (c) All except Park are places of worship.

31. (d) Icecream, Burger and Pizza are eatable, but Juice is drink-able, so Juice is odd one out.

32. (b) Bird can fly but rest dog, cat and monkey can not fly.

33. (a) Ship is a water transport.

34. (d) Fish is odd one because fish lives in water and rest live on land.

Level-2

1. (c) All except (c) are birds, while tiger is an animal.

2. (b) All except (b) are places of worship.

3. (c) All except (c) are used by doctors only.

4. (c) All except (c) are junk foods.

5. (c) All except (c) are used for playing.

6. (c) All except (c) are footwears.

7. (d) Except option (d), the line divides the circle into two equal halves.

8. (b) All except (b) has four squares.

9. (d) Only (d) has a square at the centre.

10. (c) All except (c) has only one small figure enclosed in large figure.

11. (c) Only (c) has 3 shaded strips unlike the others which have only two shaded strips.

12. (a) S is a picture of bread jam. Rest are the pictures of cake.

13. (a) S is standing alone but P, Q, and R are groups of two children.

14. (c) Apple is a fruit. Rest are classroom articles.

15. (b) Except (b), in all other options digits have been repeated.

16. (b) All others except (b) are odd numbers.

17. (c) Except (c), in all others, zero is in middle place.

18. (d) Except (d), in all other pairs numbers are in ascending order.

19. (c) In all other pairs, the sum of two numbers is 8.

20. (c) In all other groups first and third letters are the same.

21. (d) In all other groups first and second letters are consecutive.

22. **(b)** All other groups are in lowercase.

23. **(c)** All other groups are in uppercase.

24. **(a)** All other groups contain first and third letters in uppercase and second letter in lower case.

25. **(d)** All except Mango are flowers.

26. **(c)** All except Lizard are water animals.

27. **(c)** All except Horse are young ones of animals.

28. **(d)** All except aeroplane run on roads.

29. **(c)** All except tree are parts of plants.

30. **(d)** Option (d) is the odd one out.

31. **(b)** Option (b) is the odd one out.

32. **(c)** Except 15, all others are divisible by 10.

33. **(d)** Figure (d) is exactly the same as the given figure (X).

Ranking Test

OBJECTIVES

- To enhance structural and locational abilities.
- To trace out specific mentioned positions according to a certain given pattern.

INTRODUCTION

Position or Ranking is a place of something in a certain given conditions.

Type I:

- Identify the position of an object/a person from the left end or right end and rank them from the top or from the bottom.

Type II:

- In this type, identify positions of two persons/objects by interchanging.

Type III:

- Identify the position of an object/a person with respect to the position or rank of other person.

Type IV:

- Identify the position of an object/a person after removing some object/ person from the series.

Steps to Solve

★ **Step 1:** See carefully all items given in the figure.

★ **Step 2:** Identify the position of an object/ a person from left end or right end.

★ **Step 3:** Think and choose the right option.

Examples:

1. The position of the ice-cream in the circle is ______________ .

   (a) 3rd from the left end   (b) 6th from the left end

   (c) 4th from the right end   (d) In the centre

Ans. (b)

Circled ice-cream is 6th from the left end.

2. The 4th flower from the right end is flower ______________.

   (a) E   (b) D   (c) F   (d) C

Ans. (a)

It is clearly shown from the given flowers that E is fourth from the right end.

3. Which flower is fourth to the right of flower R?

   (a) S   (b) G   (c) F   (d) E

(Olympiad)

Ans. (b)

Flower G is fourth to the right of flower R.

4.   If the table is removed from the arrangement shown below, then which item is third to the left of the fourth item from the right end?

(a)   (b)   (c)   (d)

(Olympiad)

Ans. (a)

Stapler is third to the left of the fourth item from the right end.

5.   Study the given pictures carefully.

Which letter is fourth to the left of the third letter from the right end?

(a) O   (b) T   (c) A   (d) L

(Olympiad)

Ans. (c)

Letter A is fourth to the left of the third letter from the right end.

1. The 5th fish from the left end is ____________.

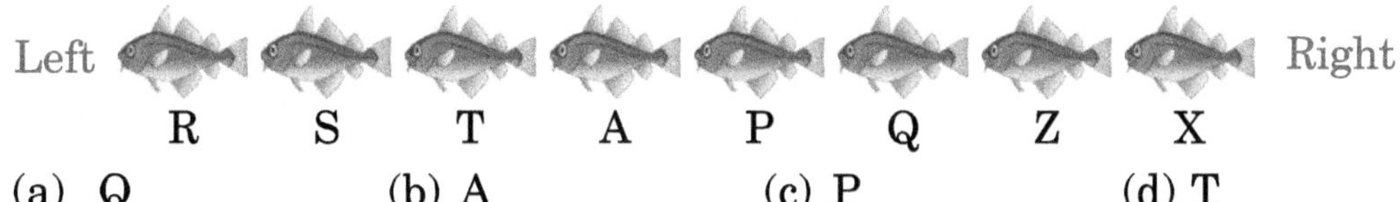

(a) Q   (b) A   (c) P   (d) T

Direction (Qs. 2-4): Answer the following questions.

2. Dev is just before ____________.

(a) Aanya   (b) Raghu   (c) Anu   (d) Pari

3. Anu is just after ____________.

(a) Pari   (b) Aanya   (c) Juhi   (d) Dev

4. Who is in the middle of Tom and Dev?

(a) Aanya   (b) Jojo   (c) Raghu   (d) Anu

5. The 2nd teddy bear from the right end is ____________.

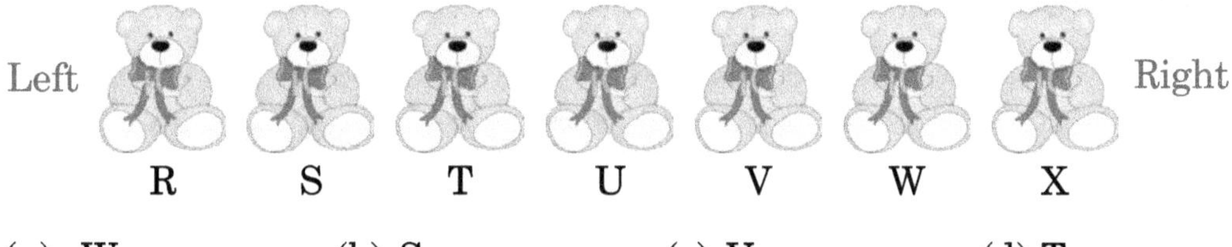

(a) W   (b) S   (c) V   (d) T

6. The ____________ is 4th from the right end.

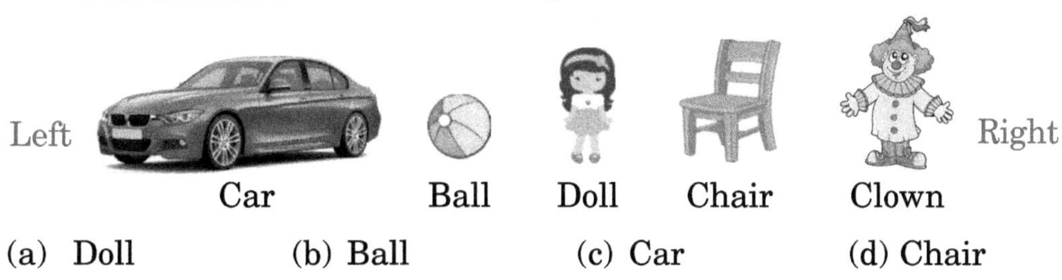

(a) Doll   (b) Ball   (c) Car   (d) Chair

Direction (Qs. 7-11): Observe the given figure carefully and answer the questions given below:

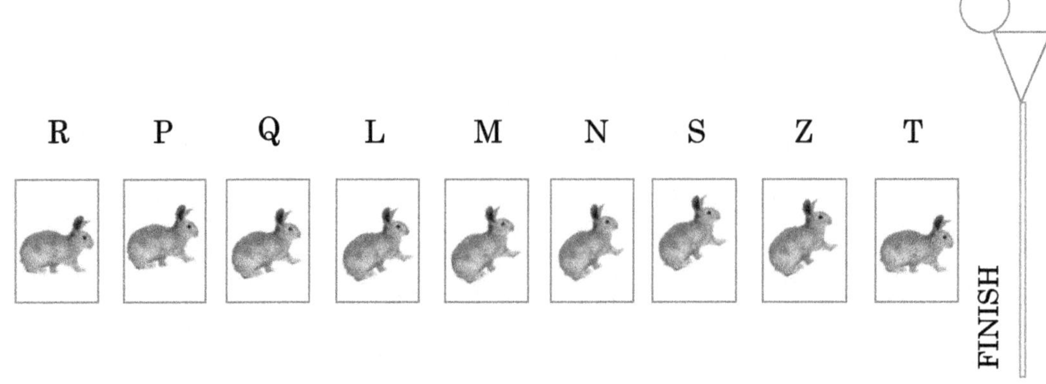

7. Rabbit _____________ is at the second position.

    (a) P   (b) Z   (c) S   (d) Q

8. Rabbit _____________ is at the third position.

    (a) Z   (b) N   (c) S   (d) Q

9. Rabbit _____________ is first from the finish line.

    (a) T   (b) R   (c) P   (d) Z

10. Rabbit _____________ is last from the finish line.

    (a) R   (b) P   (c) Q   (d) L

11. Rabbit _____________ comes after L but before P.

    (a) M   (b) P   (c) Q   (d) L

Direction (Qs. 12-14): Fill in the blanks:

12. Aarav is between ____________ and ____________.

(a) Sahil, Avni (b) Kavya, Anamika

(c) Sahil, Kavya (d) Anamika, Sahil

13. Rahul is climbing just after ____________.

(a) Sahil (b) Avni (c) Atul (d) Anamika

14. Anamika is climbing just before ____________.

(a) Aarav (b) Atul (c) Kavya (d) Sahil

15. What is the number on the 5th shirt from the left end?

Left 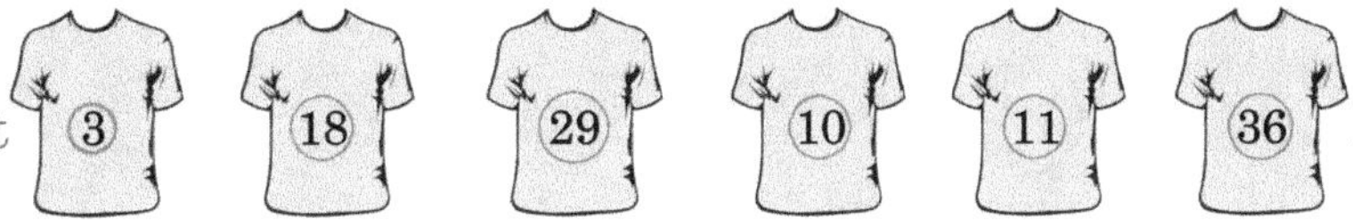
3
18
29
10
11
36
Right

(a) 18 (b) 11 (c) 29 (d) 36

16. If P buys the ticket for R, then ____________ girls are standing behind R.

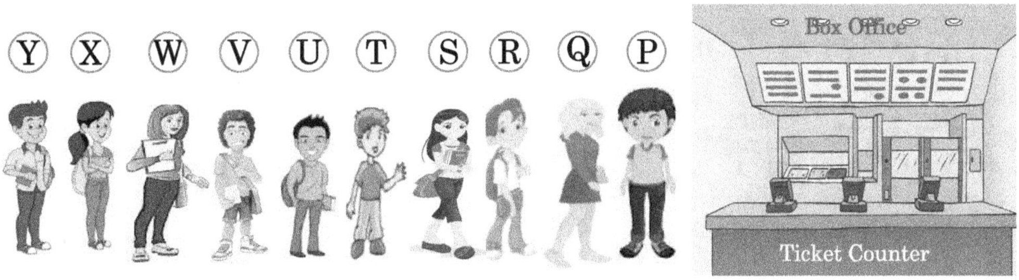
Y
X
W
V
U
T
S
R
Q
P
Box Office
Ticket Counter

(a) 4 (b) 5 (c) 6 (d) 3 (Olympiad)

17. The 5th person from the right end is ____________.

Left 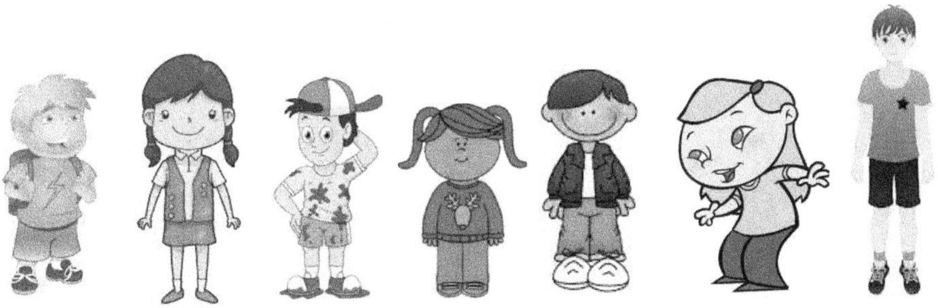

Arun Megha Nitin Priya Raj Beena Amit

(a) Megha (b) Nitin (c) Raj (d) Priya

(Olympiad)

18. On which position is Garima?

(a) 1st   (b) 2nd   (c) 3rd   (d) 4th

(Olympiad)

19. If there is no table in the picture the chair is now the ____________ item from the left end.

(a) 5th   (b) 4th   (c) 3rd   (d) 2nd

Direction (Qs. 20 - 21): Observe the following series of letters and answer the given questions.

Left	W	Q	E	T	V	Y	R	U	O	A	G	S	D	Right

20. Which letter will be 4th from the left?

(a) R   (b) T   (c) A   (d) G

21. Which letter will be in the middle?

(a) Y   (b) T   (c) R   (d) U

22. If today is Monday, when would be Sunday.

(a) Yesterday   (b) Tomorrow

(c) Day after tomorrow   (d) Day before Yesterday

23. C U B A E D E D A B E B A U

If all the As are dropped from the above arrangement, which of the following will be fifth from the left end of the above arrangement?

(a) D   (b) C   (c) U   (d) B

24. In a row there are six student standing and waiting for the bus. If we interchange the 3rd one with the 2nd then what will be the rank of the 3rd student from left in the newly formed sequence?

(a) 2   (b) 3   (c) 4   (d) 5

25. In the series given below if we add 2 to each number then what would be the sixth number from the right of the new series?

Left ←   6 9 5 2 4 1 3 6 7 5   → Right

(a) 13   (b) 6   (c) 9   (d) 11

26. In a series of trees, one tree is on 4th place from the either side of the row. So, how many trees are there in a row.

(a) 10   (b) 7   (c) 8   (d) 9

27. In a row of seven students, Mukul stands at the right end of the row and in between Mukul and Anand there are two students then what will be Anand's position from the right end?

(a) 4   (b) 5   (c) 2   (d) 1

28. In a series of 9 students, Amar ranks 5 from the left. What will be his position from right?

(a) 5   (b) 6   (c) 4   (d) 3

29. Which one is the sixth house from the left end?

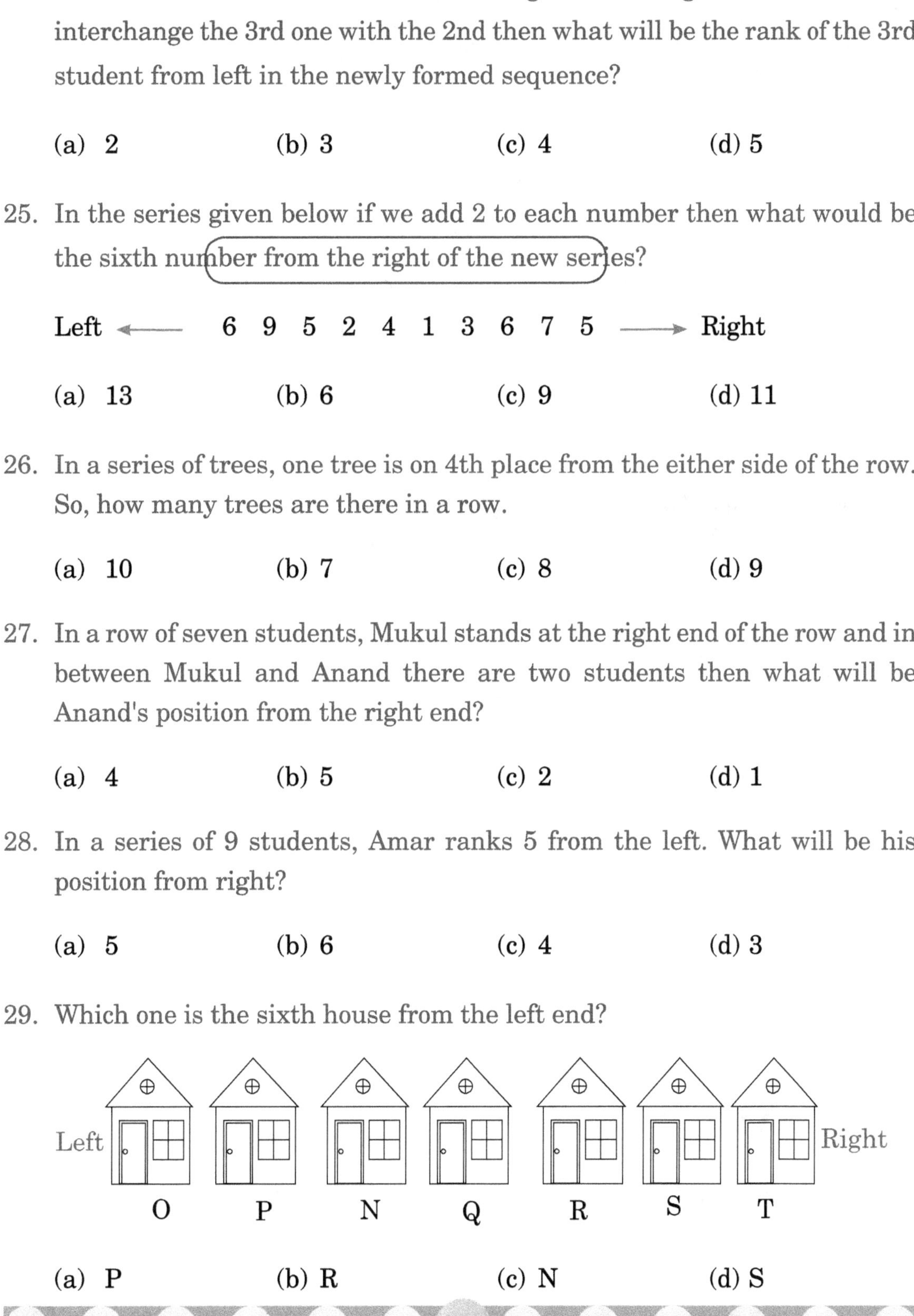

(a) P   (b) R   (c) N   (d) S

30. _____ is the longest and _____ is the shortest in the given figure.

(2018)

(a) Crayon, Paint Brush (b) Pencil, Paint Brush

(c) Pencil, Crayon (d) Paint Brush, Crayon

31. _____ is standing last in the queue. **(2018)**

(a) Latika (b) Naksh (c) Ashima (d) Ansh

32. Which of the following items costs the most? (2019)

(a)  (b)  (c)  (d)

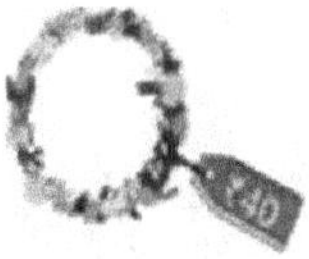

33. _____ is the shortest and _____ is the longest item in the given figure.

(2019)

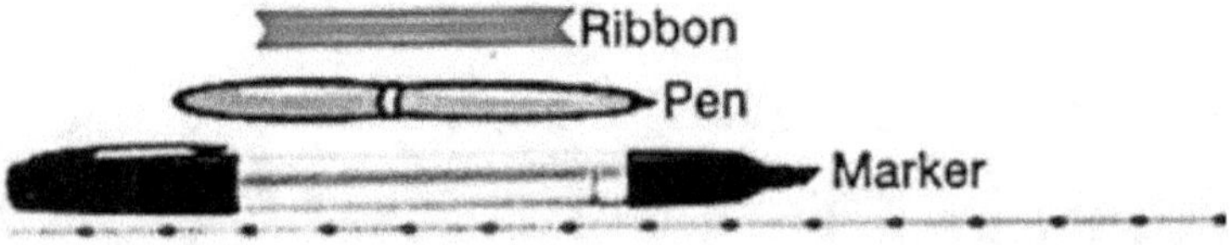

(a) Ribbon, Maker (b) Pen, Marker

(c) Pen, Ribbon (d) Ribbon, Pen

34. Who is at the first position?   (2020)

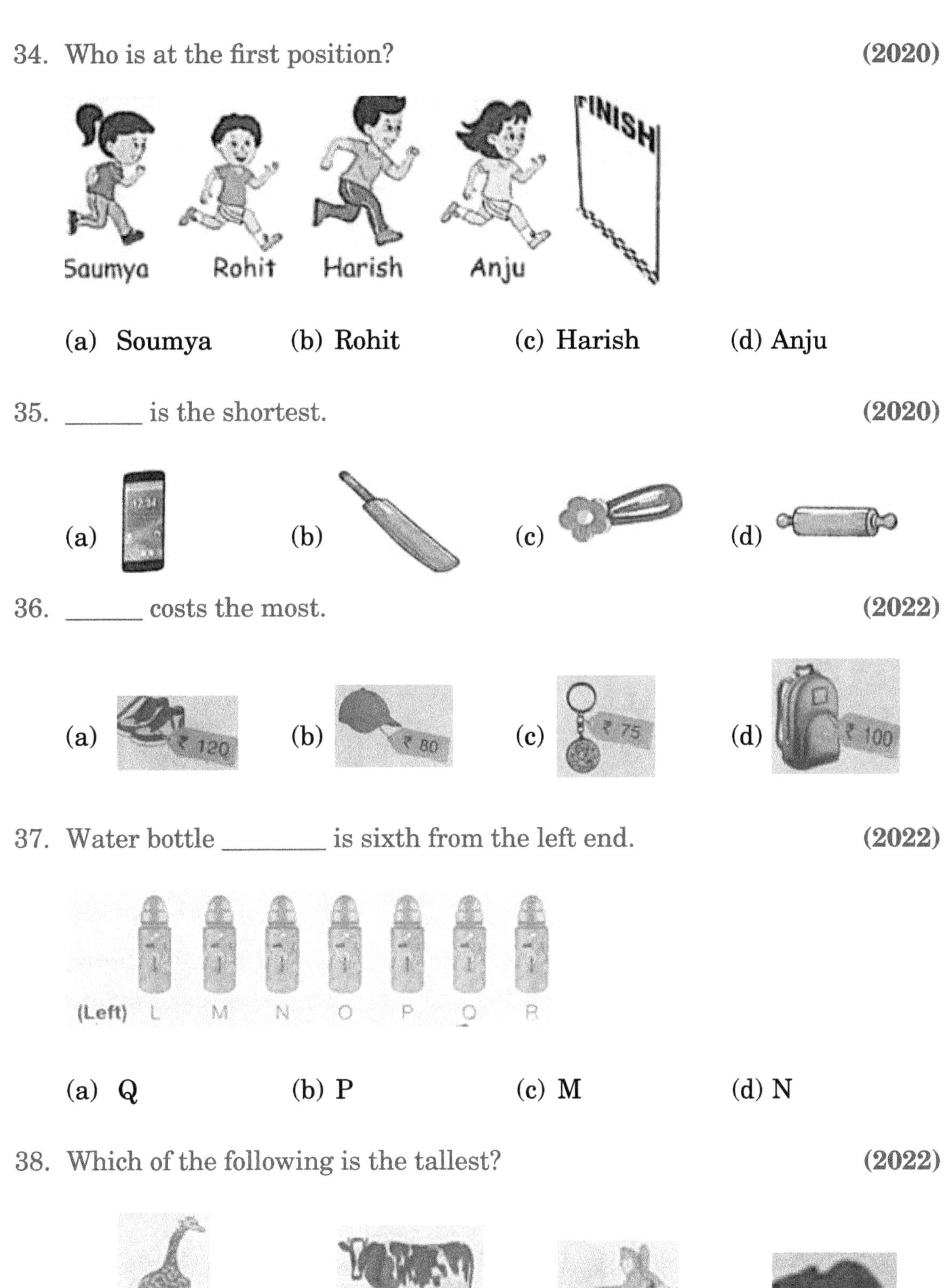

(a) Soumya   (b) Rohit   (c) Harish   (d) Anju

35. ______ is the shortest.   (2020)

(a)   (b)   (c)   (d)

36. ______ costs the most.   (2022)

(a)   (b)   (c)   (d)

37. Water bottle ________ is sixth from the left end.   (2022)

(a) Q   (b) P   (c) M   (d) N

38. Which of the following is the tallest?   (2022)

(a)   (b)   (c)   (d)

39. Tomato _______ is third from the right end.   **(2022)**

(Left)   D   E   F   G   H   I   J   K

(a) H   (b) F   (c) E   (d) I

LEVEL-2

1. The 5th letter from the right end is ____________.

Left	A	C	E	G	L	N	R	T	W	Z	Right

(a) C   (b) L   (c) R   (d) N

2. The 8th number from the left end is ____________.

Left	5	7	9	3	1	2	6	10	20	4	Right

(a) 10   (b) 9   (c) 7   (d) 20

3. Which is the fifth letter from the right end in the given word?

Left S U N F L O W E R S Right

(a) O   (b) W   (c) F   (d) L

4. Subtract the 2nd number from the left from the 1st number from the left end and you will get the ____________ number from the right end.

Left	10	6	4	3	1	Right

(a) 1st (b) 2nd (c) 3rd (d) 4th

5. Which alphabet comes in the middle of the following given word?

T E A C H E R

(a) A   (b) H   (c) R   (d) C

6. Add the 2nd number from the left to the 1st number from the left end and you will get the ______________ number from the right end.

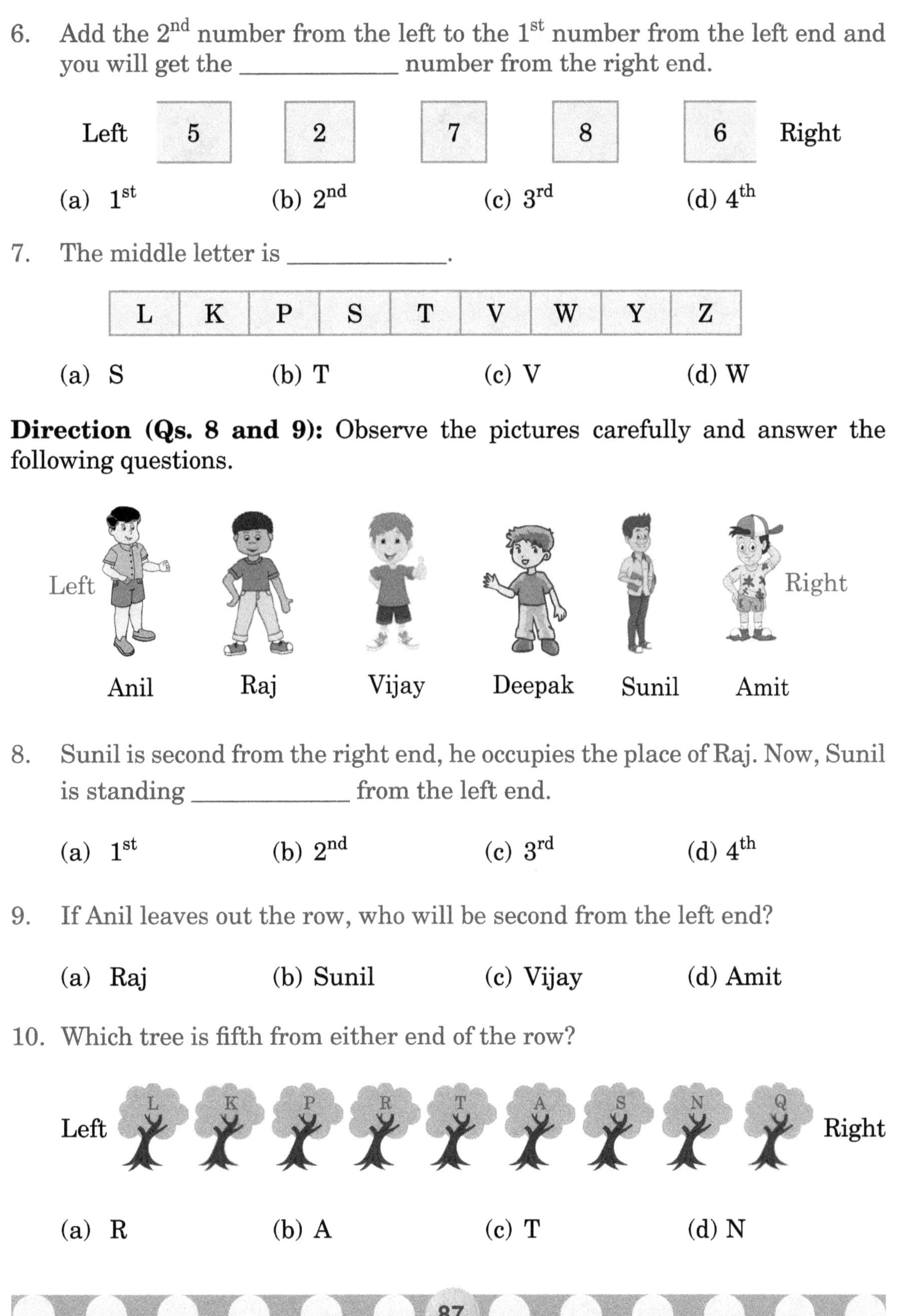

| Left | 5 | 2 | 7 | 8 | 6 | Right |

(a) 1st　　　　(b) 2nd　　　　(c) 3rd　　　　(d) 4th

7. The middle letter is ______________.

| L | K | P | S | T | V | W | Y | Z |

(a) S　　　　(b) T　　　　(c) V　　　　(d) W

Direction (Qs. 8 and 9): Observe the pictures carefully and answer the following questions.

8. Sunil is second from the right end, he occupies the place of Raj. Now, Sunil is standing ______________ from the left end.

(a) 1st　　　　(b) 2nd　　　　(c) 3rd　　　　(d) 4th

9. If Anil leaves out the row, who will be second from the left end?

(a) Raj　　　　(b) Sunil　　　　(c) Vijay　　　　(d) Amit

10. Which tree is fifth from either end of the row?

(a) R　　　　(b) A　　　　(c) T　　　　(d) N

11. Penguin is second from the left end, what is its position from the right end?

(a) 5th   (b) 6th   (c) 4th   (d) 2nd

12. The 6th doll from the right end is ______________.

(a) U   (b) Q   (c) R   (d) W

13. The position of the dice in the circle is ______________.

(a) 4th from the left   (b) 3rd from the left

(c) 4th from the right   (d) In the centre

Direction (Qs. 14 & 15): Observe the picture carefully and answer the following questions.

14. Which child is nearest to the house?

(a) Raman   (b) Raj   (c) Rana   (d) Rahul

15. Which child is farthest to the house?

   (a) Raj   (b) Rana   (c) Raman   (d) Rahul

16. Which gift is 4th from the left and 7th from the right?

Left   A   B   C   D   E   F   G   H   I   J   Right

   (a) E   (b) G   (c) D   (d) C

Direction (Qs. 17 & 18): Answer the following questions on the basis of given series.

Left | T | S | R | A | Z | U | K | L | M | N | P | Q | X | Right

17. The 6th letter from the left end is ______________.

   (a) U   (b) K   (c) L   (d) M

18. The 3rd letter from the right end is ______________.

   (a) Q   (b) P   (c) Q   (d) R

Direction (Qs. 19 & 20): Observe the given picture carefully and answer the following questions:

Left   L   K   S   U   T   P   L   Right

19. Which bear is fifth from right end?

   (a) S   (b) K   (c) U   (d) P

20. Which bear is second from left end?

   (a) K   (b) P   (c) T   (d) S

21. Which is the sixth letter from the left end in the given word?

Left (A E R O P L A N E) Right

   (a) A   (b) O   (c) L   (d) P

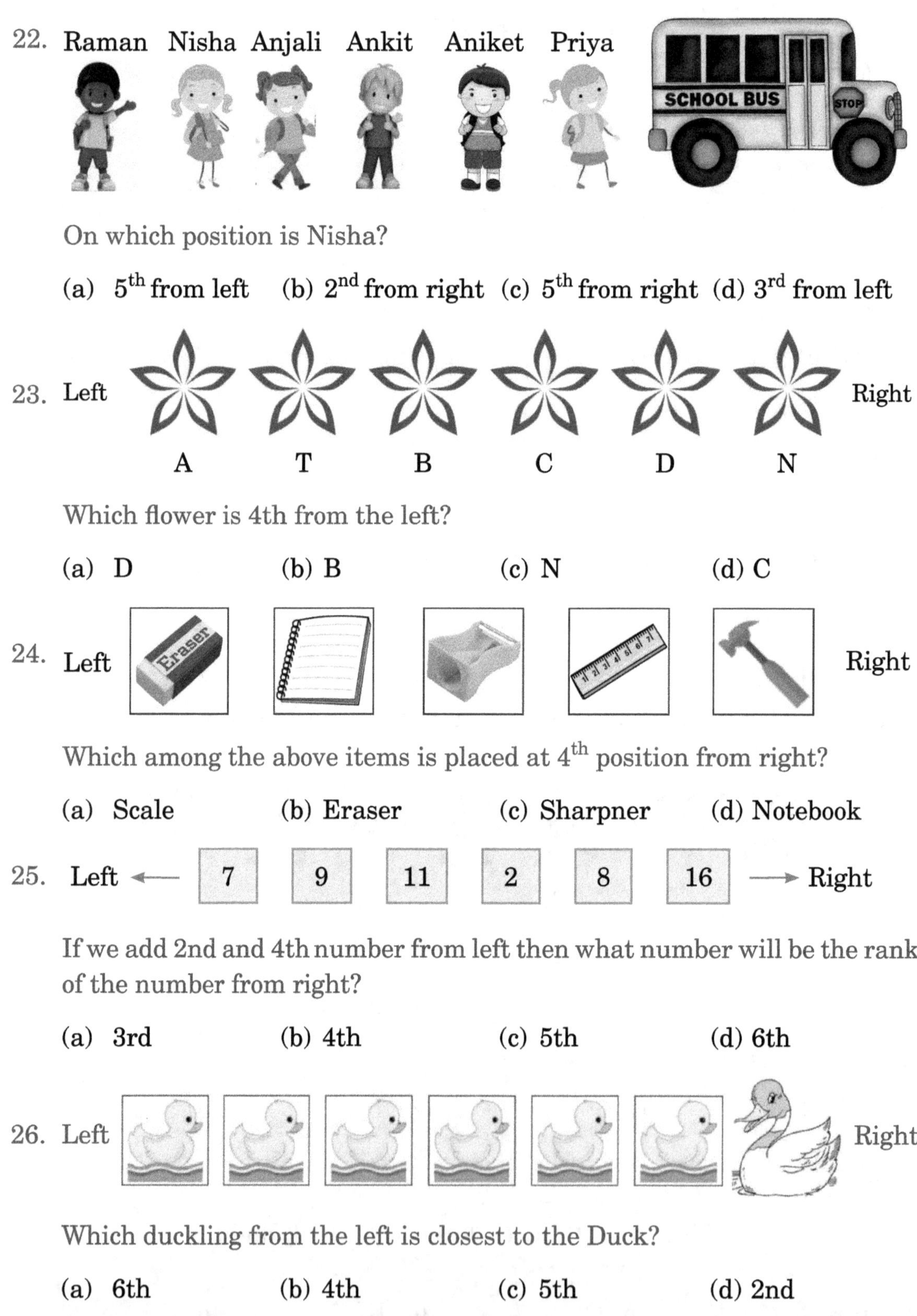

22. Raman   Nisha   Anjali   Ankit   Aniket   Priya

On which position is Nisha?

(a) 5th from left   (b) 2nd from right   (c) 5th from right   (d) 3rd from left

23. Left   A   T   B   C   D   N   Right

Which flower is 4th from the left?

(a) D   (b) B   (c) N   (d) C

24. Left   Right

Which among the above items is placed at 4th position from right?

(a) Scale   (b) Eraser   (c) Sharpner   (d) Notebook

25. Left ← 7   9   11   2   8   16 → Right

If we add 2nd and 4th number from left then what number will be the rank of the number from right?

(a) 3rd   (b) 4th   (c) 5th   (d) 6th

26. Left   Right

Which duckling from the left is closest to the Duck?

(a) 6th   (b) 4th   (c) 5th   (d) 2nd

27. There are some items given below. If we interchange the position of the items placed in second and fifth position from left then which item will be placed in fifth position from right?

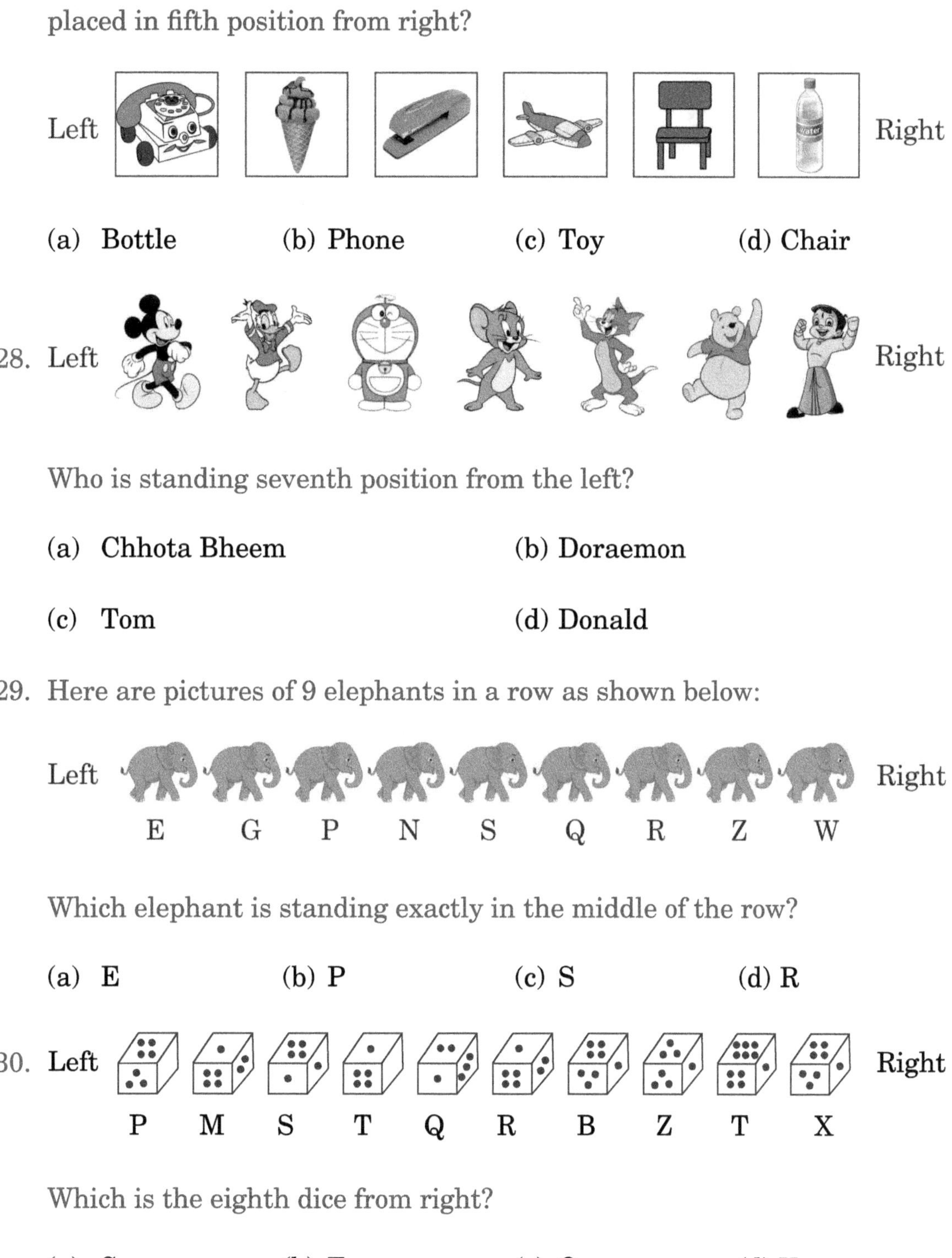

(a) Bottle   (b) Phone   (c) Toy   (d) Chair

28. **Left** ... **Right**

Who is standing seventh position from the left?

(a) Chhota Bheem   (b) Doraemon

(c) Tom   (d) Donald

29. Here are pictures of 9 elephants in a row as shown below:

Left   E   G   P   N   S   Q   R   Z   W   **Right**

Which elephant is standing exactly in the middle of the row?

(a) E   (b) P   (c) S   (d) R

30. **Left** ... P   M   S   T   Q   R   B   Z   T   X   **Right**

Which is the eighth dice from right?

(a) S   (b) T   (c) Q   (d) X

31. Kite _______ is 4th from the right end in the arrangement given below.

(2021)

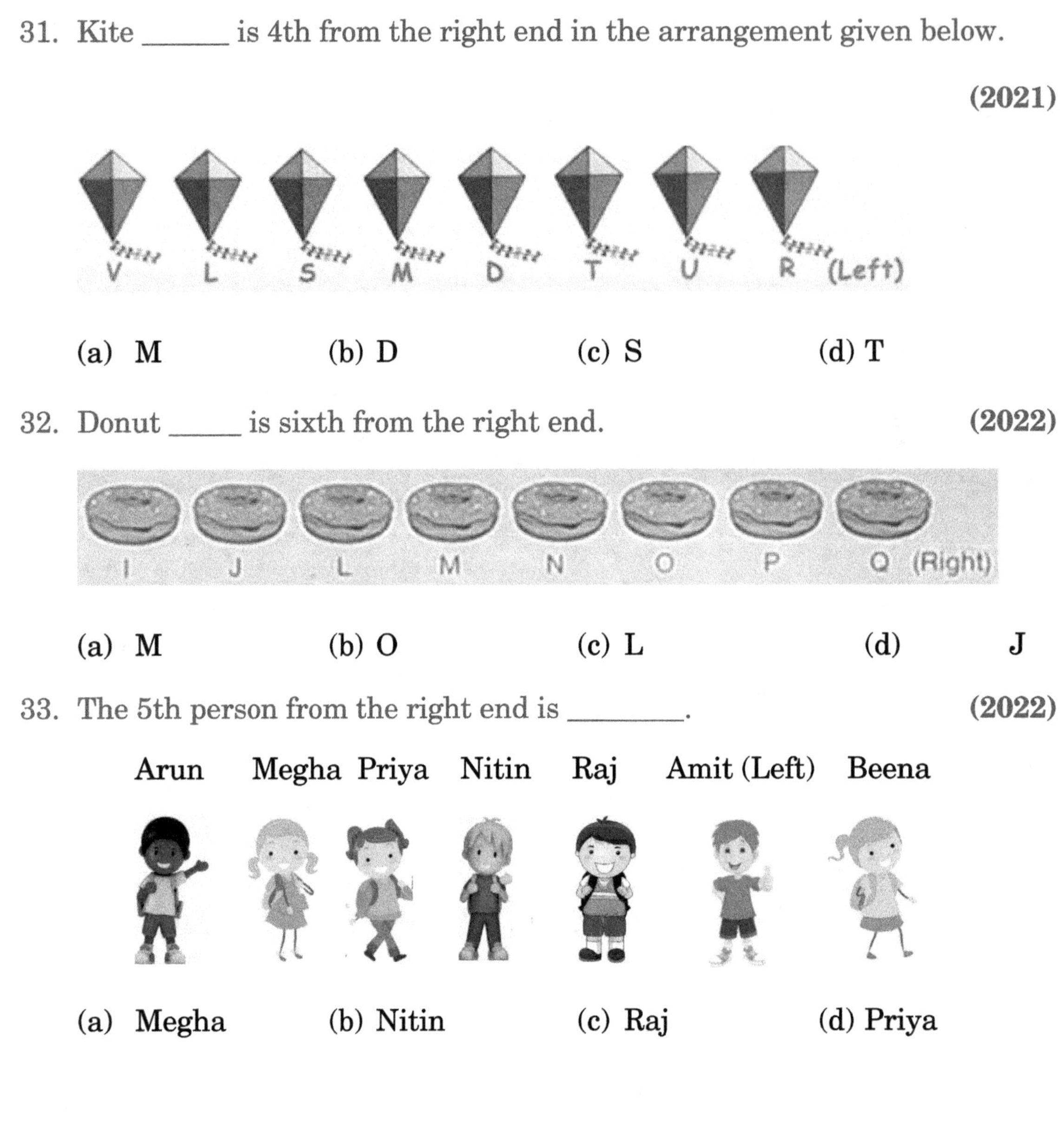

(a) M   (b) D   (c) S   (d) T

32. Donut _______ is sixth from the right end.   **(2022)**

(a) M   (b) O   (c) L   (d)   J

33. The 5th person from the right end is _________.   **(2022)**

(a) Megha   (b) Nitin   (c) Raj   (d) Priya

Level-1

1. (c) Fish P is the fifth from the left end.

2. (b) Dev is just before Raghu.

3. (a) Anu is just after Pari.

4. (c) Raghu is in the middle of Tom and Dev.

5. (a) The 2nd teddy bear from the right end is W.

6. (b) The ball is fourth from the right end.

7. (b) Rabbit Z is at the second position.

8. (c) Rabbit S is at the third position.

9. (a) Rabbit T is first from the finish line.

10. (a) Rabbit R is last from the finish line.

11. (c) Rabbit Q comes after L but before P.

12. (c) Aarav is between Sahil and Kavya.

13. (b) Rahul is climbing just after Avni.

14. (c) Anamika is climbing just before Kavya.

15. (b) Number 11 is on the 5th shirt from the left end.

16. (d) If P buys the ticket for R, then 3 girls are standing behind R.

17. (b) The 5th person from the right end is Nitin.

18. (b) Garima is on 2nd position.

19. (a) If there is no table in the picture the chair is now the 5th item from the left end.

20. (b) Given series is:

Left   W   Q   E   (T)   V   Y   R   U   O   A   G   S   D   Right

4th

T is 4th from the left.

21. (c)

Left   W   Q   E   T   V   Y   (R)   U   O   A   G   S   D   Right

Middle

R will be in the middle.

22. (a) Yesterday.

23. (a) The new arrangement will be:

C U B E (D) E D B E B U

5th from the Left

24. (a)

The new position of the third student will be 2nd from the left.

25. (b)

Old Series	6	9	5	2	(4)	1	3	6	7	5	+ 2
New Series	8	11	7	4	6	3	5	8	9	7	

Hence, the number appears in the sixth position of the new series will be 6.

26. (b) Number of trees in a row is

$$= 3 + 1 + 3$$
$$= 7$$

27. (a) 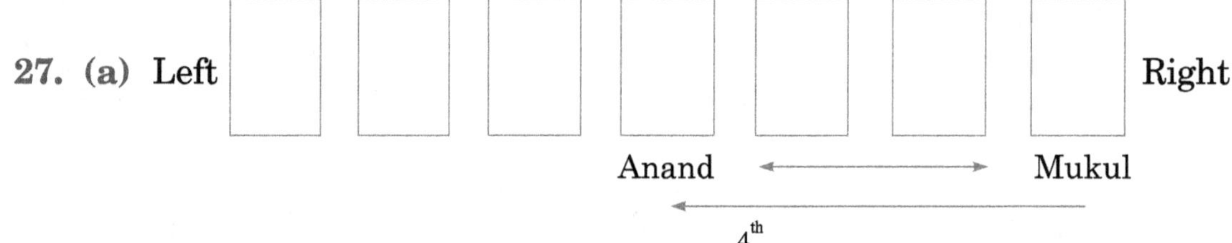

So, Anand will be on 4th position from the left end.

28. (a) 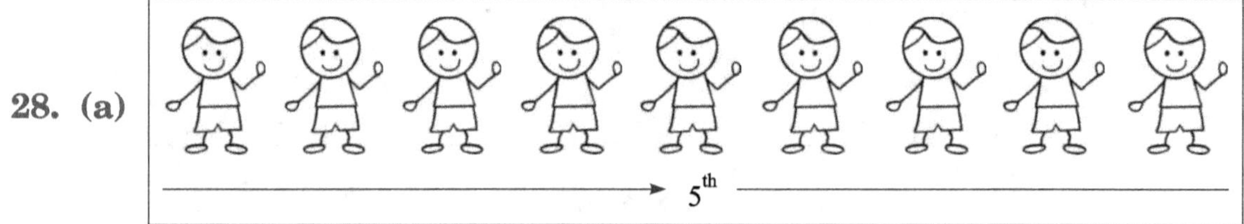

The total number of students = 9.

and Amar is 5th from left.

So, from right there are = $9 - 5 = 4$ Students after/before him.

Hence, his position is 5th from the right also.

29. (d) S is the Sixth house from left.

30. (d) Paint brush is the longest in length and Cragon is the shortest in length among given in figure.

31. (b) Naksh is standing behind of all. So, Naksh is standing last in the queue.

32. (d) ₹ 20 < ₹ 25 < ₹ 35 < ₹ 40

So, the item cost ₹ 40 is most costly.

33. (a) Length of Ribbon is the shortest among given itmes.

Length of marker is the longest among given items.

34. (d) 'Anju' is ahead from Harish, Rohit and Saumya.

So, 'Anju' is at the first position.

35. (c) Hair clip < Mobile < Rolling pin < Bat

So, Hair clip is the shortest.

36. (a) Shoes costs the most, because

₹ 120 > ₹ 100 > ₹ 80 > ₹ 75

37. (a) Bottle L is at left end.

So, bottle Q is sixth from the left end.

38. (a) Order according their heights,

Giraffe ⟩ Cow ⟩ Robbit ⟩ Rat

So, Giraffe is the tallest.

39. (d)

Level-2

1. (d) The given series is:

Left	A	C	E	G	L	N	R	T	W	Z	Right
						5	4	3	2	1	

The 5th letter from the right end is N.

2. (a) The given series is

Left	5	7	9	3	1	2	6	10	20	4	Right
	1	2	3	4	5	6	7	8			

The 8th number from the left end is 10.

3. (a) The given word is:

Left	S	U	N	F	L	O	W	E	R	S	Right
						5	4	3	2	1	

The fifth letter from the right end is O.

4. **(c)** 1st number from the left end is 10

2nd number from the left end is 6

The result is $10 - 6 = 4$

4 is the 3rd number from the right end.

5. **(d)** The given word is:

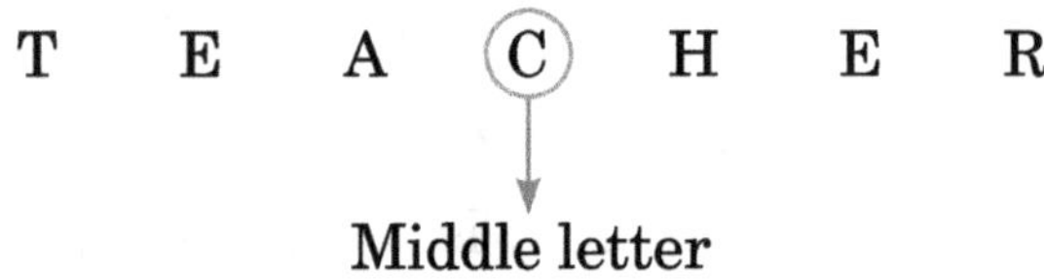

The middle letter is C.

6. **(c)** 2nd number from the left end is 2

1st number from the left end is 5

Result is $= 5 + 2 = 7$

7 is the 3rd number from the right end.

7. **(b)** The given series is:

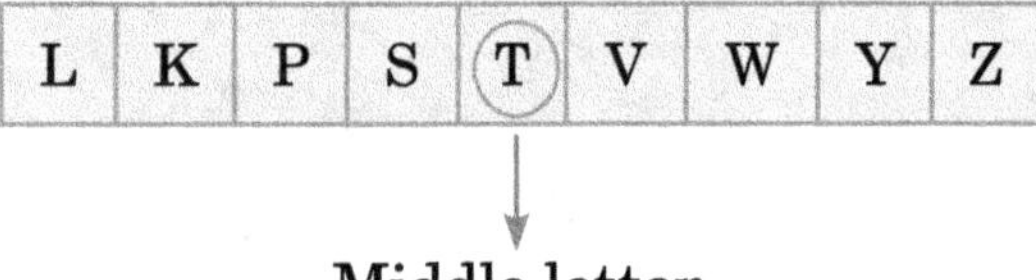

The middle letter is T.

8. **(b)** He is standing 2nd from the left end.

9. **(c)** If Anil leaves out the row, Vijay will be second from the left end.

10. **(c)** T tree is fifth from either end of the row.

11. **(a)** Penguin position from the right end is 5th.

12. **(c)** The 6th doll from the right end is R.

13. **(b)** The position of the dice in the circle is 3rd from the left.

14. **(a)** Raman is nearest to the house.

15. **(b)** Rana is farthest to the house.

16. **(c)** Gift D is 4th from the left and 7th from the right.

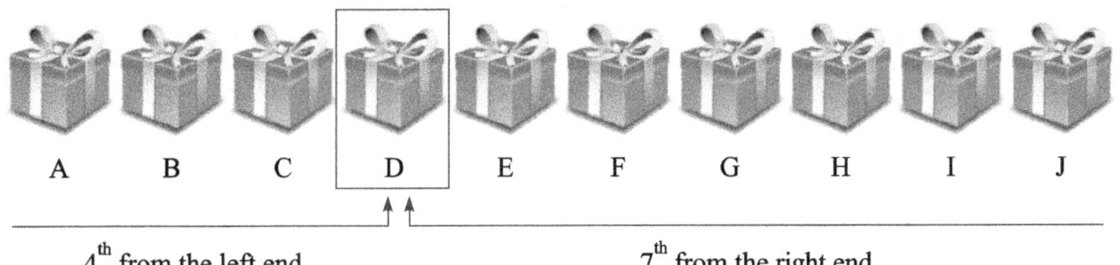

| A | B | C | D | E | F | G | H | I | J |

4th from the left end   7th from the right end

17-18. The given series is

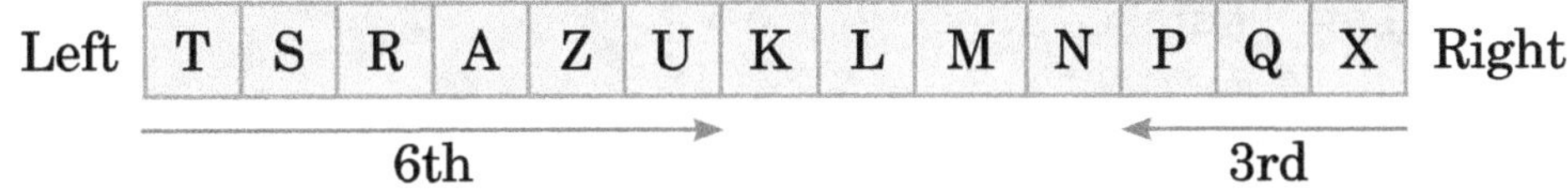

Left T S R A Z U K L M N P Q X Right

6th   3rd

17. (a) The 6th letter from the left end is U.

18. (b) The 3rd letter from the right end is P.

19. (a) Bear S is fifth from the right end.

20. (a) Bear K is second from the left end.

21. (c)

A E R O P Ⓛ A N E

1 2 3 4 5 6

Left   Right

22. (c)

23. (d) Flower C is 4th from the left.

24. (d) The Notebook is placed at the fourth position from right.

25. (b)

Left $\longleftarrow$ 7   9   11   2   8   16 $\longrightarrow$ Right

             1st 2nd 3rd 4th

2nd number from left = 9

4th number from left = 2

The result = 9 + 2 = 11

11 is the 4th number from right.

26. (a) The sixth duckling from the left is closest to the duck.

27. (d) The second item in the row from left is Ice cream.

The fifth item in the row from left is Chair.

If we interchange their positions then the item on 5th position from right will be the chair.

28. (a) Chhota Bheem is standing seventh position from the left.

29. (c) As there are nine elephants in the row, the elephant in the 5th position will be exactly in the middle position and it is occupied by 'S'.

30. (a) 'S' is the eighth dice from right.

31. (a) As kite V is at right end, so kite M is 4th from the right end.

32. (c) As Q is at right end, So Donut L is sixth from right end.

33. (d) Amit is at right end.

So, Priya is the 5th person from the right end.

Problem-Solving

OBJECTIVES

- Students will identify different problem solving styles and methods.

- They will apply methods to specific problems.

- A problem-solving approach can be used to encourage students to make generalization about rules and concepts.

- It develops students confidence in their own ability to think mathematically.

INTODUCTION

Problem solving is a process of working through details of a problem to reach a solution.

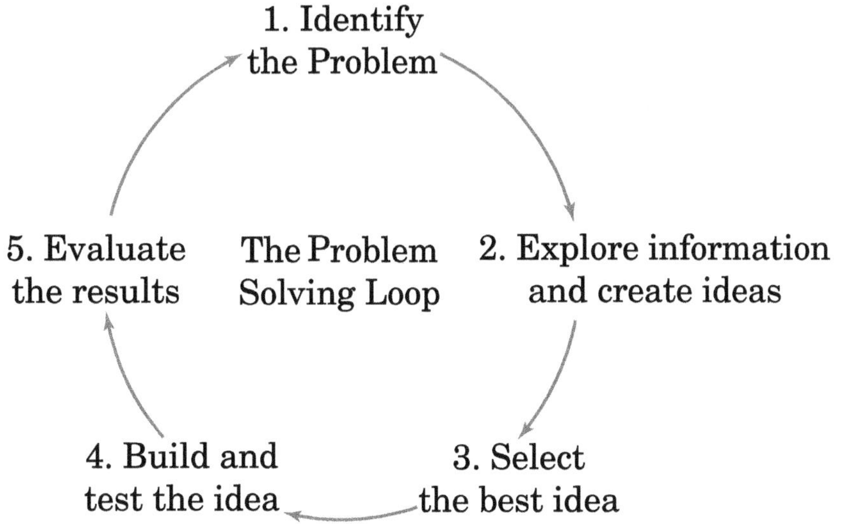

- Students will learn the use of one piece of information in the problem.
- They will organise the given information.

Examples:

1. Rihana plucks 5 flowers in her garden. The 1st flower is pink. The 2nd flower is white. The 3rd flower is pink. If this pattern continues, what colour is the 5th flower?

   (a) White (b) Pink (c) Red (d) Yellow

Ans. (b) The pattern is as follows:

1st flower	2nd flower	3rd flower	4th flower	5th flower
Pink	White	Pink	White	Pink

So, the colour of the 5th flower is Pink.

2. There are 2 bikes and 2 cars in a parking lot. How many wheels do they have in all?

   (a) 16 (b) 8

   (c) 24 (d) 12

Ans. (d) A bike has 2 wheels.

   2 bikes have 2 + 2 = 4 wheels

   A car has 4 wheels

   2 cars have = 4 + 4 = 8 wheels

   Total wheels = 4 + 8 = 12

3. Misha went to the grocery store. She bought 18 packs of cookies and 12 packs of noodles. How many packs of groceries did she buy in all?

   (a) 12 (b) 26

   (c) 30 (d) 18

Ans. (c) 18 + 12 = 30

   So, She bought 30 packs of groceries in all.

4. Jay had 14 marbles in his collection. He lost 6 marbles. How many marbles does he have now?

(a) 20   (b) 14   (c) 6   (d) 8

Ans. (d) $14 - 6 = 8$

He now has 8 marbles

5. • Lina said, "My number is the same as the number of fingers on my two hands."

    • Mohit said, "My number is 4 less than Lina's."

    What is Mohit's number?

(a) 5   (b) 6   (c) 7   (d) 10

Ans. (b) Lina's number = Fingers in two hands = 10

Mohit's number = $10 - 4 = 6$

LEVEL-1

1. Amit is taller than Bunny and Bunny is taller than Chetan. Who is tallest among them?

   (a) Chetan   (b) Bunny   (c) Amit   (d) None of these

2. Sonia needs some eggs to make a cake. Eggs are not more than five and not less than five. How many eggs she needs to buy?

   (a) 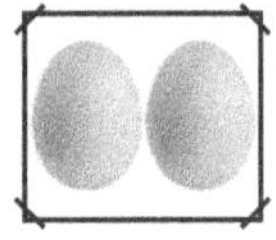   (b)    (c) 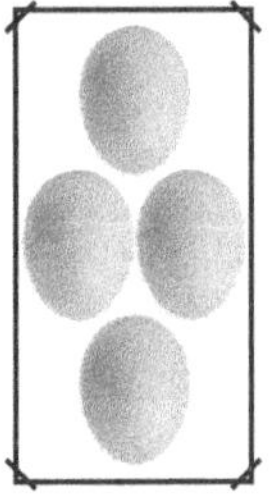   (d) 

3. Anu has 5 biscuits, Charu has some biscuits. Together they have 7 biscuits. How many biscuits does Charu have?

   (a) 2   (b) 4   (c) 6   (d) 3

4. In the given figure, how many dots are there in the circle but not in the rectangle?

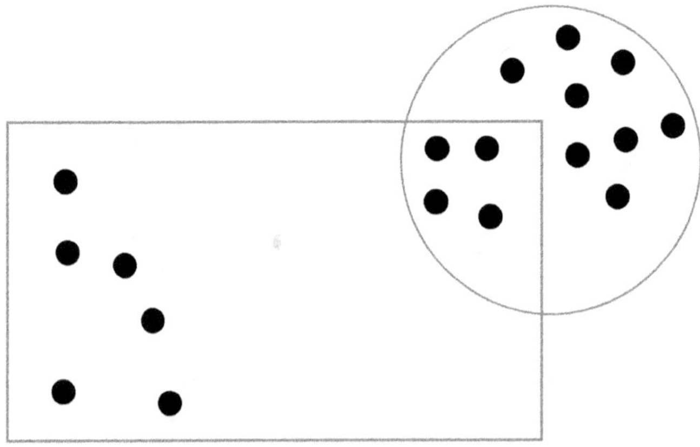

   (a) 8   (b) 12   (c) 6   (d) 7

5. Lata went from her house to Madhav's house, then they went to school. How much distance is travelled by Lata?

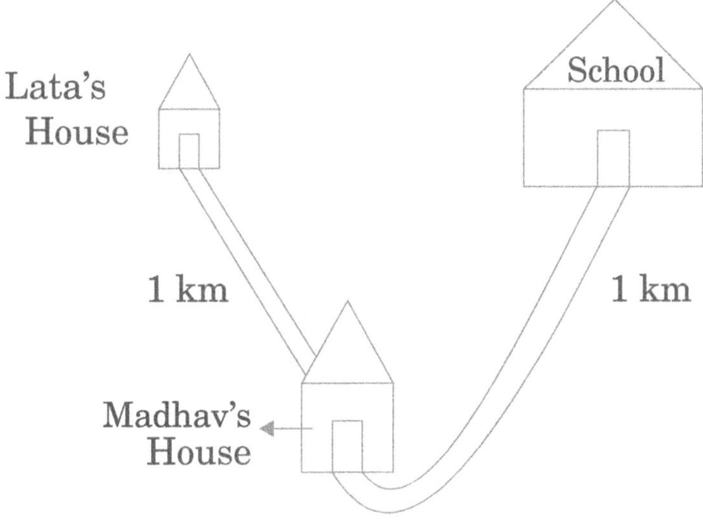

(a) 2 km　　　　(b) 3 km　　　　(c) 1 km　　　　(d) 15 km

6. There are 10 people in the rope skipping race, 5 fell down. How many people did not fall?

(a) 2　　　　(b) 5　　　　(c) 1　　　　(d) 3

7. In the given figure, how many flowers are there in the triangle as well as in the square?

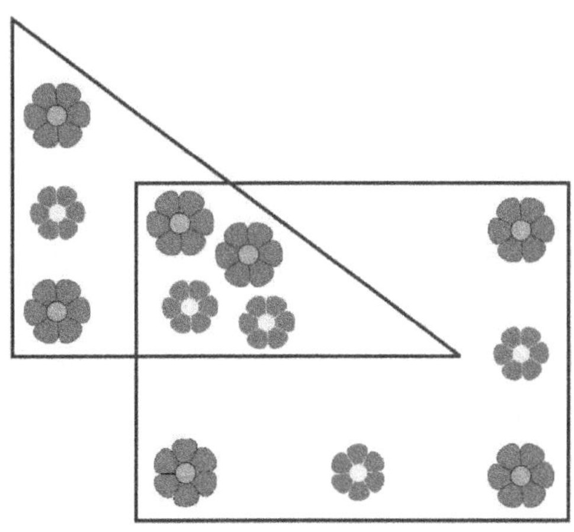

(a) 5　　　　(b) 4　　　　(c) 3　　　　(d) 6

Direction (Qs. 8 & 9): Three friends Rahul, Nikhil and Virat went to the zoo. Virat saw an elephant after both Rahul and Nikhil. Rahul saw the elephant second.

8. Who saw the elephant first?

    (a) Rahul   (b) Virat

    (c) Nikhil   (d) Cannot be determined

9. Who saw the elephant last?

    (a) Virat   (b) Rahul

    (c) Nikhil   (d) Cannot be determined

10. Sheena has 16 friends. She took 7 of them to the movie. How many friends couldn't go to the movie?

    (a) 9   (b) 6   (c) 8   (d) 10

11. Meeta ate 3 Pastries, Johnny ate 5 Pastries, and Grandma ate 7 Pastries. How many Pastries did Johnny and Grandma eat altogether?

    (a) 7   (b) 12   (c) 14   (d) 20

Direction (Qs. 12 & 13): Shalu, Kesha, Rehana and Pari each likes different colours. Rehana likes pink colour. Shalu does not like yellow colour. Pari likes orange colour and Kesha does not like red colour.

12. Who likes red colour?

    (a) Pari   (b) Shalu   (c) Rehana   (d) Kesha

13. Who likes yellow colour?

    (a) Kesha   (b) Pari   (c) Rehana   (d) Shalu

14. Tripti ate 4 apple pies and 6 blueberry pies. How many pies did Tripti ate?

    (a) 5   (b) 7   (c) 4   (d) 10

15. Neena had 8 flowers in her garden. Two of them plucked. Now she has __________ flowers.

    (a) 6   (b) 5   (c) 2   (d) 1

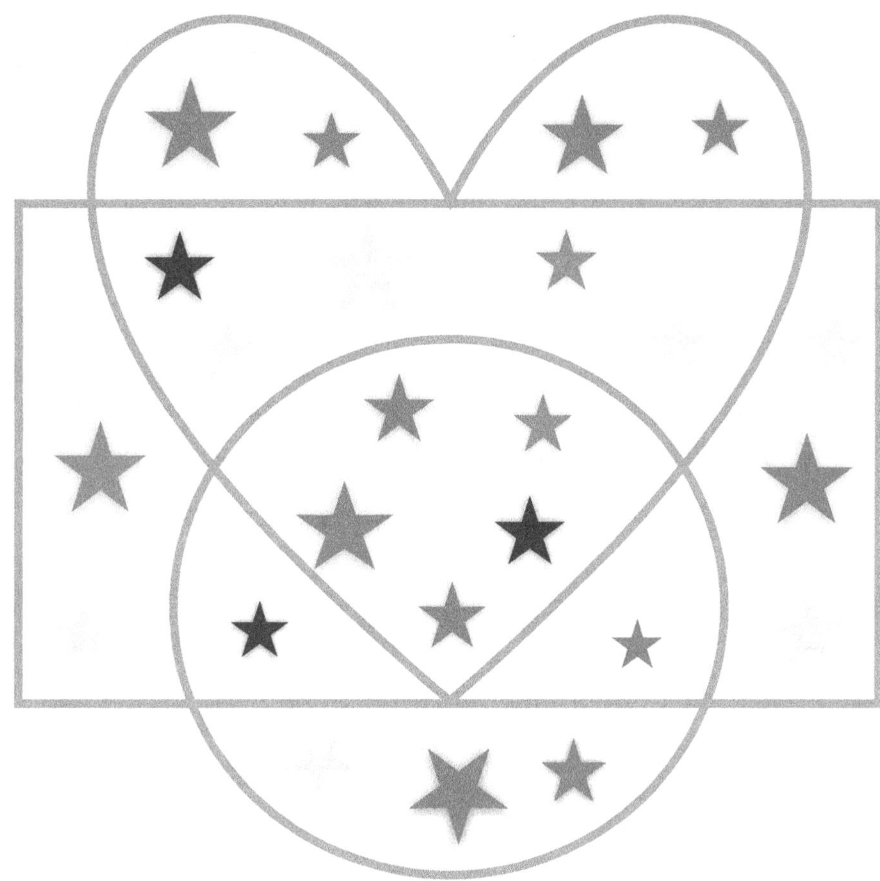

16. How many stars are there in the heart but not in the rectangle/circle?

    (a) 14   (b) 10   (c) 5   (d) 4

17. How many stars are there in rectangle as well as in circle but not in heart?

    (a) 5   (b) 2   (c) 7   (d) 10

18. How many stars are there in the given figure?

    (a) 20   (b) 22   (c) 24   (d) 26

19. Whack-a-worm is a gaming machine and Shreya is playing on it. There are 48 worms in total. Shreya whacked 26 worms. How many worms did she miss?

    (a) 28   (b) 22   (c) 30   (d) 10

20. Shreya cooked 50 burgers. She ate 20 burgers. How many burgers was she left with?

    (a) 50 – 30   (b) 50 – 20   (c) 50 + 30   (d) 50 + 20

21. Jayesh sold 16 hot dogs with Mustard. He sold 14 hot dogs with relish. How many hot dogs here sold by Jayesh altogether?

    (a) 10   (b) 12   (c) 30   (d) 35

Direction (Qs. 22 & 23): Study the information carefully to answer the questions.

Pinki, Ridhima, Raghav and Mohit are sitting around a dining table facing the centre. Pinki is sitting just right to the Ridhima. Ridhima is sitting just right to the Mohit. Raghav is sitting between Pinki and Mohit.

22. Who is sitting just left of Raghav?

    (a) Mohit   (b) Pinki

    (c) Ridhima   (d) Cannot be determined

23. Who is sitting just right of Mohit?

    (a) Raghav   (b) Ridhima

    (c) Pinki   (d) Cannot be determined

24. There were 35 brinjals in the contest. The judges picked 4 brinjals as finalists. How many brinjals were not finalists?

    (a) 30   (b) 31   (c) 20   (d) 32

25. Monster Deriff made Tony scream 28 times. Siya screamed 18 times. How many times did they scream altogether?

    (a) 26   (b) 46   (c) 56   (d) 36

26. Which of the following items can Aaryan buy from the given amount of money?   (2019)

(a)   (b)   (c)   (d)

27. If Tarun's birthday is on second Saturday of August 20XX, then on which date will Tarun celebrate his birthday? **(2019)**

AUGUST 20XX

Sun	Mon	Tue	Wed	Thu	Fri	Sat
			1	2	3	4
5	6	7	8	9	10	11
12	13	14	15	16	17	18
19	20	21	22	23	24	25
26	27	28	29	30	31	

(a) 12th August   (b) 11th August   (c) 10th August   (d) 18th August

28. If Kartik's birthday falls on 4th Tuesday of January 20XX, then on which date will he celebrate his birthday? **(2020)**

JANUARY 20XX

Sun	Mon	Tue	Wed	Thu	Fri	Sat
			1	2	3	4
5	6	7	8	9	10	11
12	13	14	15	16	17	18
19	20	21	22	23	24	25
26	27	28	29	30	31	

(a) 14th January (b) 7th January   (c) 28th January (d) 27th January

29. Nimit's birthday falls on 2nd Saturday of November 20XX. On which date is Nimit's birthday **(2020)**

NOVEMBER 20XX

Sun	Mon	Tue	Wed	Thu	Fri	Sat
1	2	3	4	5	6	7
8	9	10	11	12	13	14
15	16	17	18	19	20	21
22	23	24	25	26	27	28
29	30					

(a) 7th November   (b) 8th November

(c) 14th November   (d) 15th November

30. Palak's school's annual day function is on 3rd Saturday of May 20XX. On which date is the school's annual day function? **(2022)**

MAY 20XX						
Sun	Mon	Tue	Wed	Thu	Fri	Sat
	1	2	3	4	5	6
7	8	9	10	11	12	13
14	15	16	17	18	19	20
21	22	23	24	25	26	27
28	29	30	31			

(a) 19th May   (b) 20th May   (c) 13th May   (d) 27th May

LEVEL-2

1. Ram has five fruits with him: Banana, Apple, Guava, Mango, Pineapple. He wants to eat a fruit which:

– Has "e" in its name

– Its name is a 5 letter word

Which fruit should he eat?

(a) Apple   (b) Banana   (c) Guava   (d) Mango

2. When was the car sold?

   A. Month in which the car was sold starts with M.

   B. Name of the month is of 5 letters.

   (a) May   (b) March   (c) Monday   (d) None

3. Ana has 4 chocolates. If she eats one chocolate, how many chocolates are left?

   (a) 4   (b) 3   (c) 5   (d) 0

Direction (Qs. 4 & 5): Three friends A, B and C participate in a race. C finishes after both A and B. A finishes second.

4. Who won the race?

   (a) A   (b) B

   (c) C   (d) Cannot be determined

5. Who came last in the race?

(a) A   (b) B

(c) C   (d) Cannot be determined

6. There are 10 dogs and cats in the store. 5 of the pets are dogs. 3 of the cats are white. How many cats are there?

(a) 2   (b) 3   (c) 4   (d) 5

7. Raj needs 20 cherries to make a pie. Which two boxes does he buy?

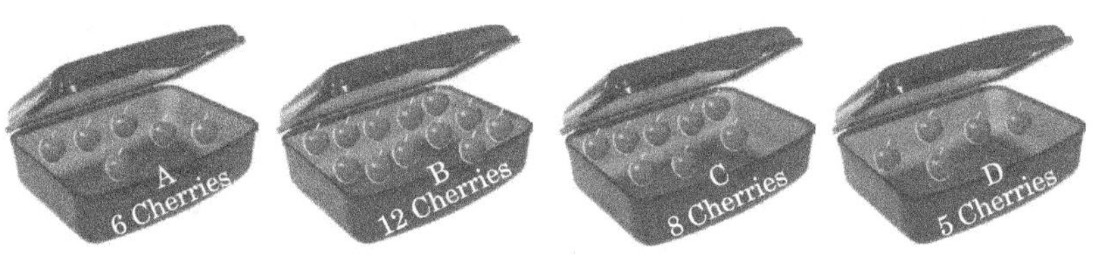

(a) A and B   (b) B and C   (c) C and D   (d) A and D

8. Joseph can go swimming, to the zoo or to the circus. It is too cold to swim. He is tired of going to the zoo. Where does Joseph go?

(a) Zoo   (b) Circus

(c) Swimming pool   (d) Cannot be determined

Direction (Qs. 9-11): There are three houses labelled with numbers. Read the given statements and answer the following questions.

Statements:

Binny: My name is Binny. I live between Bobby and Billy.

Billy: My house is red. I don't live in house number 3.

Bobby: My house is blue. Binny is my neighbour.

9. Whose house colour is green?

    (a) Binny   (b) Billy   (c) Bobby   (d) None

10. Who lives in house No. 3?

    (a) Binny   (b) Billy   (c) Bobby   (d) None

11. Who is the neighbour of Billy?

    (a) Binny   (b) Bobby   (c) Both   (d) None

Direction (Qs. 12 & 13): Emily, Bea and Ryan, each lives in different cities. Emily does not live in Delhi and Mumbai. Bea does not live in Jaipur and Delhi.

12. Where does Emily live?

    (a) Delhi   (b) Mumbai   (c) Jaipur   (d) None

13. Who does not live in Mumbai?

    (a) Emily   (b) Bea

    (c) Ryan   (d) Emily and Ryan

Direction (Qs. 14 & 15): Raj, Dev and Manav are going to beach, each using a different mode of transportation.

- Dev drives the car.

- Manav hates motorcycle.

14. Who drives motorcycle?

    (a) Raj   (b) Dev   (c) Manav   (d) No one

15. Who drives boat?

    (a) Raj   (b) Dev   (c) Manav   (d) No one

16. Mary, Frank, Bob and Juhi all went out for the night party. Mary danced with Bob.

    Who is the dance partner of Frank?

    (a) Mary   (b) Bob   (c) Juhi   (d) None

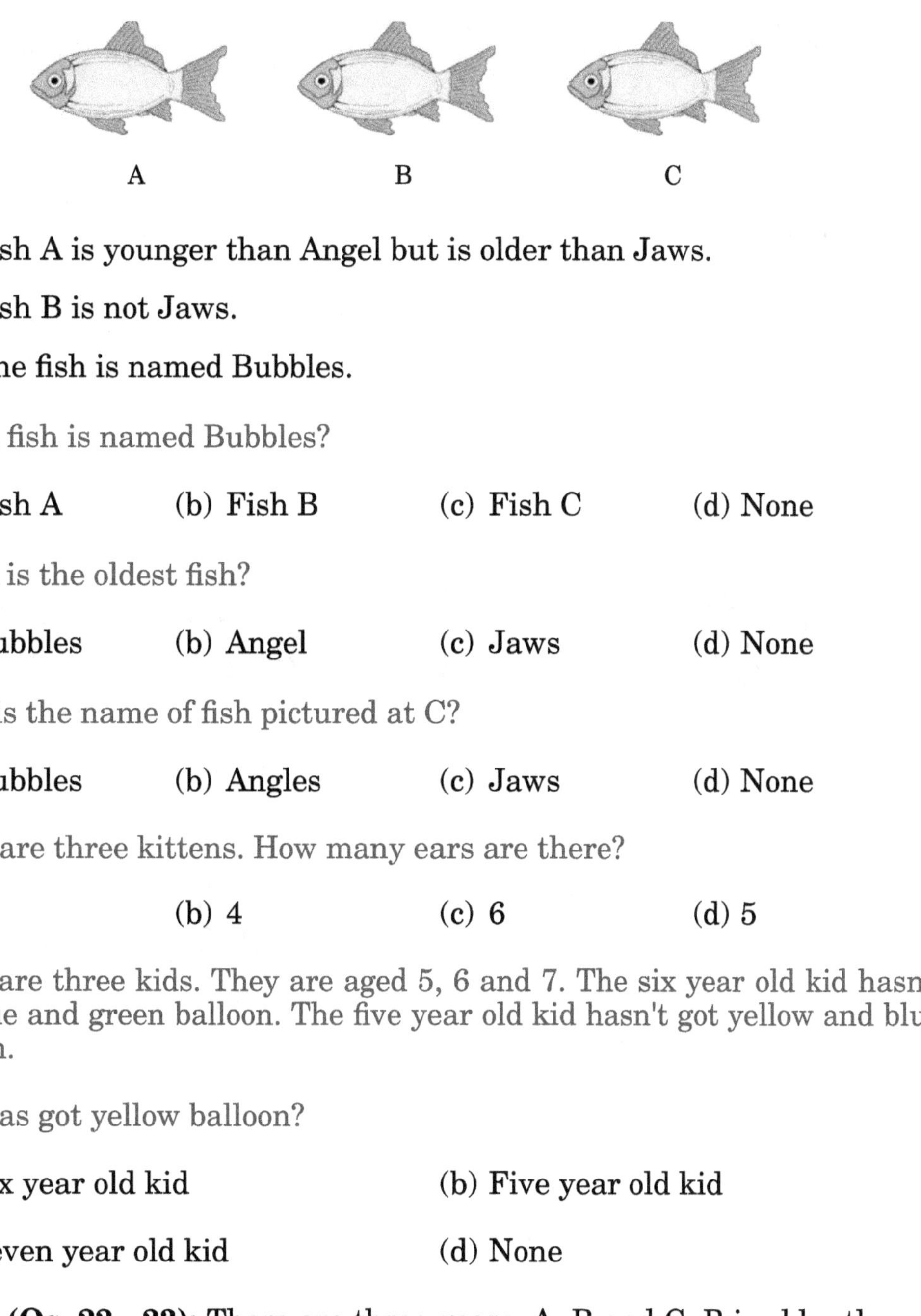

- Fish A is younger than Angel but is older than Jaws.
- Fish B is not Jaws.
- One fish is named Bubbles.

17. Which fish is named Bubbles?

    (a) Fish A   (b) Fish B   (c) Fish C   (d) None

18. Which is the oldest fish?

    (a) Bubbles   (b) Angel   (c) Jaws   (d) None

19. What is the name of fish pictured at C?

    (a) Bubbles   (b) Angles   (c) Jaws   (d) None

20. There are three kittens. How many ears are there?

    (a) 8   (b) 4   (c) 6   (d) 5

21. There are three kids. They are aged 5, 6 and 7. The six year old kid hasn't got blue and green balloon. The five year old kid hasn't got yellow and blue balloon.

    Who has got yellow balloon?

    (a) Six year old kid   (b) Five year old kid

    (c) Seven year old kid   (d) None

Direction (Qs. 22 - 23): There are three geese, A, B and C. B is older than C and younger than A.

22. Who is the youngest?

    (a) A   (b) B   (c) C   (d) None

23. Who is the oldest?

(a) A   (b) B   (c) C   (d) None

24. Raj, Amit and Dev are sitting in a row. Raj is sitting between Amit and Dev. Which of the following is the correct order?

(a) | Raj | Amit | Dev | (b) | Dev | Amit | Raj |

(c) | Amit | Raj | Dev | (d) | Raj | Dev | Amit |

25. Four friends are celebrating their birthdays.

The candles on the cake show their ages.

Who is the oldest among them.

(a) Ankit   (b) Ruchi   (c) Parul   (d) Anu

26. Given two baskets show the number of apples.

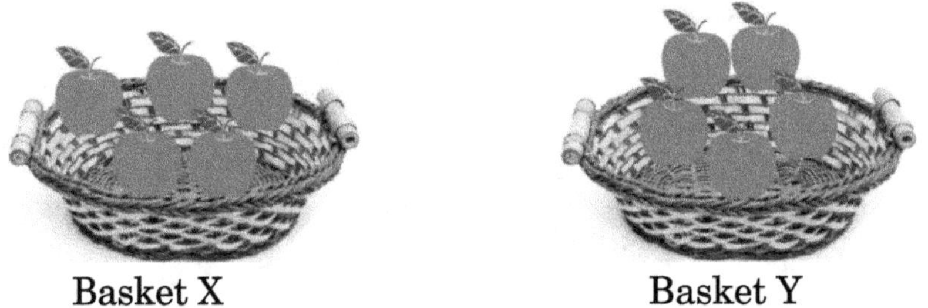

Basket X   Basket Y

Which of the following statements is correct?

(a) Basket X has more apples than Basket Y.

(b) Basket X has one apple less than basket Y.

(c) Basket Y has more apples than Basket X.

(d) Both Baskets X and Y have equal apples.

Direction (Qs. 27 - 28): Study the following information carefully and answer the questions given below.

Bunty, Dev and Manav are sitting around a circle facing the centre. Dev is sitting between Bunty and Manav. Manav is sitting first right to Bunty.

27. Who is sitting to the left of Dev?

    (a) Bunty   (b) Manav   (c) Both   (d) None

28. Who is sitting to the left of Bunty?

    (a) Dev   (b) Manav   (c) Both   (d) None

29. Ankita, Priyanka, Monika and Sunita have apples as shown below:
                                                                    (2022)

Ankita   Priyanka   Monika   Sunita

Who has apples more than 9 but less than 11?

(a) Ankita   (b) Priyanka   (c) Monika   (d) Sunita

30. Which one of the following boxes has the same number of spoons? **(2022)**

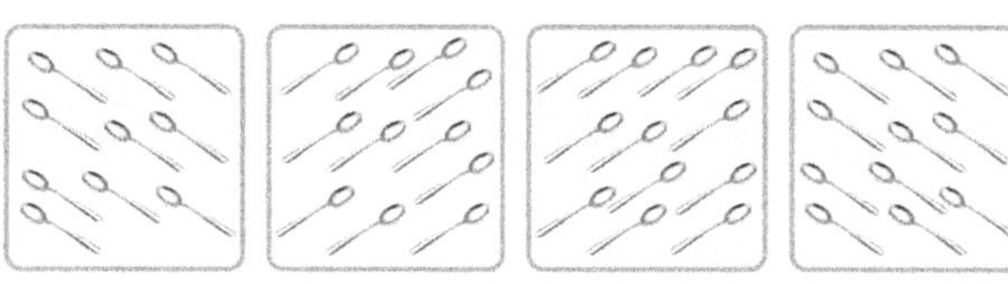

Box (1)   Box (2)   Box (3)   Box (4)

(a) Box (1) and box (3)   (b) Box (2) and box (4)

(c) Box (1) and box (2)   (d) Box (3) and box (4)

Level-1

1. **(c)** Amit is the tallest among them.

2. **(d)** Sonia needs to buy five eggs.

3. **(a)** Total biscuits = 7

   Anu has biscuits = 5

   Charu has = 7 – 5 = 2

   So, (a) is the correct answer.

4. **(a)** There are 8 dots in the circle but not in the rectangle.

5. **(a)** Distance between Lata's home to Madhav's home

   = 1 km

   Distance between Madhav's home to school = 1 km

   Distance covered by Lata

   = 1 + 1 = 2 km

   So, the correct answer is (a).

6. **(b)**

   Number of people in race = 10

   Number of people fell down = 5

   Number of people did not fall = 10 – 5

   = 5

7. **(b)** There are 4 flowers in the triangle as well as in the square.

8. **(c)** Nikhil > Rahul > Virat

      (I)   (II)   (III)

   So, Nikhil saw the elephant first.

9. **(a)** Virat saw the elephant last.

10. **(a)** Sheena has 16 friends and with seven of her friends she went to movie. The rest 16 – 7 = 9 friends couldn't go to movies.

11. **(b)**

   Johnny ate = 5 Pastries

   Grandma ate = 7 Pastries

   Altogether = 5 + 7 = 12 Pastries

(12-13):

	Pink	Red	Orange	Yellow
Shalu		✓		
Kesha				✓
Rehana	✓			
Pari			✓	

12. **(b)** Shalu likes red colur.

13. **(a)** Kesha likes yellow colour.

14. **(d)**

   Tripti ate = 4 apple pies

   Tripti ate = 6 blueberry pies

   Total = 4 + 6 = 10 pies

15. **(a)**

   Neena had = 8 flowers

   Plucked = 2 flowers

   Now she has = 8 – 2 = 6 flowers

16. **(d)** There are 4 stars in the heart but not in rectangle/circle.

17. **(b)** There are 2 stars in rectangle as well as in the circle but not in heart.

18. (c) There are 24 stars in the given figure.

19. (b)

Total number of worms = 48

Shreya whacked = 26 worms

Total number of worms she missed

$$= 48 - 26 = 22$$

20. (b)

Number of cooked = 50
burgers

Number of burgers = 20
eaten by Shreya

Number of burgers = 50 – 20 = 30
needed by her to
complete the total

So, She was left 30 burgers.

21. (c)

Number of Mustard = 16
hot dogs sold by
Jayesh

Number of Relish = 14
hot dogs sold by
Jayesh

Altogether = 16 + 14 = 30

(22-23):

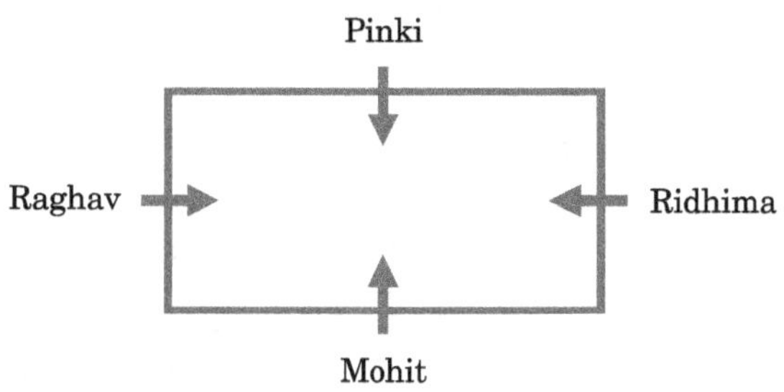

22. (b) Pinki is sitting just left of Raghav.

23. (b) Ridhima is sitting just right of Mohit.

24. (b)

Total number of = 35
brinjals in the
contest

Number of brinjals = 4
that were picked as
finalists

Total number of = 35 – 4 = 31
brinjals not finalised
in the contest are

25. (b)

Monster Deriff made = 28 times
Tony scream

Siya screamed = 18 times

Number of times they = 28 + 18 = 46
screamed altogether

26. (c) The total money is Rs 85. Therefore, only book can be bought from that much amount.

27. (b)

28. (c) 1st Tuesday falls on ⇒ 7 January

2nd Tuesday falls on ⇒ 7 + 7 = 14 January

3rd Tuesday falls on ⇒ 14 + 7 = 21 January

4th Tuesday falls on ⇒ 21 + 7 = 28 January

So, Kartik will celebrate his birthday on 28th January.

29. (c) 1st Saturday on = 7th November

2nd Saturday on = 14th November

So, Nimit's birthday date is 14th November.

30. (b) 20th May is the third Saturday of May.

Level-2

1. (a) Apple has "e" in its name and it is a five letter word.

2. (b) March has 5 letters.

3. (b) Ana has 4 – 1 = 3 chocolates.

4. (b) B > A > C

   (I) (II) (III)

B won the race.

5. (c) C came last in the race.

6. (d) Total pets = 10

Number of dogs = 5

Number of cats =10 – 5 = 5.

7. (b) Number of cherries in Box B = 12

Number of cherries in Box C = 8

Total cherries = 12 + 8 = 20.

8. (b) Joseph goes to circus.

(9-11) :

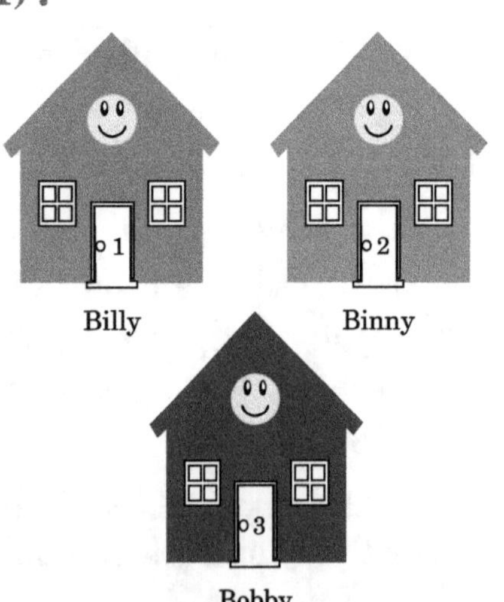

9. (a)

House Number - 1 ⇒ Billy → Red colour

House Number - 2 ⇒ Binny → Green colour

House Number - 3 ⇒ Bobby → Blue colour

10. (c) Bobby lives in House number 3.

11. (a) Binny is the neighbour of billy.

(12-13) :

Person	Places
Emily	Jaipur
Bea	Mumbai
Ryan	Delhi

12. (c) Emily does not live in Delhi and Mumbai, hence she lives in Jaipur.

13. (d) So, Emily and Ryan do not live in Mumbai.

(Qs 14-15):

People	Transport
Raj	Motorcycle
Dev	Car
Manav	Boat

14. (a) Raj drives motorcycle.

15. (c) Manav drives boat.

16. (c) Mary was the partner of Bob.

So, Juhi was the partner of Frank.

(17-18):

Fish B > Fish A > Fish C

(Angel) (Bubbles) (Jaws).

17. (a) Fish A is named Bubbles.

Fish B is named Angel.

Fish C is named Jaws.

18. (b) Fish B is the oldest fish.

19. (c) The name of fish pictured at C is Jaws.

20. (c) One kitten has 2 ears.

Three kitten has $2 + 2 + 2 = 6$ ears.

21. (a) Six years old kid has Yellow balloon.

(22-23): A > B > C

22. (c) C is the youngest.

23. (a) A is the oldest.

24. (c) | Amit | Raj | Dev | is correct.

25. (b) Ruchi is oldest among them.

26. (d) Both Basket X and Y have 5 apples each.

(27-28):

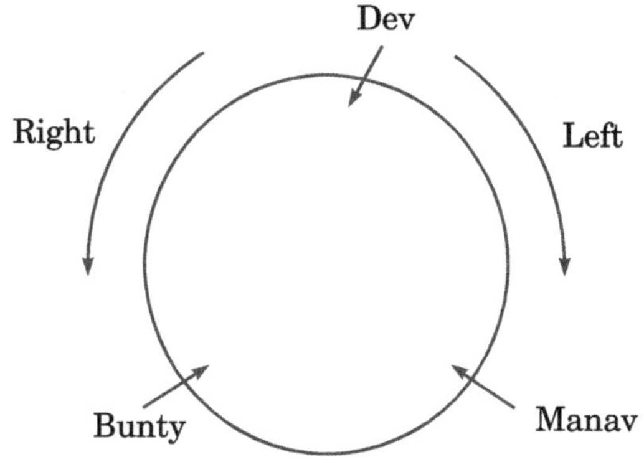

Circular Arrangement

27. (b) Manav is sitting left of Dev.

28. (a) Dev is sitting left of Bunty.

29. (b) Ankita has 8 apples.

Priyanka has 10 apples. $\rightarrow 9 < 10 < 11$.

Monika has 11 apples.

Sunita has 9 apples.

So, Priyanka has apples more than 9 but less than 11.

30. (b) Box (1) has 10 spoons.

Box (2) has 11 spoons.

Box (3) has 12 spoons.

Box (4) has 11 spoons.

So, Box (2) = Box (4) = 11 spoons.

Estimation

CHAPTER 7

OBJECTIVES

- Students will involve in estimating real-life quantities such as distances, areas and volumes.
- Estimation allows students to make judgements about how much time, money, food..... they will need.
- In estimation, students use their mathematical reasoning which ultimately saves time and money.

INTRODUCTION

Estimation is a rough calculation of the value, number, quantity, or extent of something.

Examples:

1. How many sweets are there in the box? Estimate.

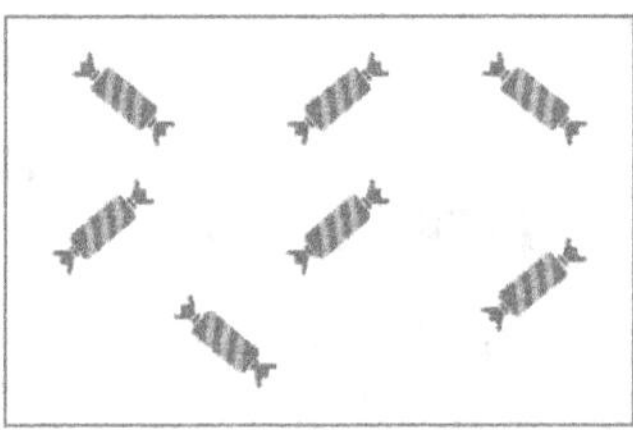

   (a) 6   (b) 7   (c) 8   (d) 9

Ans. (b) There are 7 sweets in the box

2. Reha went to the zoo and saw some Giraffes and Alligators. She made a picture graph of the animals at the zoo:

| Alligators | | | | | | | |
| Giraffes | | | | | | | |

Which animal did she see fewer of ?

(a) Alligators   (b) Giraffes   (c) Both   (d) None of them

Ans. (b) Count the number of each animal in the graph. She saw 7 Alligators and 3 Giraffes. So, she saw fewer Giraffes.

3.   Which bus is the shortest among them?

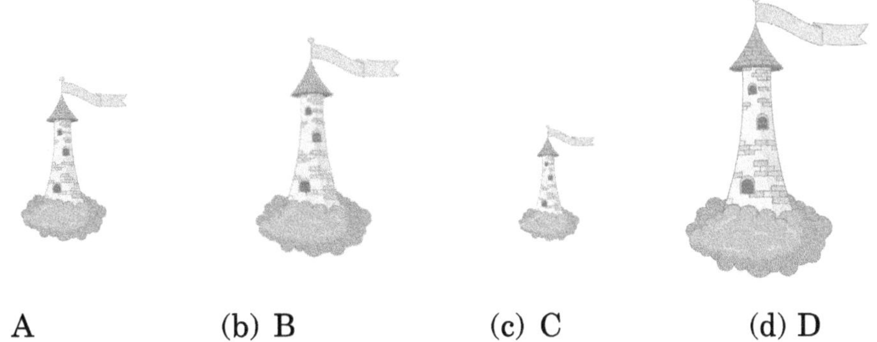

(a) P   (b) Q   (c) R   (d) S

Ans. (d) Bus S is shortest among them.

4.   Which tower is taller than B?

(a) A   (b) B   (c) C   (d) D

Ans. (d) Tower D is taller than B.

5.   Estimate the weight of an eraser.

(a) 2 g   (b) 2 kg   (c) 200 g   (d) 5 kg

Ans. (a) The estimated weight of a rubber is 2 g.

LEVEL-1

1. Which sofa is longest among them?

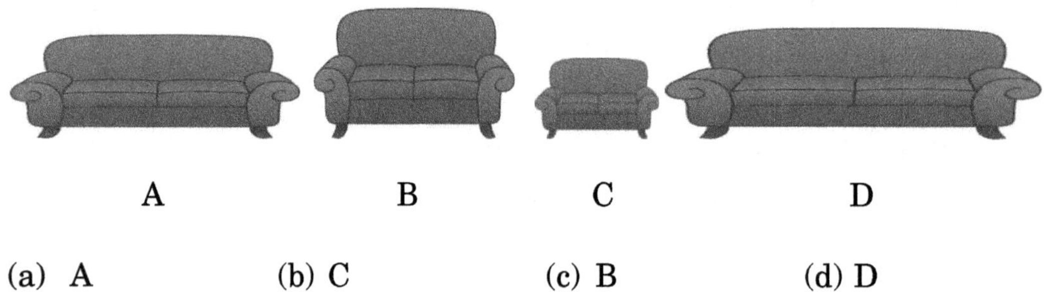

    A   B   C   D

  (a) A   (b) C   (c) B   (d) D

2. Raj's candy basket has 3 gumballs, 5 chocolates, 6 jelly beans. Raj has fewer lollipops than gumballs. How many lollipops are there in Raj's candy basket?

  (a) 6   (b) 4   (c) 3   (d) 2

3. Which bug is smaller than bug G?

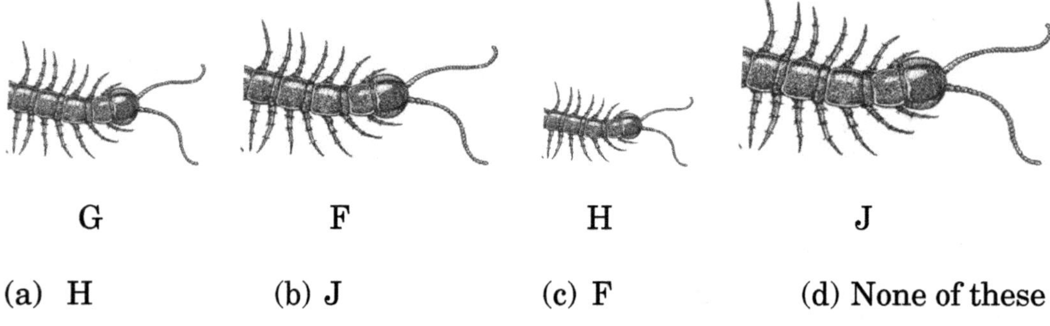

    G   F   H   J

  (a) H   (b) J   (c) F   (d) None of these

4. The wild animal park has 5 lions. It has more tigers than lions. How many tigers does the wild animal park have?

  (a) 4   (b) 3   (c) 5   (d) 6

5. Estimate the weight of a pen.

  (a) 10 g   (b) 5 kg   (c) 10 kg   (d) 500 g

6. Which shape is most in numbers?

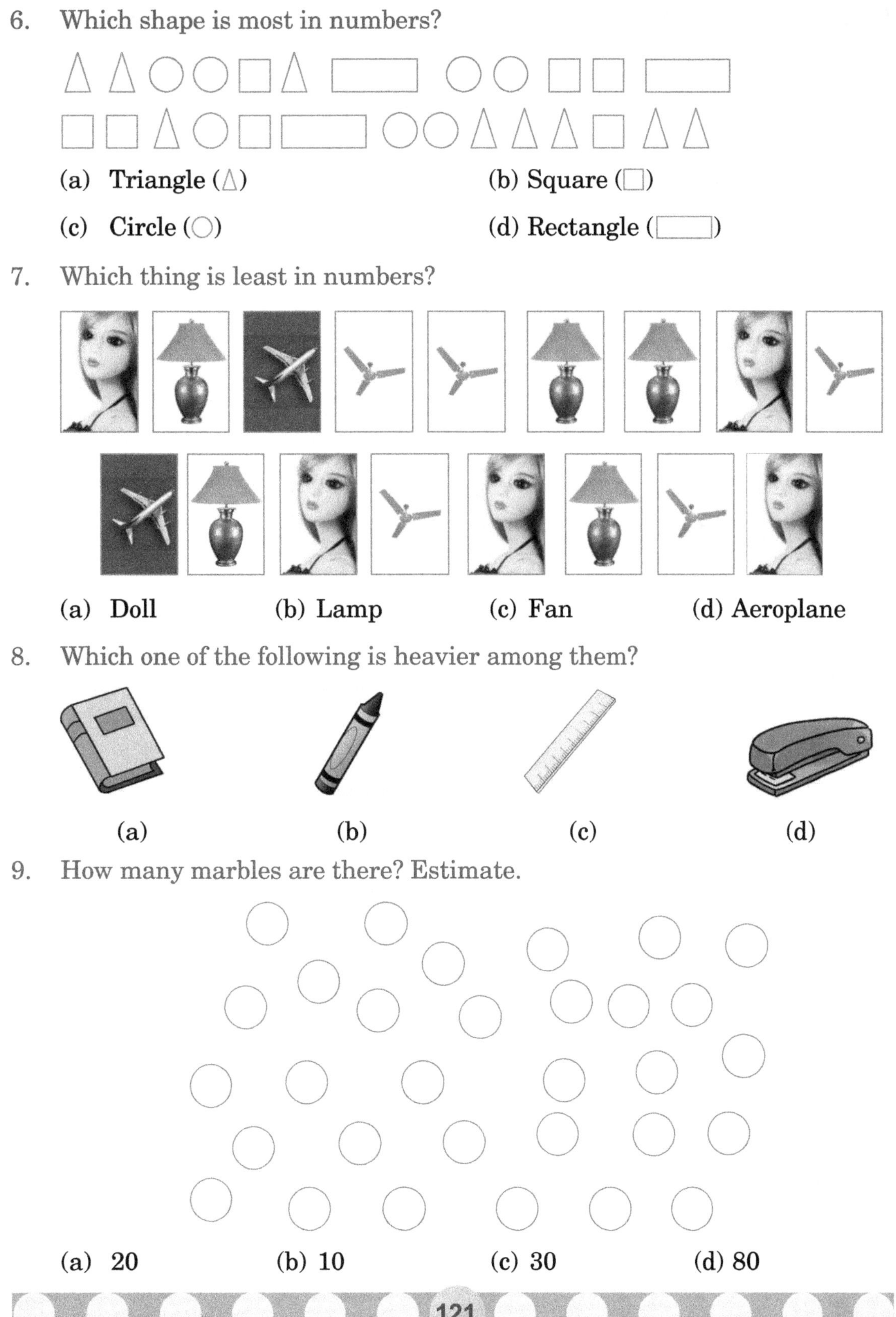

(a) Triangle (△)   (b) Square (□)

(c) Circle (○)   (d) Rectangle (▭)

7. Which thing is least in numbers?

(a) Doll   (b) Lamp   (c) Fan   (d) Aeroplane

8. Which one of the following is heavier among them?

(a)   (b)   (c)   (d)

9. How many marbles are there? Estimate.

(a) 20   (b) 10   (c) 30   (d) 80

Direction (Qs. 10 & 11): Estimate the time of each activity given below:

10. To cook dinner
    (a) about 3 second
    (b) about 1 day
    (c) about 1 minute
    (d) about 1 hour

11. To drink a glass of milk
    (a) about 4 hours
    (b) about 10 seconds
    (c) about 3 days
    (d) about 30 minutes

12. Which of the following holds more water in it?

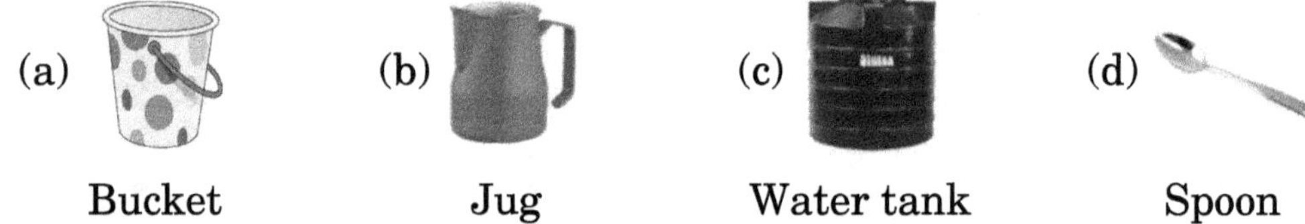

| (a) Bucket | (b) Jug | (c) Water tank | (d) Spoon |

13. Which one of the following is lightest among them?

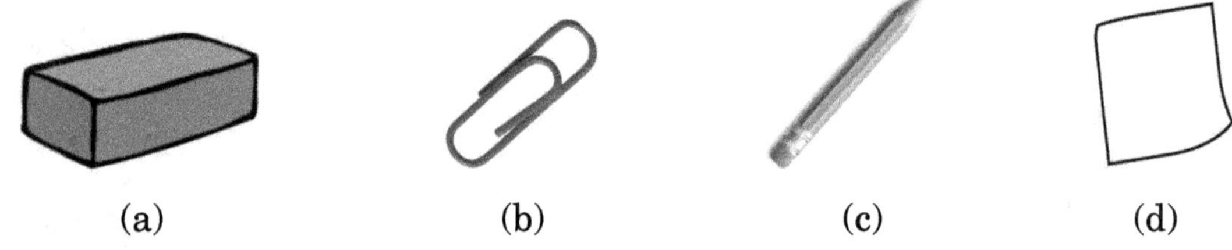

(a)   (b)   (c)   (d)

14. Observe the picture, which of the following statement is correct?

    (a) The teddy bear is as heavy as the book.
    (b) The teddy bear is lighter than the book.
    (c) The teddy bear is heavier than the book.
    (d) None of these

15. How many flowers are there? Estimate.

   (a) Around 20   (b) Around 30   (c) Around 60   (d) Around 80

Directions (Qs. 16-18): Estimate the weight of each object.

16. Book 

   (a) 3 kg   (b) 40 kg   (c) 3 g   (d) 9 g

17. Apple 

   (a) 10 g   (b) 7 g   (c) 7 gm   (d) 100 gm

18. Mobile phone 

   (a) 15 g   (b) 150 kg   (c) 100 g   (d) 20 kg

19. Which is the best estimate for the weight of a strawberry ?

    (a) 1 kg   (b) 500 gms   (c) 25 gms   (d) 1 gm

20. Which is the best estimate for the weight of a car?

    (a) 1000 kg   (b) 100 g   (c) 10 kg   (d) 500 kg

21. Which is the best estimate for the weight of a television set?

    (a) 15 gms   (b) 1 kg   (c) 15 kg   (d) 1 ton

22. Which is the best estimate for the weight of a DVD disc?

    (a) 5 kgs   (b) 1 kg   (c) 500 gm   (d) 15 gm

23. What is the approximate weight of your school bag packed with books ?

   (a) 50 gms   (b) 5 kgs   (c) 50 kgs   (d) 20 kgs

24. Which of the following will be the heaviest ?

   (a) A tennis ball   (b) A cricket (cork) ball

   (c) A football   (d) A table tennis ball

25. Which of the following is arranged in the correct order of weight (from light to heavy)?

   (a) Badminton racket, Cricket bat, Hockey stick

   (b) Hockey stick, Badminton racket, Cricket bat

   (c) Hockey stick, Cricket bat, Badminton racket

   (d) Badminton racket, Hockey stick, Cricket bat

26. Which of the following amount is enough to buy the given toy guitar?

(2021)

(a)    (b) 

(c)    (d) 

LEVEL-2

1. Which of the following is arranged in the correct order of weight (from light to heavy)?

   (a) Motorcycle, Truck, Car   (b) Car, Motorcycle, Truck

   (c) Motorcycle, Car, Truck   (d) Truck, Car, Motorcycle

Direction (Qs. 2 & 3): Observe the pictures given below and answer the questions that follow.

2. How many boxes can the truck occupy?

   (a) 6   (b) 8   (c) 12   (d) 16

3. How many elephants can the truck occupy ?

   (a) 1   (b) 4   (c) 6   (d) 2

Direction (Qs. 4-7): Choose the best answer.

4. My bedroom's length is less than

   (a) 10 metres   (b) 10 centimeters

   (c) 1 metre   (d) 500 millimeters

5. The height of my classroom is more than

   (a) 100 metres   (b) 10 metres   (c) 2 metres   (d) 50 feet

6. Who covers the most distance in 10 minutes ?

   (a) Elephant   (b) Deer   (c) Horse   (d) Tiger

7. Who covers the most distance in an hour ?

   (a) Helicopter   (b) Rocket   (c) Aeroplane   (d) Bullet Train

8. Flower L is shorter than __________ and __________.

B   C   L   M

(a) B and M   (b) M and C   (c) B and C   (d) None of these

9. Who is farthest from the house among them?

(a) Pihu   (b) Misha   (c) Golu   (d) Rinku

10. The day before today is __________, if tomorrow will be Monday.

Yesterday	Today	Tomorrow
?		Monday

(Olympiad)

(a) Sunday   (b) Saturday   (c) Tuesday   (d) Friday

11. __________ is the lightest.

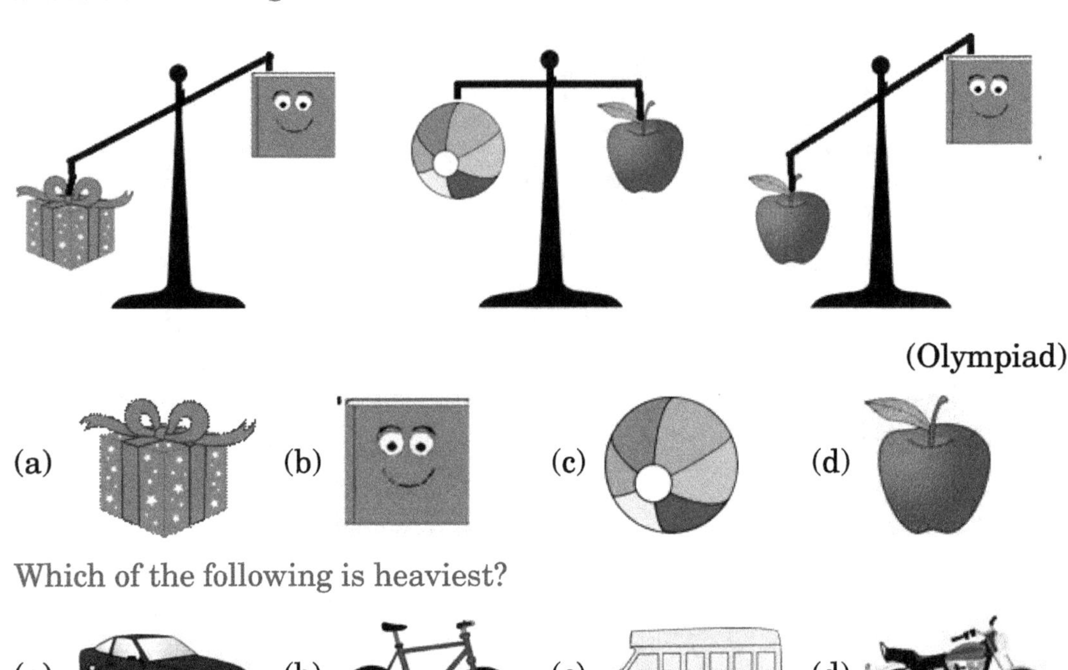

(a) (b) (c) (d)

12. Which of the following is heaviest?

(a) (b) (c) (d)

13. The activity shown here is occurring in the __________.

(a) Morning   (b) Afternoon   (c) Evening   (d) Night

14. Identify the shortest thread.

(a)   (b)   (c)   (d)

15. __________ is the heaviest.

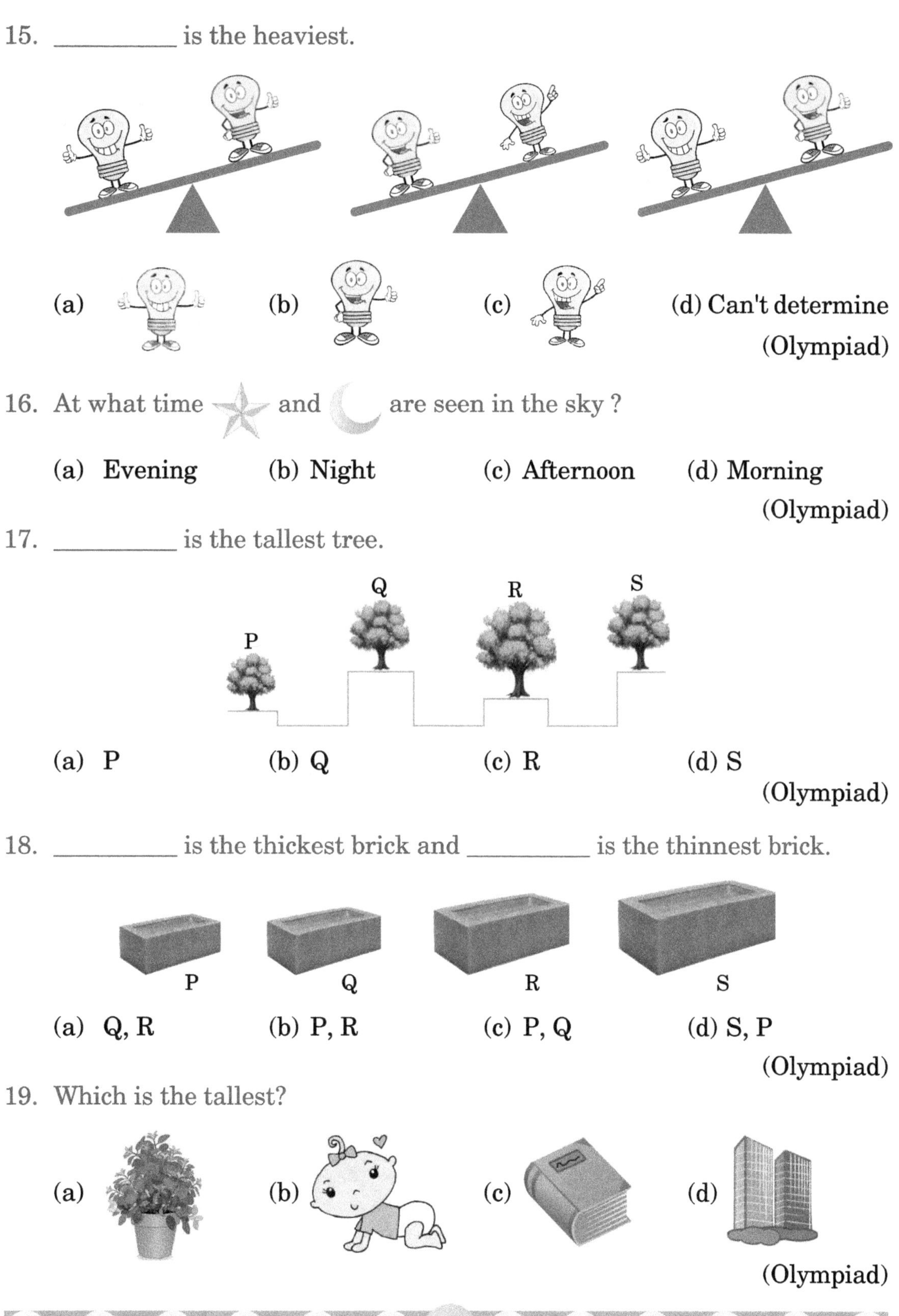

(a)   (b)   (c)   (d) Can't determine
(Olympiad)

16. At what time ⭐ and 🌙 are seen in the sky ?

(a) Evening   (b) Night   (c) Afternoon   (d) Morning
(Olympiad)

17. __________ is the tallest tree.

(a) P   (b) Q   (c) R   (d) S
(Olympiad)

18. __________ is the thickest brick and __________ is the thinnest brick.

(a) Q, R   (b) P, R   (c) P, Q   (d) S, P
(Olympiad)

19. Which is the tallest?

(a)   (b)   (c)   (d)
(Olympiad)

20. The watermelon is ___________ apples in the given figure.

(a) Heavier than   (b) Lighter than

(c) As heavy as   (d) Can't be determined

(Olympiad)

21. Raju's family is having __________ in the __________.

(a) Breakfast, Morning   (b) Dinner, Night

(c) Tea, Evening   (d) Lunch, Afternoon

(Olympiad)

22. Which is the thickest?

(a)    (b)    (c)    (d)

(Olympiad)

23. Which is the lightest?

(a) 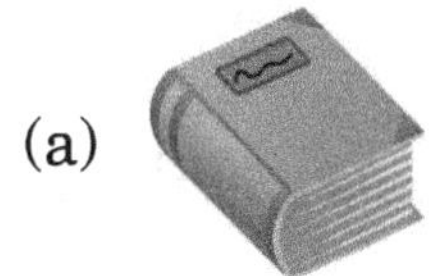　　(b) 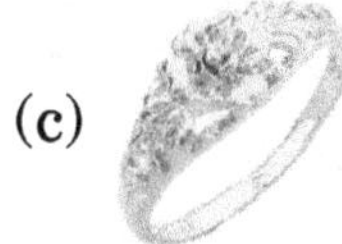　　(c) 　　(d)

(Olympiad)

24. Kunal is sleeping in the __________ .

(a) Night　　　(b) Morning　　　(c) Evening　　　(d) Afternoon

(Olympiad)

25. The grapes are __________ bananas in the given figure.

(a) Heavier than　　　　　　(b) Lighter than

(c) As heavy as　　　　　　(d) Can't be determined

(Olympiad)

Level-1

1. (d) Sofa D is longest among them.

2. (d) There are 2 lollipops in Raj's candy basket.

3. (a) Bug H is smaller than bug G.

4. (d) There are 6 tigers in the wild animal park.

5. (a) The weight of a pen is 10 g.

6. (a) Triangle ($\triangle$) is most in numbers.

7. (d) Aeroplane is least in number.

8. (a) Book is heavier among them.

9. (c) There are 31 marbles.

10. (d) About 1 hour.

11. (b) About 10 seconds.

12. (c) Water tank holds more water.

13. (d) Paper is lightest among them.

14. (b) The teddy bear is lighter than the book.

15. (b) There are around 30 flowers.

16. (a) The estimated weight of a book is 3 kg.

17. (d) The estimated weight of an apple is 100 gm.

18. (c) The estimated weight of a mobile phone is 100 g.

19. (c) 25 gms

20. (a) 1000 kg

21. (c) 15 kg

22. (d) 15 gm

23. (b) 5 kgs

24. (b) A cricket ball

25. (d) Badminton racket, Hockey stick, Cricket bat

26. (c) ₹ 77 is less than ₹ 100 So ₹ 100 rupees not is enough to buy the guitar.

1. (c) Motorcycle, Car, Truck

2. (d) The truck can occupy two boxes widthwise and two boxes heightwise and four boxes lengthwise.

   So total boxes = 4 × 2 × 2 = 16

3. (b) The truck can occupy one baby elephant widthwise and four lengthwise.

   So total baby elephants
   = 1 × 4 = 4.

or

4. (a) 10 metres

5. (c) 2 metres

6. (d) Tiger

7. (b) Rocket

8. (c) Flower L is shorter than B and C.

9. (c) Golu is farthest from the house.

10. (b)

Yesterday	Today	Tomorrow
Saturday	Sunday	Monday

   The day before is Saturday, if tomorrow will be Monday.

11. (b)  is the lightest.

12. (c) is the heaviest.

13. (a) The activity shown there occurring in the morning.

14. (a) Figure (a) is the shortest thread.

15. (a)

16. (b)

17. (c)

18. (d)

19. (d)

20. (a)

21. (b)

22. (c)

23. (b)

24. (a)

25. (b)

Spatial Understanding

INTRODUCTION

Spatial understanding is an organised knowledge of objects including oneself in a given space. Spatial understanding also involves understanding of these objects when there is a change of position and form.

Questions asked in this chapter are based on following topics.

Inside / Outside, Above / Below, Top / Bottom, Far / Near, On / Under, Thick / Thin and Few More

Examples:

1. Number of balls inside the net is ____________.

    (a) 7   (b) 6   (c) 5   (d) 2

Ans. (a) Number of balls inside the net is 7.

2. Number of apples outside the box is ____________.

    (a) 2   (b) 8   (c) 3   (d) 4

Ans. (c) Number of apples outside the box is 3

3. How many flowers are outside the vase?

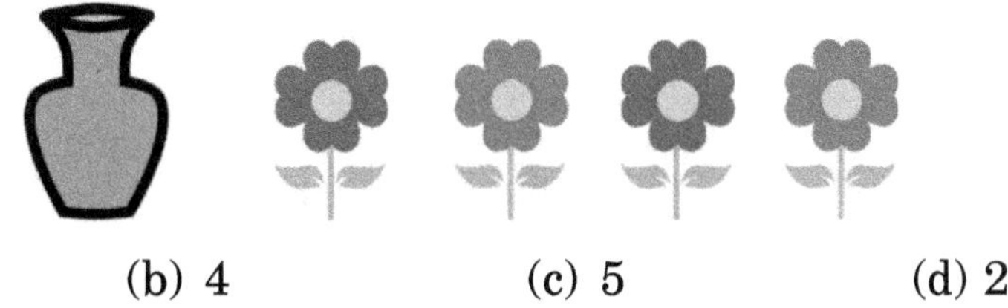

    (a) 3   (b) 4   (c) 5   (d) 2

Ans. (b) 4 flowers are outside the vase.

Direction (Examples 4 and 5): Observe the picture carefully and answer the following questions.

4. How many children are there inside the bus?

    (a) 2   (b) 3   (c) 1   (d) 4

Ans. (d) There are 4 children inside the bus.

5. How many children are standing outside the bus?

    (a) 5   (b) 7   (c) 3   (d) 0

Ans. (a) There are 5 children standing outside the bus.

1. How many balls are there outside the box?

(a) 12   (b) 15   (c) 3   (d) 20

2. How many students are there outside the bus?

(a) 7   (b) 5   (c) 4   (d) 9

3. How many birds are sitting on the tree?

(a) 4   (b) 3   (c) 2   (d) 6

Direction (Qs. 4 & 5): Observe the following picture carefully and answer the following questions.

4. How many apples are on the ground?

   (a) 7   (b) 5   (c) 8   (d) 3

5. How many apples are on the middle tree?

   (a) 12   (b) 13   (c) 16   (d) 18

6. How many creatures are on the jar?

   (a) 7   (b) 3   (c) 2   (d) 6

Direction (Qs. 7-9): Study the following picture carefully and answer the following questions.

7. How many birds are flying in the picture?

    (a) 3 (b) 2 (c) 4 (d) 5

8. How many hens are near the house?

    (a) 3 (b) 2 (c) 4 (d) 5

9. How many hens are far from the house?

    (a) 3 (b) 2 (c) 4 (d) 5

Direction (Qs. 10 - 11): Study the following picture carefully and answer the following questions.

10. How many students are there in the second row?

    (a) 3   (b) 5   (c) 4   (d) 6

11. How many students have raised their hands in the class?

    (a) 5   (b) 4   (c) 6   (d) 3

12. Where is the cat sitting?

    (a) Behind the first table   (b) Between the tables

    (c) Under the second table   (d) On the first table

13. Match the following:

Group A	**Group B**
(1)	(A) Between
(2)	(B) Behind
(3)	(C) On
(4)	(D) Under

    (a) 1-C, 2-D, 3-A, 4-B   (b) 1-C, 2-A, 3-D, 4-B

    (c) 1-A, 2-D, 3-B, 4-C   (d) 1-C, 2-B, 3-D, 4-B

14. __________ cherries are on the tree and __________ cherries are under the trees.

   (a) 20, 11   (b) 20, 14   (c) 18, 16   (d) 20, 12

                                                              (Olympiad)

15. The birds in the given image are flying __________ the house.

   (a) Inside   (b) Above   (c) Below   (d) Under

                                                              (Olympiad)

16. How many mangoes are there in the figure?   **(2020)**

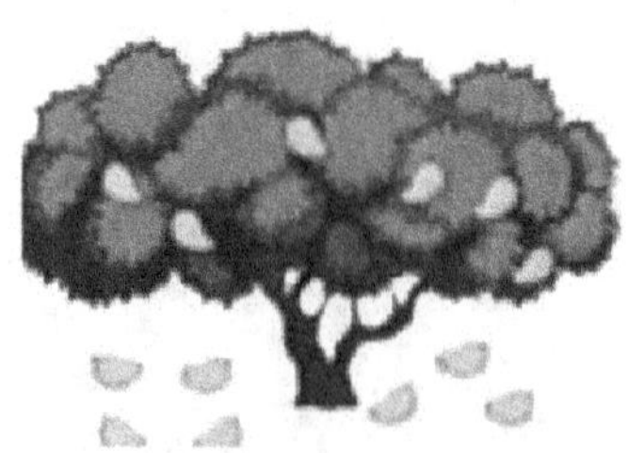

   (a) 10   (b) 12   (c) 15   (d) 13

17. ________ is kept on the table.   **(2020)**

(a) Cake   (b) Cat   (c) Ball   (d) Birthday cap

18. There are ________ laddoos inside the tiffin box.   **(2022)**

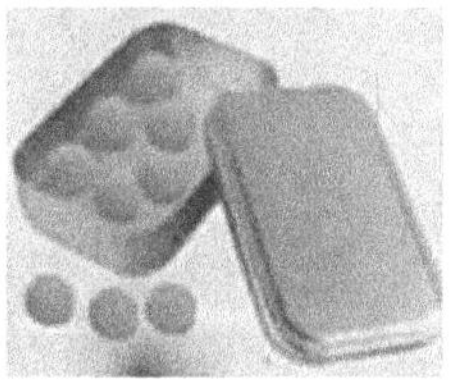

(a) 6   (b) 3   (c) 9   (d) 7

LEVEL-2

Direction (Qs. 1-3): Study the following picture carefully and answer the following questions.

1. How many kids are playing volleyball on the beach?

(a) 4   (b) 6   (c) 2   (d) 3

2. How many kids are flying kites in the picture?

(a) 2   (b) 3   (c) 1   (d) 0

3. How many kids are inside the life tube?

(a) 2   (b) 1   (c) 3   (d) 0

Direction (Qs. 4-6): Study the following picture carefully and answer the following questions.

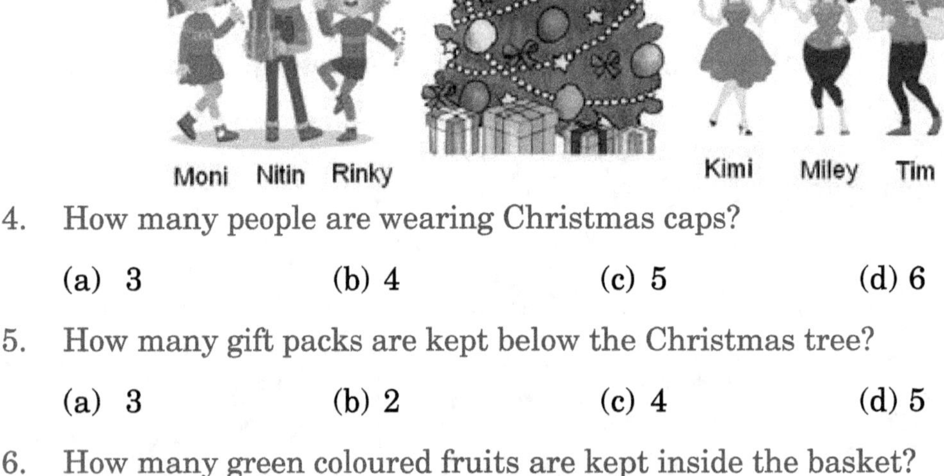

4. How many people are wearing Christmas caps?

(a) 3   (b) 4   (c) 5   (d) 6

5. How many gift packs are kept below the Christmas tree?

(a) 3   (b) 2   (c) 4   (d) 5

6. How many green coloured fruits are kept inside the basket?

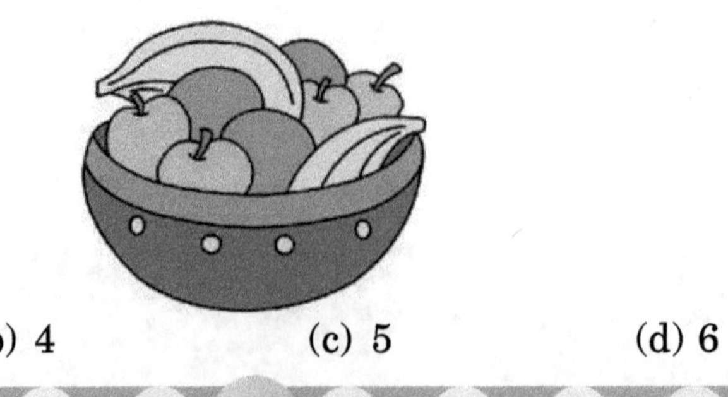

(a) 3   (b) 4   (c) 5   (d) 6

Direction (Qs. 7-10): Study the following picture carefully and answer the following questions.

7. Which of the following statements is/are correct?

    (a) Heffalump is sitting between Piglet and Tigger.

    (b) Tigger is standing in between Piglet and Pooh.

    (c) Piglet is standing in front of the table.

    (d) Pooh is sitting on the table.

8. Number of cup cakes on the table are _________.

    (a) 2   (b) 4   (c) 5   (d) 3

9. Which of the following statements is/are correct?

    (a) There are two glasses of milk on the table.

    (b) Altogether there are 7 members in the party.

    (c) There are five cup cakes on the table.

    (d) There are two chairs behind the table.

10. Number of butterflies flying over Pooh and Piglet are _________.

    (a) 4   (b) 5   (c) 2   (d) 3

Direction (Qs. 11 & 12): Study the following pictures carefully and answer the following questions.

11. Number of ducklings inside the pond are _________.

    (a) 4   (b) 2   (c) 5   (d) 3

12. Number of ducklings outside the pond are _________.

    (a) 4   (b) 7   (c) 5   (d) 2

Direction (Qs. 13-15): Study the following picture carefully and answer the following questions.

13. Number of sheep near the house is/are _________.

    (a) 4   (b) 5   (c) 1   (d) 2

14. Who is standing between sheep and duck?

    (a) Cow   (b) Duck   (c) Hen   (d) Dog

15. Number of rabbits in the picture is/are _________.

    (a) 1   (b) 2   (c) 3   (d) 0

16. The goat is standing _______ the tree. **(2022)**

   (a) At   (b) In   (c) Under   (d) Above

17. Car is parked ____ the building. **(2022)**

   (a) Above   (b) Under   (c) On   (d) Outside

Level-1

1. (c) 3 balls are there outside the box.

2. (d) There are 9 students outside the bus.

3. (b) 3 birds are sitting on the tree.

4. (d) 3 apples are on the ground.

5. (a) There are 12 apples on the middle tree.

6. (c) There are 2 creatures on the jar.

7. (c) There are four birds flying in the picture.

8. (a) 3 hens are near the house.

9. (b) 2 hens are far from the house.

10. (c) 4 students are in the second row.

11. (b) 4 students have raised their hands in the class.

12. (b) Between the tables.

13. (a) 1-C, 2-D, 3-E, 4-B, 5-A

14. (d) 20 cherries are on the tree and 12 cherries are under the tree.

15. (b) The birds in the image are flying above the house.

16. (d) Mangoes in the figure = 4 + 3 + 2 + 1 + 3 = 13

17. (a) Only 'Cake' is kept on the table and rest are not on the table.

18. (a) There are 6 laddoos inside the tiffin box and 3 laddoos outside the tiffin box.

Level-2

1. (c) 2 kids playing volleyball on the beach.

2. (a) 2 kids are flying kites in the picture.

3. (b) Only one kid is inside the life tube.

4. (b) 4 people are wearing Christmas caps.

5. (c) 4 gift packs are kept below the Christmas tree.

6. (b) 4 green coloured fruits are kept inside the basket.

7. (b) Tiger is standing in between Piglet and Pooh.

8. (a) 2 cup cakes on the table.

9. (d) There are two chairs behind the table.

10. (c) 2 butterflies are flying over Pooh and Piglet.

11. (b) 2 ducklings are inside the pond.

12. (a) 4 ducklings are outside the pond.

13. (c) 1 sheep is near the house.

14. (d) Dog is standing between sheep and duck.

15. (a) 1 rabbit is in the picture.

16. (c)

17. (d) Car is parked out side the building.

Geometrical Shapes

OBJECTIVES

- Students will know the properties of different 2D and 3D shapes.
- Students will recognise difference between 2D and 3D shapes.
- Students will learn how to move a shape around, enlarge it, rotate it without it being changed in shape.

INTRODUCTION

Geometry is all about shapes and their properties. Geometrical shapes consists of points, lines, planes, square etc.

SHAPES AND THEIR NAMES

2D Geometrical Shapes

1. = Rectangle
2. = Square
3. = Circle
4. = Oval
5. = Triangle

3D Geometrical Shapes

= Cube

= Cuboid

= Sphere

= Cone

= Cylinder

LINES

Slanting Lines	=	
Vertical Lines	=	
Horizontal Lines	=	
Curved Lines	=	
Ray	=	

All slanting, vertical and horizontal lines are straight lines.

Examples:

Type-1: Identify Shapes

1. Which one of the following is a square?

    (a)   (b)   (c)   (d)

Ans. (b)

A square has four equal sides.

Type-2: Count Sides/Corner

2D Geometrical Figures:

Shape	Sides	Corners
Rectangle	4	4
Square	4	4
Triangle	3	3
Circle/Oval	0	0

3D Geometrical Figures:

Shape	Edges	Vertices
Cube	12	8
Cuboid	12	8
Sphere	0	0
Cone	1	1
Cylinder	2	0

2. How many corners does this shape have?

(a) 4   (b) 2   (c) 5   (d) 3

Ans. (d)

A triangle has three corners.

Type-3: Similar Shapes

3. Which shape is similar to the group of three given below?

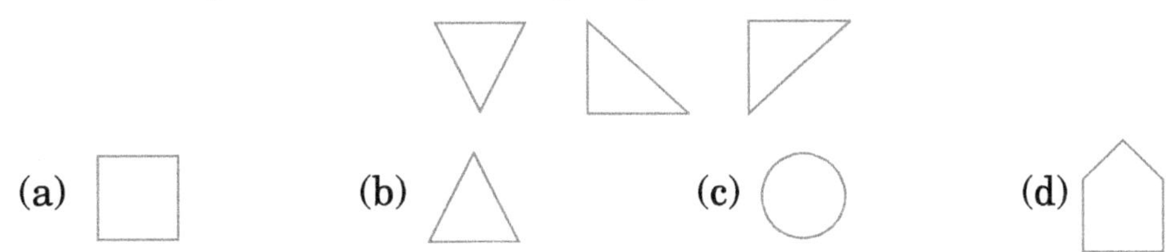

(a)   (b)   (c)   (d)

Ans. (b)

Option (b) is similar to the group of three figures. So, option (b) is the correct answer.

Type-4: Hidden Shapes

4. In which of the following figures is the shape ↑ hidden?

(a)   (b)   (c)   (d)

Ans. (c)

Option (c) has the exact hidden shape.

1. There are __________ triangles in the given figure.

   (a) 2   (b) 3   (c) 4   (d) 5

2. Which one of the following is a circle?

   (a)   (b)   (c)   (d)

3. Tick the right name of the shape that is given below.

   (a) Circle   (b) Square   (c) Triangle   (d) Rectangle

4. Which of these is a cylinder?

   (a) 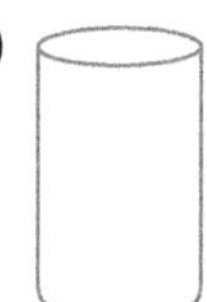   (b)   (c)    (d) 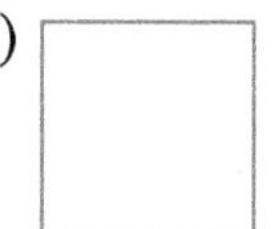

5. Riya draws a face as shown below

Count the number of circles in the face.

(a) 4   (b) 5   (c) 6   (d) 8

6. Which object is shaped like a cube?

P   Q   R   S

(a) S   (b) Q   (c) P   (d) R

7. Given is the name of a geometrical shape but some letters are missing in it. Identify the name of the shape.

_______ _______ C T A N G _______ _______

(a) Circle   (b) Rectangle   (c) Triangle   (d) Square

8. How many sides does a Triangle have?

(a) 2   (b) 3   (c) 1   (d) 0

9. How many sides does a Rectangle have?

(a) 2   (b) 4   (c) 3   (d) 5

10. How many straight lines are there in the figure given below?

(a) 6   (b) 7   (c) 10   (d) 8

11. A cone shape looks like _______________.

(a) Building   (b) Sun   (c) Pyramid   (d) Box

12. Identify the flat shape.

(a) N (b) P (c) M (d) O

13. Identify the cone shape.

P Q R S

(a) Q (b) R (c) S (d) P

14. A circle has _____________ sides or corners.

(a) 4 (b) 5 (c) 0 (d) 1

15. Which one of these can roll?

(a) (b) (c) (d)

16. A line that extended in one direction known as _____________.

(a) Line (b) Slanting line

(c) Ray (d) Sleeping line

17. An oval has _____________ sides.

(a) Five (b) Four (c) Eight (d) No

18. Which shape has more corners?

(a) P (b) R (c) Q (d) S

19. Name the shaded part of this figure.

    (a) Cylinder   (b) Square   (c) Oval   (d) Triangle

20. Which of the following is made up of 2 curved lines?

    (a) 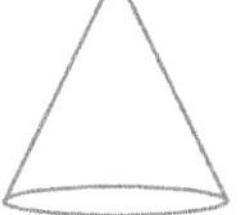   (b) 

    (c) 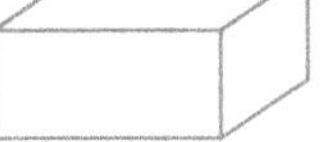   (d) 

21. How many edges a cuboid has?

    (a) 8   (b) 10   (c) 12   (d) 5

22. Match the following.

A    (i) 

B   (ii)

C 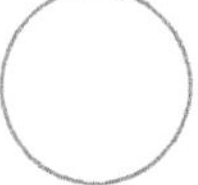   (iii)

D 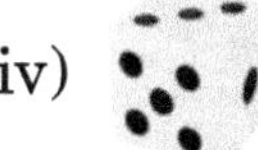   (iv)

    (a) A (iv)   B (iii)   C (i)   D (ii)
    (b) A (i)   B (ii)   C (iii)   D (iv)
    (c) A (iii)   B (iv)   C (i)   D (ii)
    (d) A (ii)   B (i)   C (iii)   D (iv)

Direction (Qs. 23-25): Observe the given figure carefully and answer the follow-ing questions.

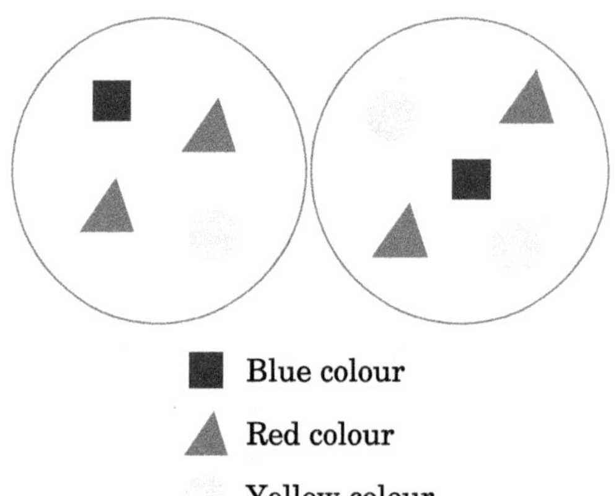

23. How many shapes are blue?

    (a) 3   (b) 6   (c) 4   (d) 2

24. How many circles are yellow?

    (a) 4   (b) 6   (c) 3   (d) 5

25. How many shapes are triangle?

    (a) 2   (b) 3   (c) 1   (d) 4

26. Name of the shape of the shaded portion is _________.

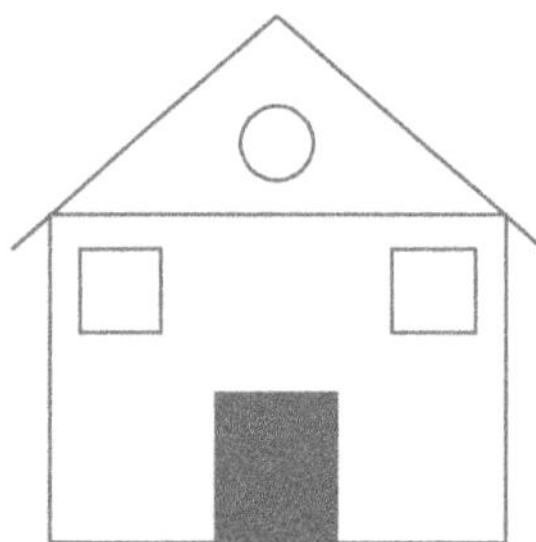

    (a) Square   (b) Rectangle   (c) Triangle   (d) Oval

27. Identify the shape of number 7 in the given figure.   **(2018)**

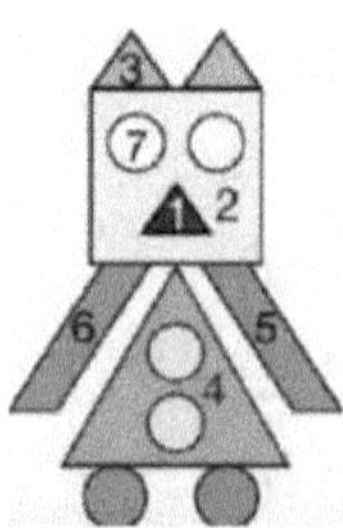

    (a) Circle   (b) Square   (c) Rectangle   (d) Triangle

28. Which of the following objects can slide but not roll?   **(2019)**

(a)   (b)    (c)    (d)

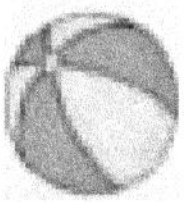

29. Which of the following objects can roll but not slide?   **(2020)**

(a)   (b)    (c) 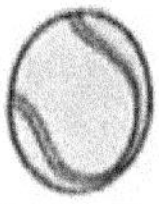   (d)

30. Which of the following objects can be used to draw a square?   **(2021)**

(a)    (b)    (c)    (d)

31. There are _______ slanting lines in the given figure.   **(2021)**

(a) 8   (b) 10   (c) 19   (d) 12

32. The number of triangles in the given figure is ______.   **(2022)**

(a) 4   (b) 5   (c) 7   (d) 6

33. Which of the following shapes is NOT present in the given figure? **(2022)**

(a) Circle   (b) Square   (c) Triangle   (d) Rectangle

34. How many squares are there in the figure given below? **(2022)**

(a) 12   (b) 14   (c) 15   (d) 17

LEVEL-2

1. Find the number of triangles in the given figure.

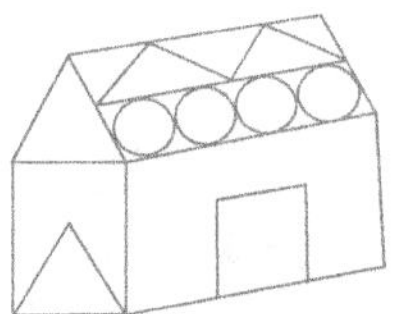

(a) 1   (b) 2   (c) 4   (d) 7

2. How many curved lines are there in the given figure?

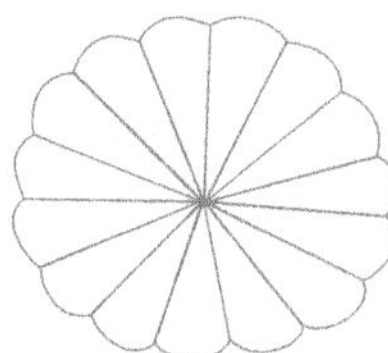

(a) 7   (b) 15

(c) 10   (d) 12

3. How many rectangles are there in the given figure?

(a) 3   (b) 4

(c) 6   (d) 2

4. Match the shapes in column I to the objects in column II.

Column I   Column II

A    1. 

B    2. 

C    3. 

D 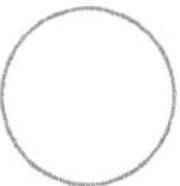   4. 

	A	B	C	D
(a)	2	3	4	1
(b)	1	3	4	5
(c)	4	3	2	1
(d)	3	2	4	1

5. Name the shape of the shaded face.

(a) Circle   (b) Triangle   (c) Square   (d) Rectangle

6. There are _______________ circles in the given figure.

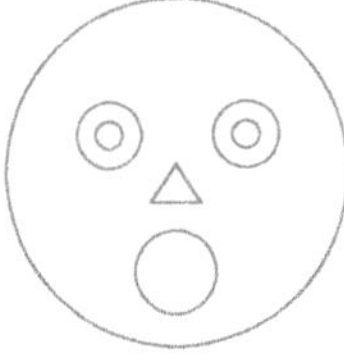

(a) 4   (b) 5   (c) 6   (d) 2

7. Study the figure carefully, which shapes are present in the figure?

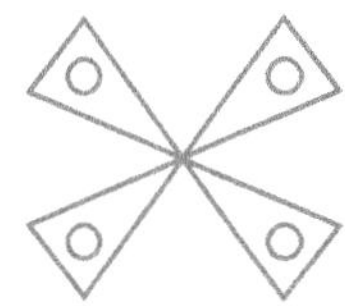

(a) Rectangle, square   (b) Triangle, circle

(c) Circle, square   (d) Rectangle, triangle

8. The figure is made up of 2 triangles and ___________.

(a) Circle   (b) Rectangle

(c) Square   (d) Oval

9. Which shape has 5 sides?

(a) 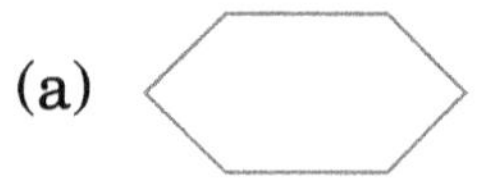   (b)    (c)    (d) 

10. How many straight lines does this figure has?

(a) 7   (b) 10   (c) 9   (d) 15

11. Look at this Yummy Pastry. How many circles does it have?

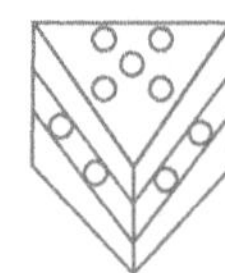

(a) 5   (b) 6   (c) 9   (d) 4

12. How many triangles are there in the given shape?

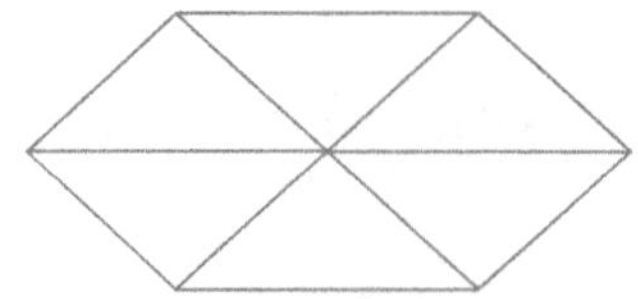

(a) 5   (b) 7   (c) 6   (d) 10

13. There are _______________ squares in the given figure.

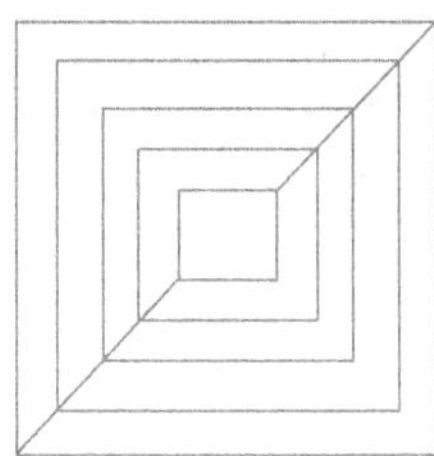

(a) 5   (b) 4   (c) 7   (d) 6

14. Match the shapes in Column I with their names in Column II.

Column I	Column II
A (rectangle face)	1. Circle
B (circle face)	2. Square
C (square face)	3. Triangle
D (triangle face)	4. Rectangle

(a) A – 4, B – 1, C – 2, D – 3   (b) A – 2, B – 3, C – 4, D – 1

(c) A – 1, B – 2, C – 3, D – 4   (d) A – 3, B – 4, C – 2, D – 1

15. Identify the object which is under the table.

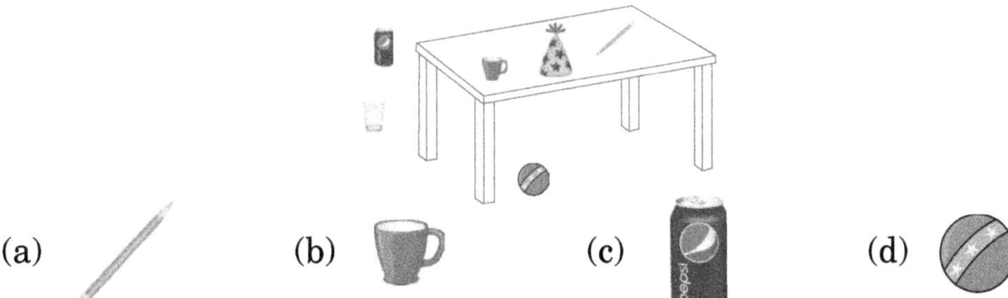

(a) (pencil)   (b) (mug)   (c) (pepsi can)   (d) (ball)

16. Choose the missing shape in the given clock.

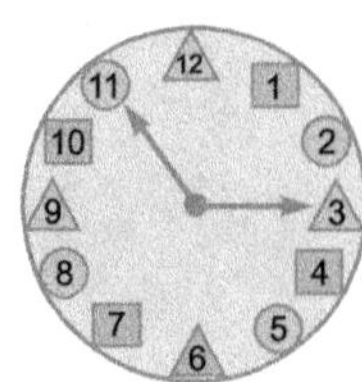

   (a) Circle   (b) Triangle   (c) Square   (d) Rectangle

(Olympiad)

17. Select the INCORRECT match.

   (a) Circle    (b) Square 

   (c) Triangle    (d) Rectangle 

(Olympiad)

18. Which of the following shapes is missing in the given image?

   (a) Rectangle   (b) Circle   (c) Triangle   (d) Square

(Olympiad)

19. There are _____________ less squares than triangles in the given figure.

   (a) 10   (b) 9   (c) 8   (d) 7

(Olympiad)

20 Identify the shapes marked as a, b and c.

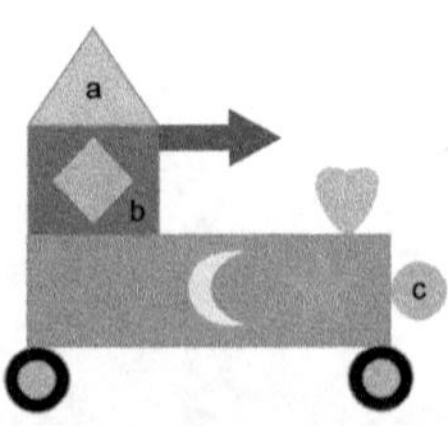

(a)	Square	Triangle	Rectangle
(b)	Triangle	Square	Circle
(c)	Triangle	Circle	Square
(d)	Square	Triangle	Circle

(Olympiad)

21. Count the number of triangles in the figure.

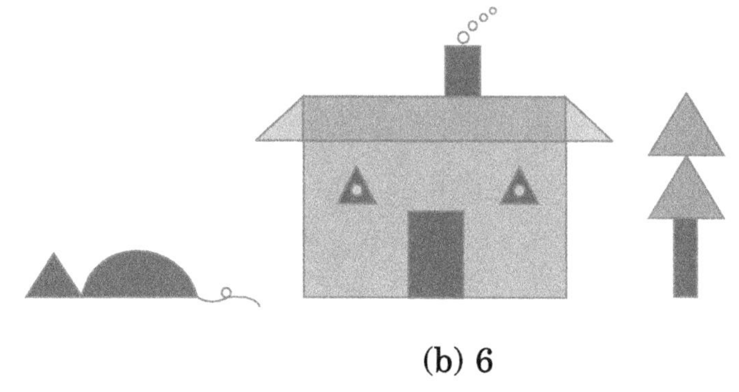

(a) 10   (b) 11   (c) 12   (d) 13

(Olympiad)

22. Shapes _____________ and _____________ will combine to form a square.

(a) P, R   (b) Q, S

(c) S, P   (d) Q, R

(Olympiad)

23. Count the number of triangles in the given figure.

(a) 5   (b) 6

(c) 7   (d) 8

(Olympiad)

24. This figure is made up of _____________ triangles.

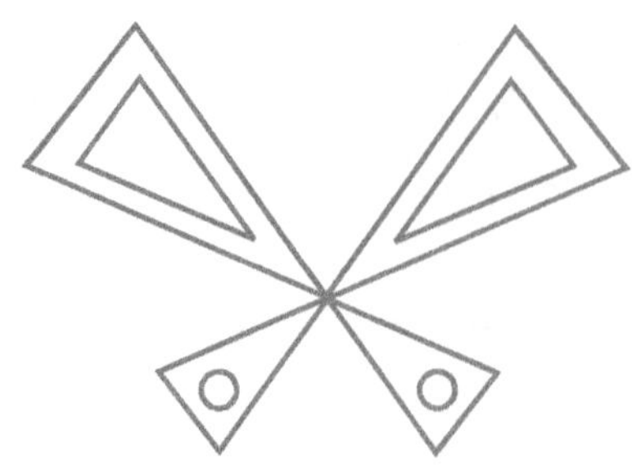

(a) 6   (b) 3   (c) 2   (d) 4

25. Name the shape which is shaded face in the given figure.

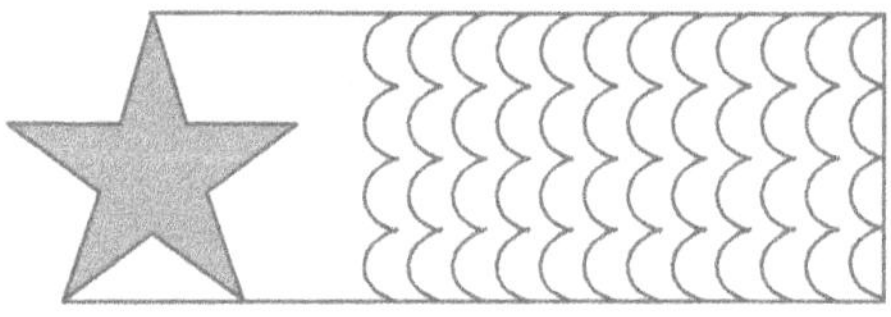

(a) Circle   (b) Star   (c) Square   (d) Triangle

26. Shapes _______ and _________ will form a square. **(2020)**

(a) P and Q   (b) P and R   (c) Q and R   (d) P and S

27. There are ______ circles in the given figure. **(2021)**

(a) 14   (b) 10

(c) 13   (d) 9

28. If Vijay's birthday is on the second Thursday of July 20XX, then on which date will Vijay celebrate his birthday? **(2022)**

July 20XX						
Sun	Mon	Tue	Wed	Thu	Fri	Sat
			1	2	3	4
5	6	7	8	9	10	11
12	13	14	15	16	17	18
19	20	21	22	23	24	25
26	27	28	29	30	31	

(a) 2nd July   (b) 9th July   (c) 16th July   (d) 23rd July

Answers and Explanations

Level-1

1. **(b)** Triangles (R_1, R_2, R_3) = 3.

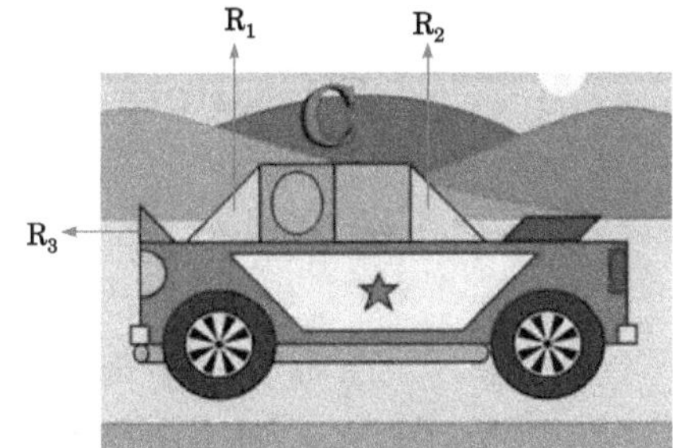

So, there are 3 triangles in the figure.

2. **(c)** It is clearly shown that option (c) is a circle.

3. **(d)** The shape given in the option (d) is a rectangle.

4. **(b)** The shape given in option (b) is a cylinder.

5. **(c)**

Circles $(C_1, C_2, C_3, C_4, C_5, C_6)$ = 6

So, there are 6 circles in the above figure.

6. **(a)** Figure S is shaped like a cube.

7. **(b)**

8. **(b)** A triangle has three sides.

9. **(b)** A rectangle has four sides.

10. **(d)** There are 8 straight lines in the given figure.

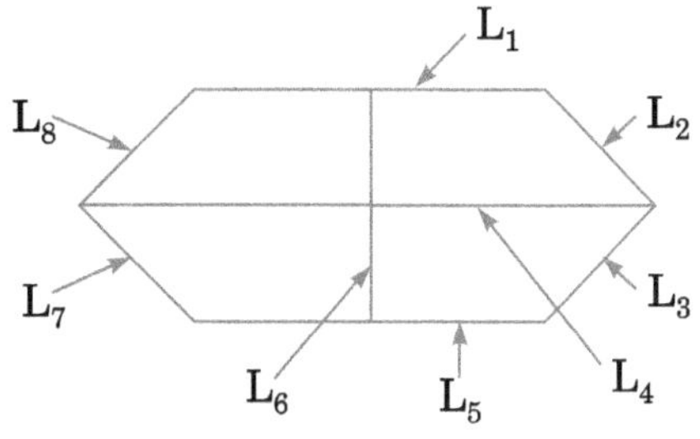

Straight lines $(L_1, L_2, L_3, L_4, L_5, L_6, L_7, L_8)$ = 8.

11. **(c)** A cone is a three-dimensional geometrical shape that looks like a Pyramid.

12. **(b)** Figure P has a flat shape.

13. **(c)** Figure 'S' has a cone shape.

14. **(c)** A circle has no corner or side.

15. **(a)** 'M' one of these can roll.

16. **(c)** A ray is extended only in one direction.

17. **(d)** An oval has no corner and no sides at all.

18. **(c)** Figure Q has more corners.

19. **(d)** The shaded portion of the figure is a triangle.

20. **(a)** Option (a) is made up of 2 curved lines.

21. **(c)** A cuboid has 12 edges.

22. **(c)** Option (c) is correct.

23. **(d)** There are 2 blue shapes in the circles.

24. **(c)** 3 circles are grey.

25. **(d)** There are 4 triangles.

26. **(b)** The name of the shape of the shaded portion is rectangle.

27. **(a)** 

It is a circle shape.

28. **(a)**

29. **(c)** 'Ball' is circular in shape. It can be rolled. Copy, gift box and Dice are not in circular shape. They can not be rolled.

30. **(d)** 31. **(b)**

32. **(d)** △ is a triangle shape.

So, there are 6 triangles in the given figure.

33. **(b)** △ – Triangle

▭ – **Rectangle**

◯ – **Circle**

But ☐ **(square) shape is not present in figure.**

34. **(d)**

Level-2

1. **(d)** 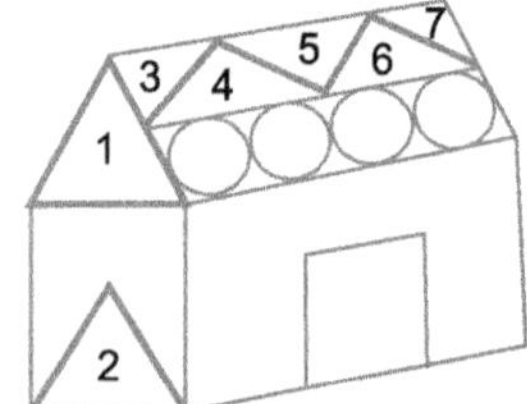

So, there are seven triangles in the given figure.

2. **(b)** 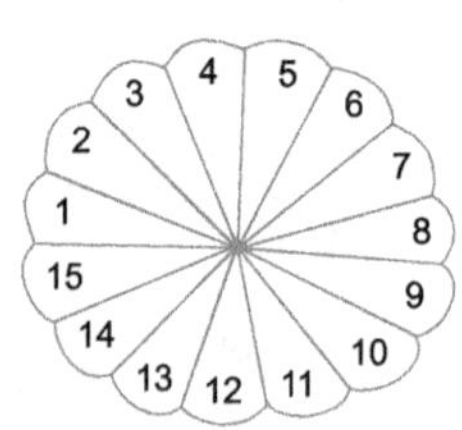

So, there are 15 curves in the given figure.

3. (a)

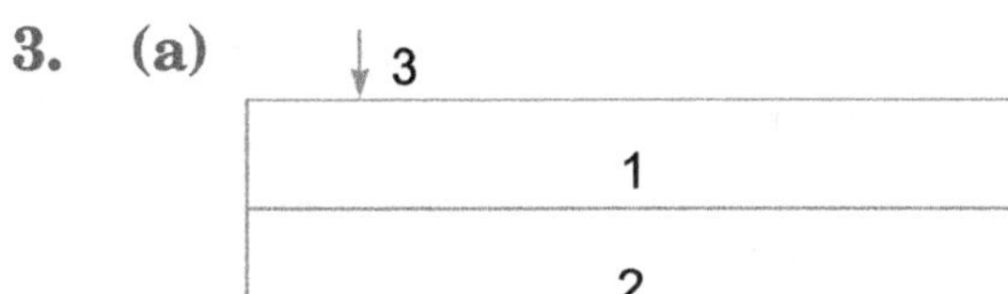

So, there are 3 rectangles in the given figure.

4. (a)

Column I   Column II

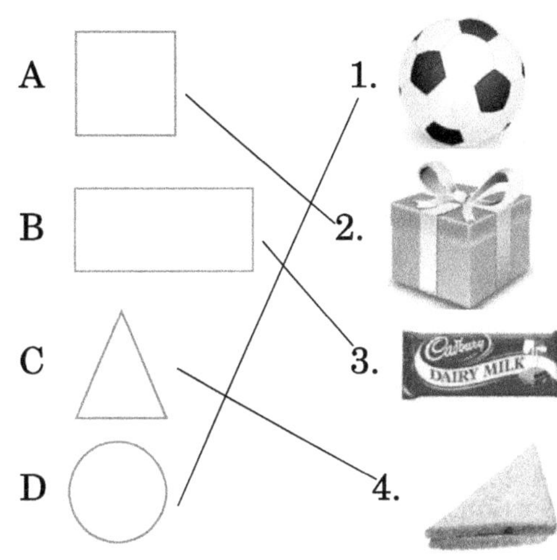

A

B

C

D

1.

2.

3.

4.

5. (b) The name of the shape of shaded face is triangle.

6. (c)

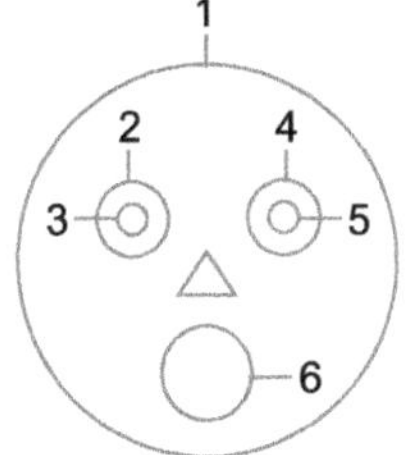

So, there are 6 circles in the given figure.

7. (b)

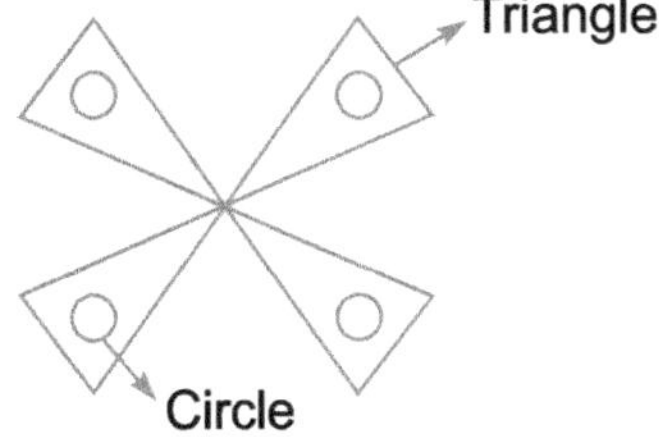

So, the given figure is the combination of triangles and circles.

8. (c)

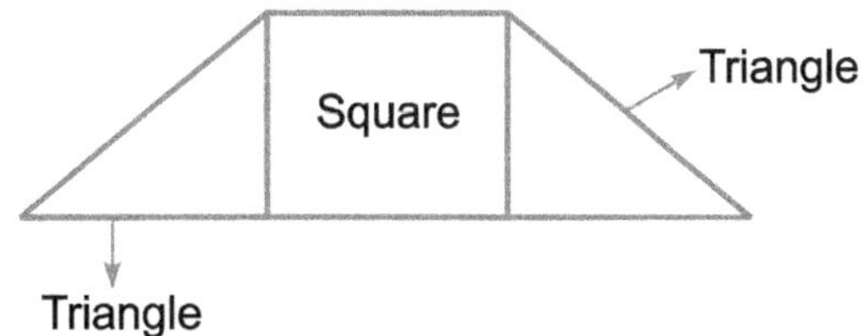

So, the figure is made up of 2 triangles and 1 square.

9. (b)

So, this shape has 5 sides.

10. (a)

So, this figure has 7 straight lines.

11. (c)

So, this Pastry has total 9 circles.

12. (c)

So, there are 6 triangles in the shape.

13. (a) 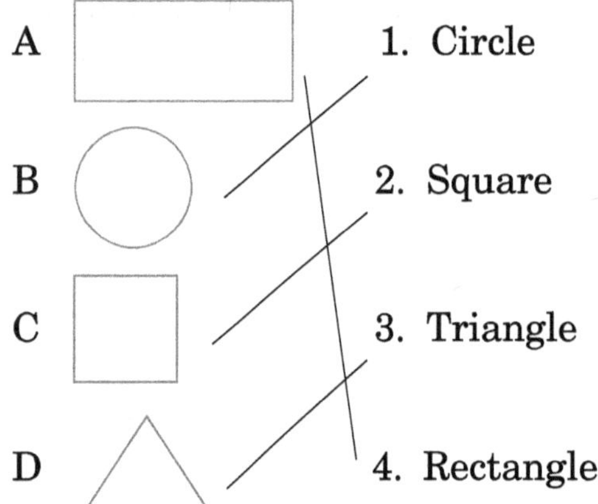

So, there are 5 squares in the figure.

14. (a)

A —   1. Circle

B —   2. Square

C —   3. Triangle

D —   4. Rectangle

So, option (a) is correct for the given matching.

15. (d) Pencil, cup and cap are kept on the table while is under the table.

16. (d) Rectangle shape is missing in the figure.

17. (b) Option (b) is incorrect match.

18. (b) Circle shape is missing in the given image.

19. (a) There are 10 less squares than triangles in the figure.

20. (b) The shapes marked as (a) Triangle, (b) Square and (c) circle.

21. (a) There are 10 triangles in the figure.

22. (b) Shapes Q and S will combine to form a square.

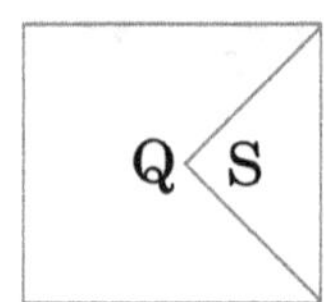

23. (c) The number of triangles in the given figure is 7.

24. (a)

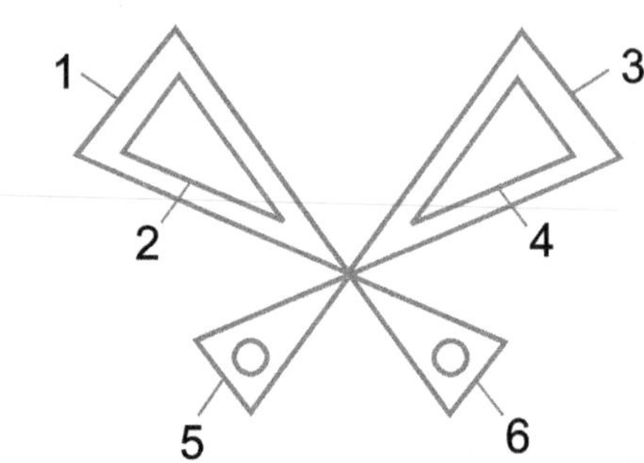

The figure is made up of 6 triangles.

25. (b) The shape which is shaded portion in the given figure is star.

26. (b)

Shapes P and R will form a square.

27. (d) There are 9 circles, 4 are oval and one shape is incompleted, circle.

28. (b)

Visual Reasoning

INTRODUCTION

Visual reasoning is the process of analyzing visual information and being able to solve problems based upon it.

Question based on Visual Reasoning:

1. Shadows

2. Views from different Sides

Shadows

A Shadow is formed where light can't reach. The larger the light source, the larger is the Shadow.

Shadows are formed where light is "blocked" by an opaque object.

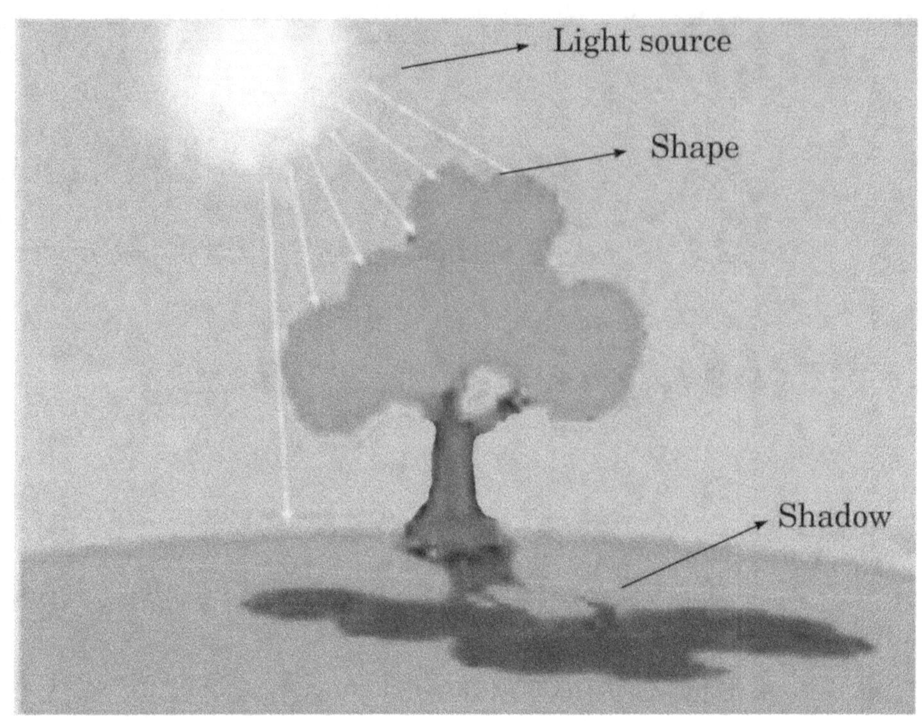

View From Different Sides

A view is a way of seeing something from a particular position. There can be different views of a thing from different sides.

Different Views of Car from Different Sides

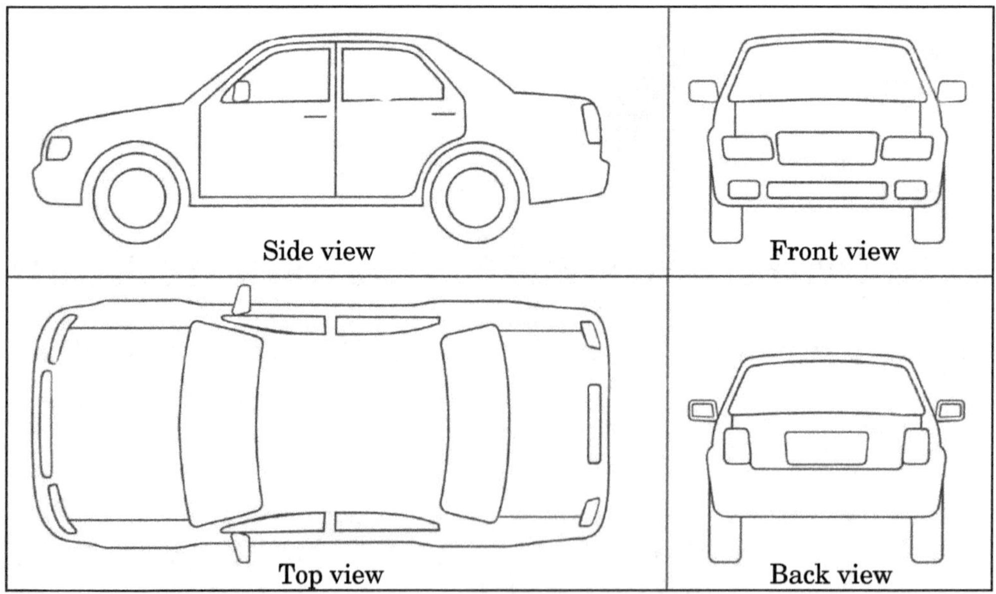

Examples:

1. Identify the shadow of the given figure (X).

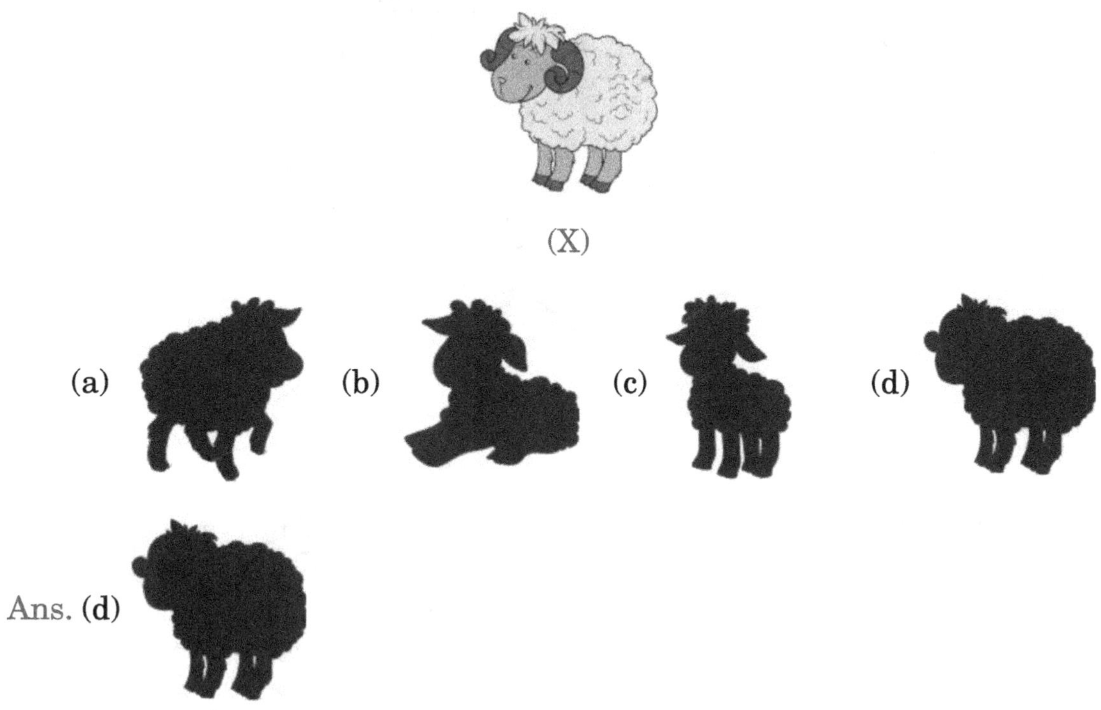

Ans. (d)

2. Which one of the following pictures of a Cap has front view?

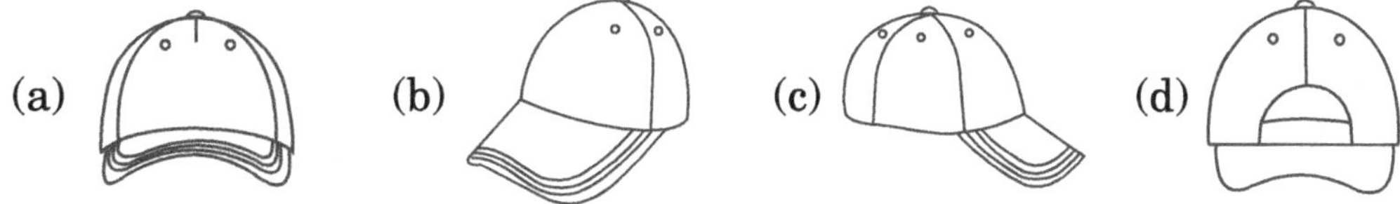

Ans. (a) Option (a) has the front view of a cap.

3. Match the shadow on the right hand side with the correct picture on the left.

C

3

D

4

E

5

Codes:

	A	B	C	D	E
(a)	4	5	3	1	2
(b)	3	2	1	4	5
(c)	2	3	5	1	4
(d)	4	1	5	3	2

Ans. (c) A-2, B-3, C-5, D-1, E-4.

4. Identify the correct shadow of the given picture (M).

(M)

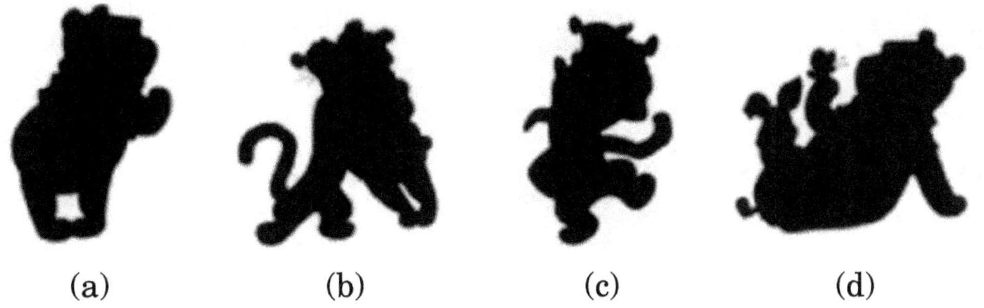

(a)   (b)   (c)   (d)

Ans. (b) Option (b) has the correct shadow of the picture (M).

5.   Identify the correct view of the picture (Y).

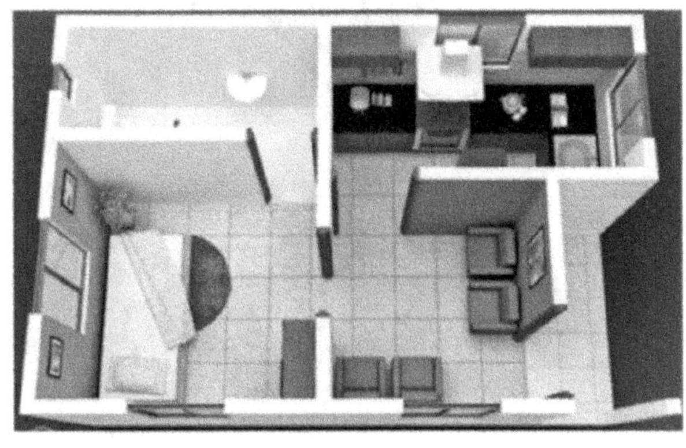

(Y)

(a) Side view   (b) Front view   (c) Back view   (d) Top View

Ans. (d) The correct view of the picture (Y) is Top view.

LEVEL-1

1. Look at the picture and identify the shadow.

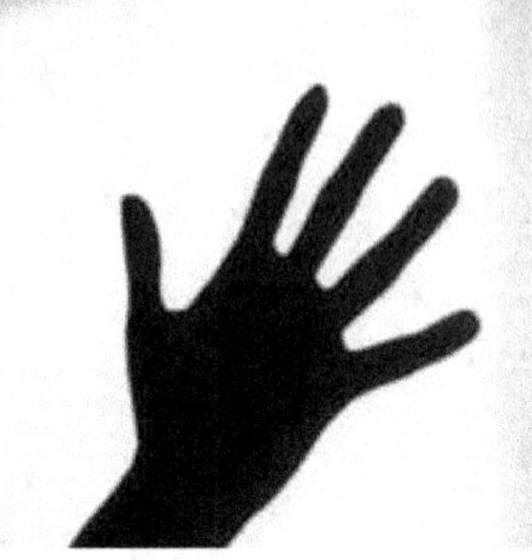

   (a) Hand   (b) Leg   (c) Nose   (d) Head

2. Match the shadow with the correct picture.

Codes:

	A	B	C	D
(a)	1	2	3	4
(b)	4	1	2	3
(c)	1	3	4	2
(d)	2	1	3	4

3. Identify the object, whose shadow is given below.

(a) A lock   (b) A key   (c) A Pin   (d) A pencil

4. 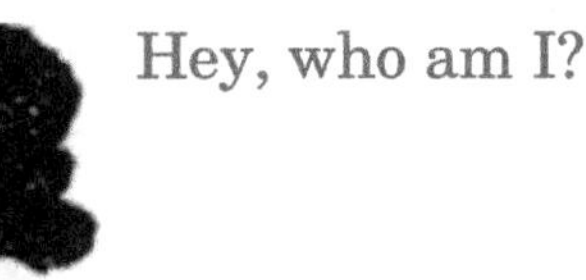 Hey, who am I?

Neil	Sammy	Nick	Dolly
(a)	(b)	(c)	(d)

5. The shadow (X) resembles ________.

(X)

(a) Drum (b) Guitar

(c) Xylophone (d) Piano

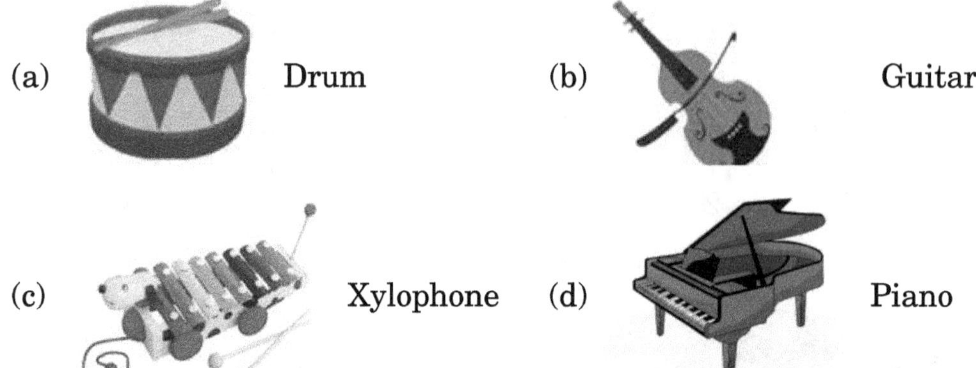

6. Match the shadows with their pictures.

A   Peacock

B   Duck

C   Penguin

D   Owl

Codes:

	A	B	C	D
(a)	Peacock	Duck	Penguin	Owl
(b)	Owl	Penguin	Peacock	Duck
(c)	Penguin	Owl	Duck	Peacock
(d)	Duck	Peacock	Owl	Penguin

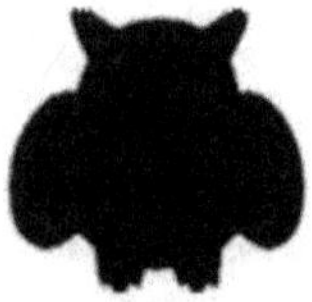

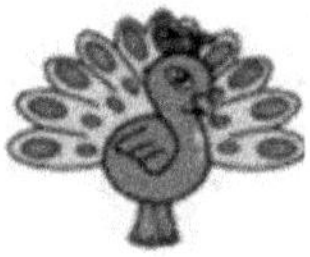

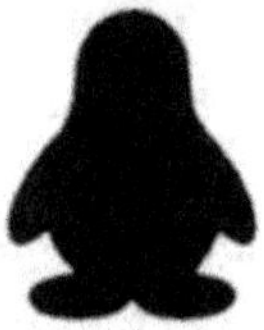

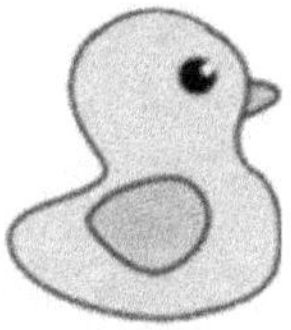

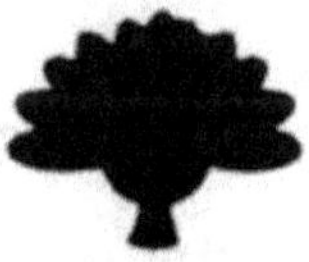

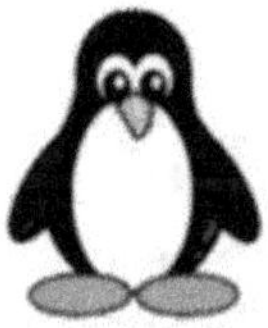

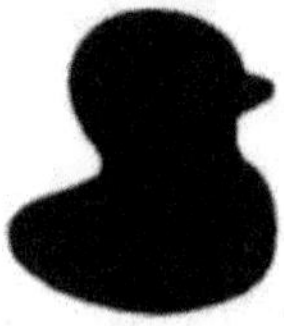

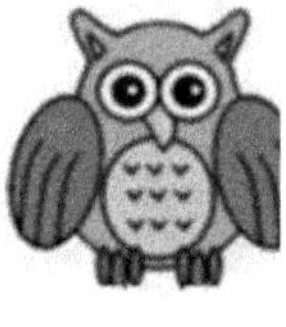

7. In the circle given below there are some pictures and their shadows. Identify among those pictures whose shadow is missing.

(a) Cow   (b) Ant   (c) Rhino   (d) Sparrow

8. The pictures of Bunnies along with their shadows are given below. Can you find the pair of bunnies which is not correctly matched?

Bunnies	Shadows

(a)   1

(b)   2

(c)   3

(d)   4

9. From the pictures given below, identify the correctly matched shadow.

A	**Duck**	1	2	3
B	Rabbit	1	2	3
C	Horse	1	2	3
D	Starfish	1	2	3

Codes:

(a) A-2, B-1, C-3, D-1   (b) A-2, B-2, C-3, D-2

(c) A-1, B-2, C-1, D-3   (d) A-3, B-3, C-2, D-1

10. Identify the animals and birds from their respective shadows.

(1)	(2)	(3)	(4)

Codes:

	Duck	Cow	Cock	Pig
(a)	1	2	3	4
(b)	2	3	1	4
(c)	3	2	4	1
(d)	4	3	2	1

11.

(a)  (b)  (c) 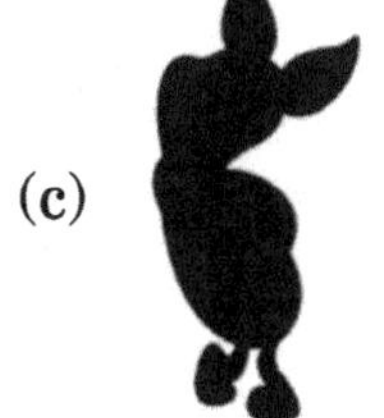 (d) 

12. Identify the exact shadow of the fish.

(a) (b) (c) (d)

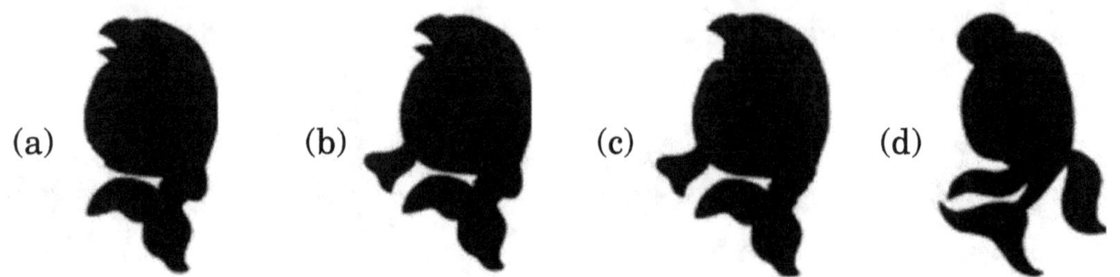

13. Match the pictures with their shadows.

	List-A	List-B	
A			1
B			2
C			3
D			4

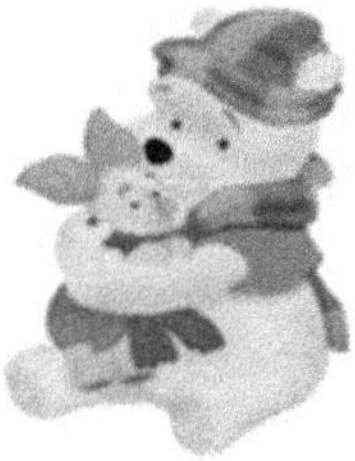

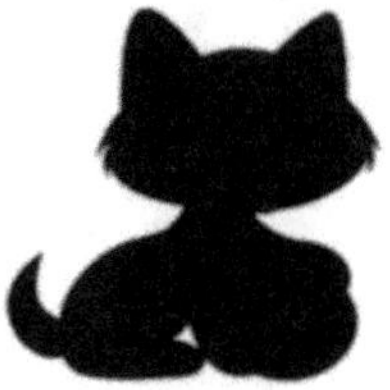

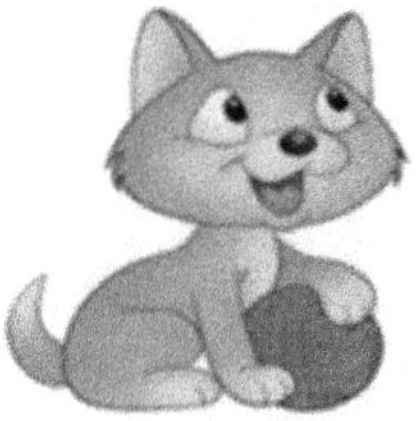

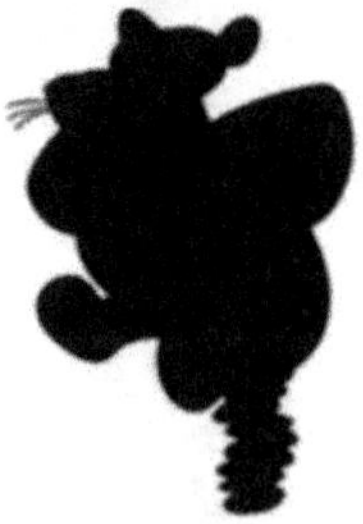

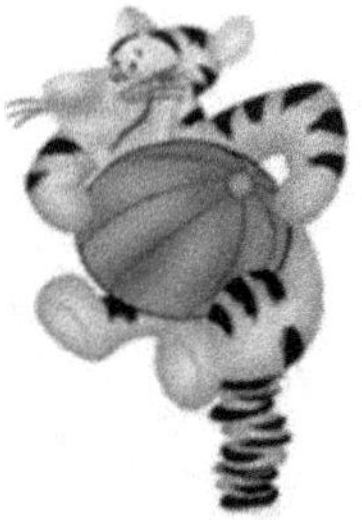

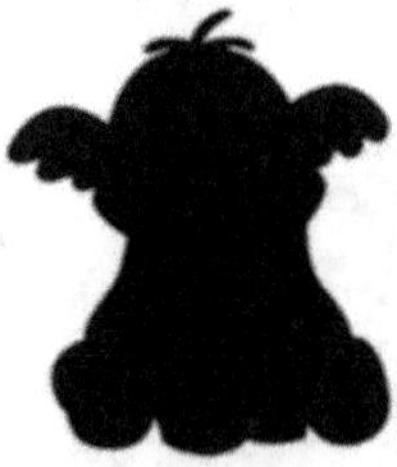

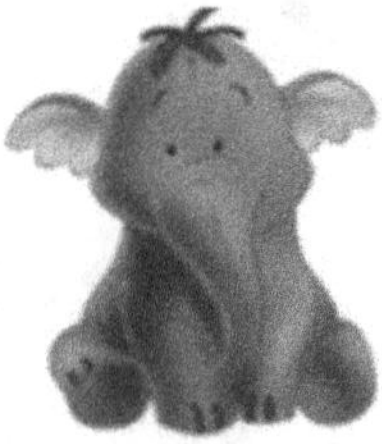

14. Identify the kitchen utensils:

Codes:

	Cup	Kettle	Spoon	Mug	Glass
(a)	4	1	2	3	5
(b)	5	4	2	3	1
(c)	2	5	3	4	1
(d)	1	5	4	3	2

15. Hey, identify my shadow, I am the famous Disney Character. Who am I?

(a) Mickey Mouse   (b) Donald Duck

(c) Harry Potter   (d) Goofy

16. Match the wild animals shadow on the left side with the correct name on the right side.

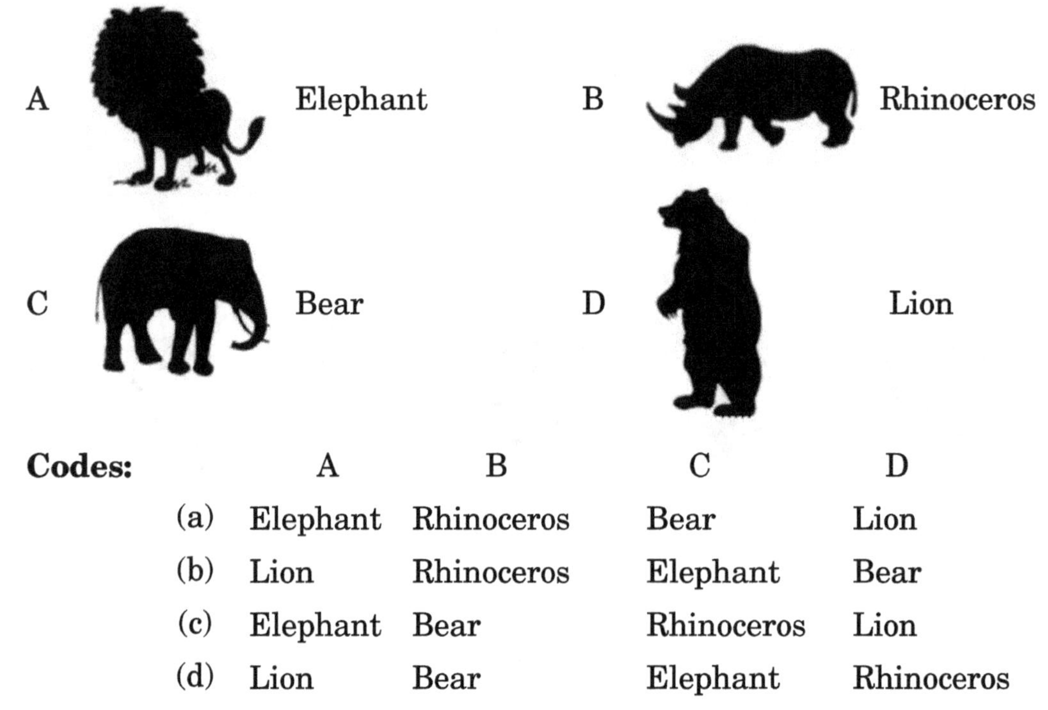

Codes:	A	B	C	D
(a)	Elephant	Rhinoceros	Bear	Lion
(b)	Lion	Rhinoceros	Elephant	Bear
(c)	Elephant	Bear	Rhinoceros	Lion
(d)	Lion	Bear	Elephant	Rhinoceros

17. Identify the picture, whose shadow is given below:

(a) Duck   (b) Cock   (c) Monkey   (d) Pig

18. There are some pictures and their shadows given below. Find out which object does not have its shadow.

Codes:

   (a)   Air craft

   (b)   Ship

   (c)   Rocket

   (d)   Kite

19. From the pictures given below identify the correctly matched shadow.

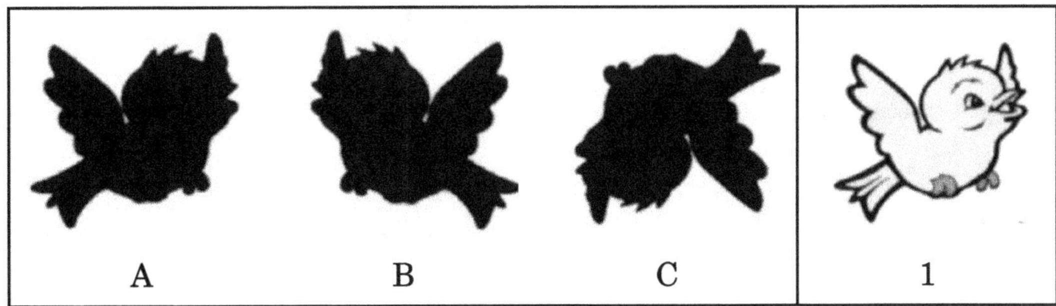

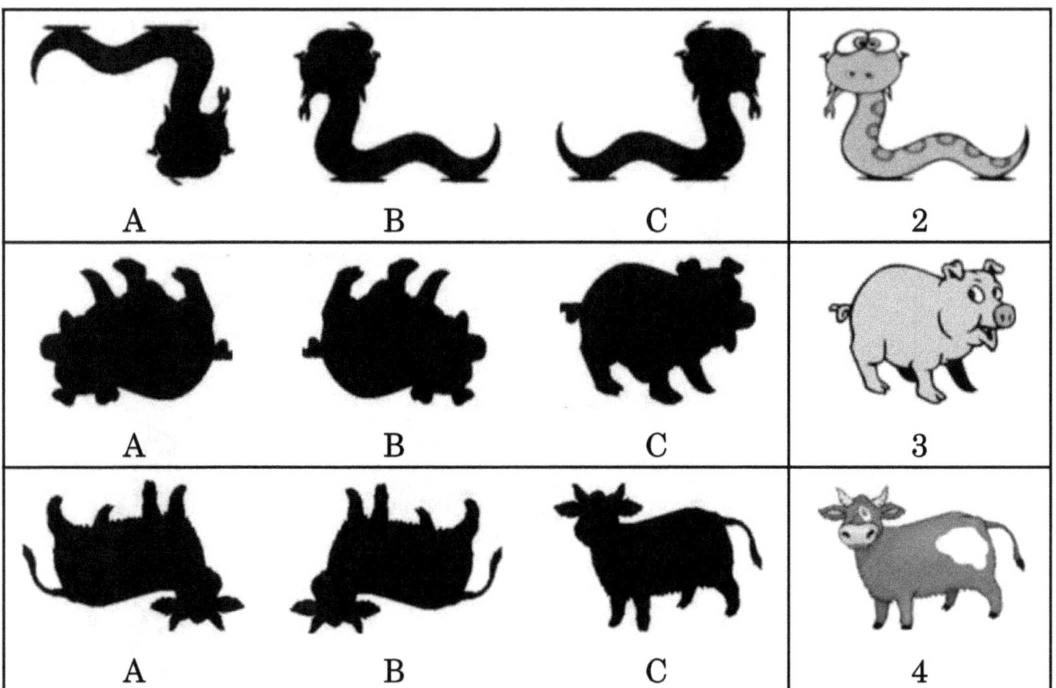

Codes:

(a) 1-B, 2-A, 3-A, 4-C	(b) 1-A, 2-B, 3-C, 4-C
(c) 1-B, 2-C, 3-B, 4-A	(d) 1-B, 2-C, 3-C, 4-A

20. Some geometrical shapes are given below. Match them with their respective shadows.

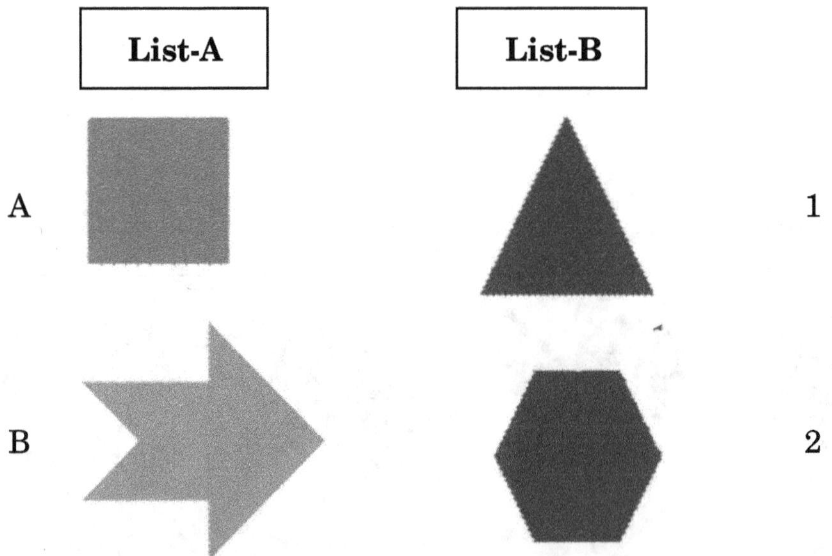

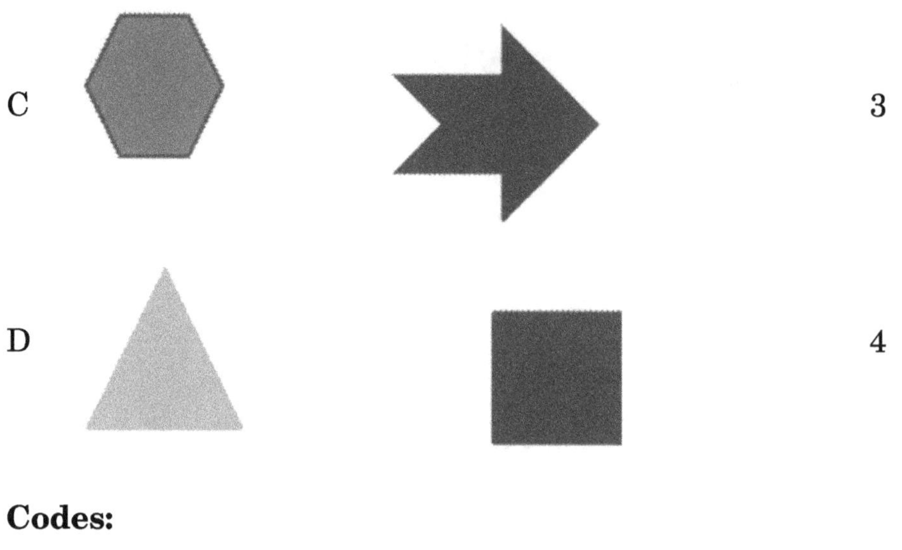

C					3
D					4

Codes:

	A	B	C	D
(a)	1	2	3	4
(b)	4	3	2	1
(c)	1	3	4	2
(d)	2	1	3	4

21. Match the following pictures with their respective shadows.

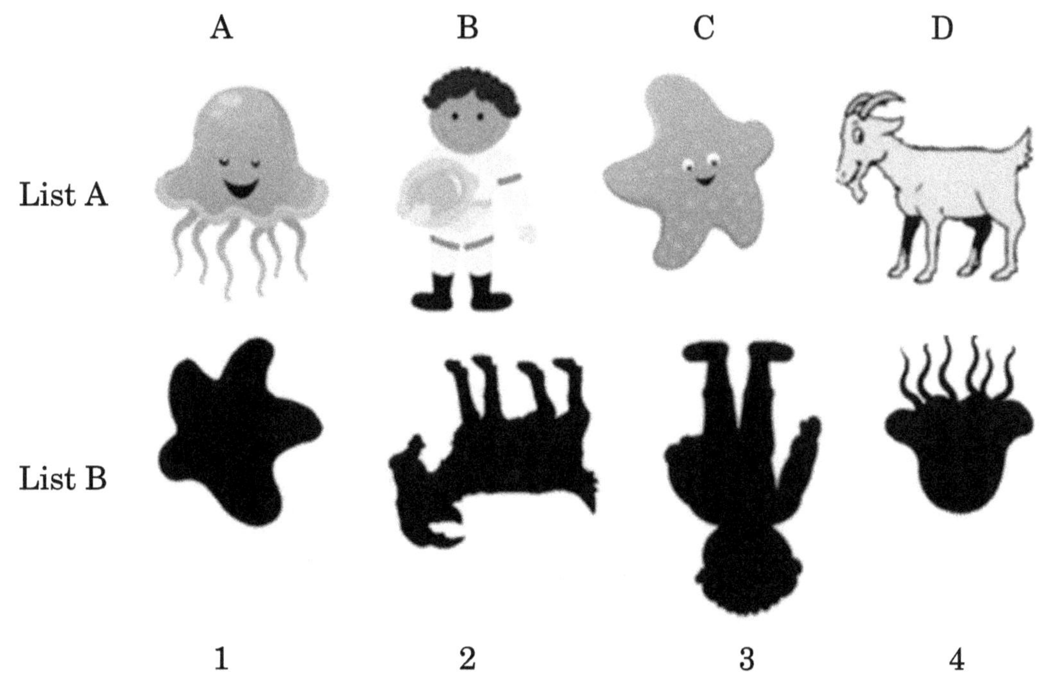

Codes:

	A	B	C	D
(a)	1	2	3	4
(b)	4	3	1	2
(c)	1	3	4	2
(d)	2	1	3	4

22. Look at the picture of a girl given below and choose the correct shadow.

(a)   (b)   (c)   (d)

23. Find the correct shadow of a parrot.

(a)   (b)   (c)   (d)

24. Match the following animals with their respective shadows which are represented in opposite manner.

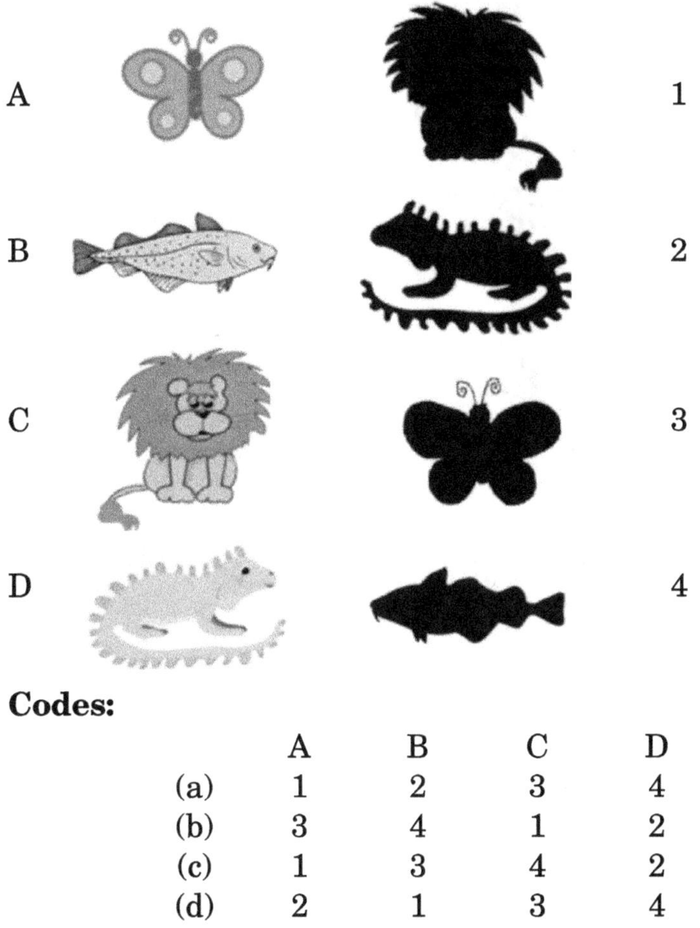

Codes:

	A	B	C	D
(a)	1	2	3	4
(b)	3	4	1	2
(c)	1	3	4	2
(d)	2	1	3	4

25. Which one of the following articles does not have a matching shadow?

(a) Slippers　　(b) Sandal　　(c) Ice cream　　(d) Gift

26. Which of the following pictures in the list A has a reverse shadow?

<table>
<tr><td>List-A</td><td>List-B</td></tr>
</table>

A   1

B   2

C   3

D   4

Codes:

(a) A-1   (b) B-2   (c) C-3   (d) D-4

27. Identify the fruits from the shadow given below.

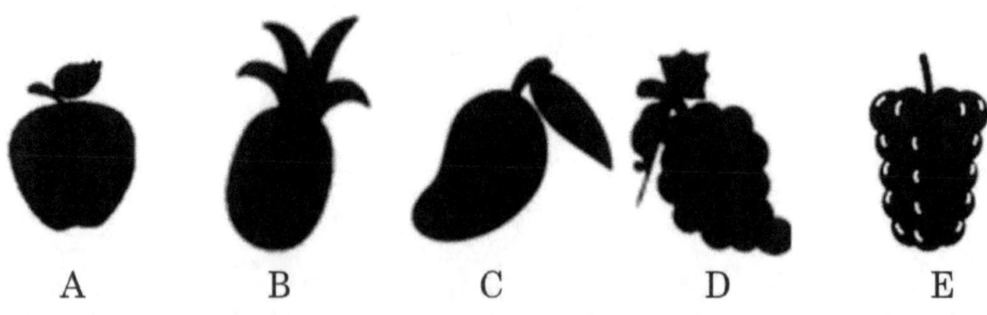

A   B   C   D   E

28. Match the following vehicles with their respective shadow in reverse pattern.

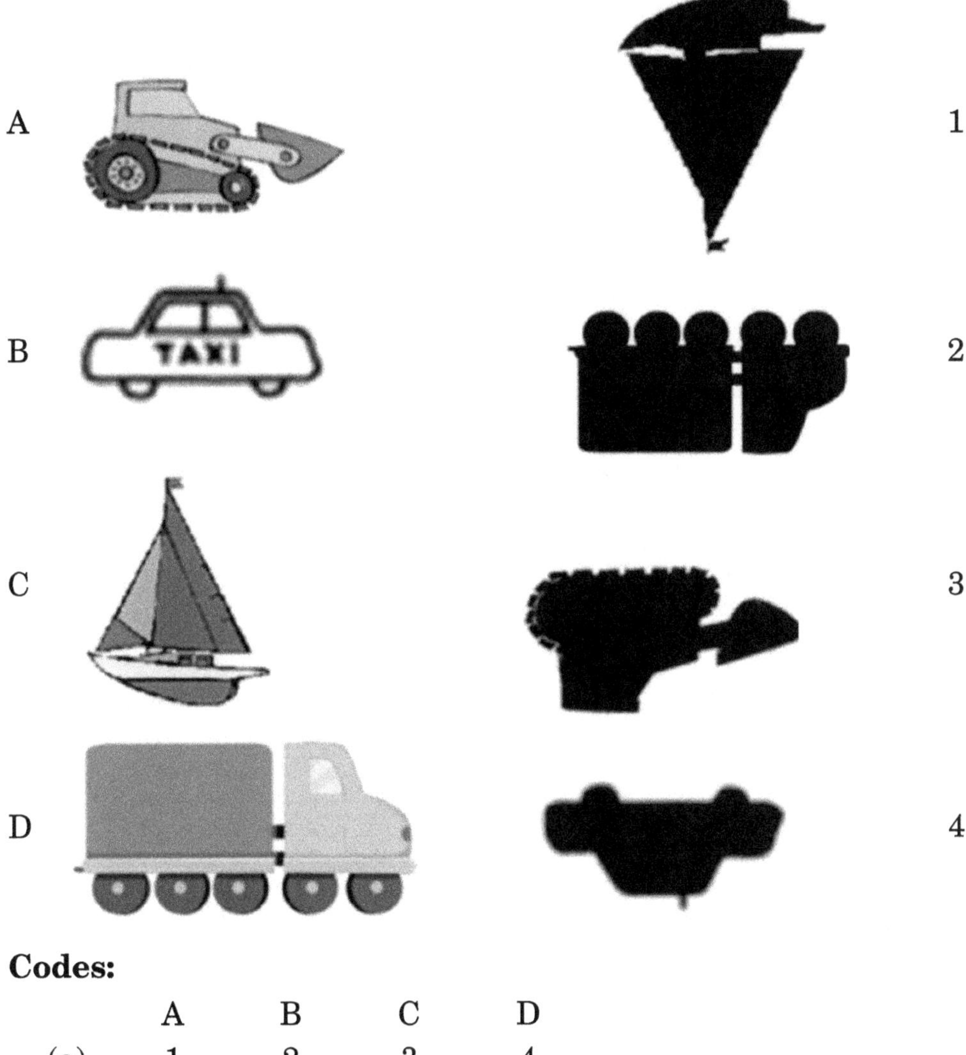

Codes:

	A	B	C	D
(a)	1	2	3	4
(b)	3	4	1	2
(c)	1	3	4	2
(d)	2	1	3	4

29. Which of the following options will complete the pattern in the given figure? **(2019)**

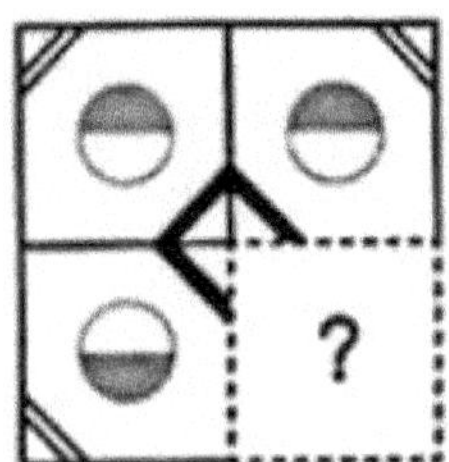

(a) 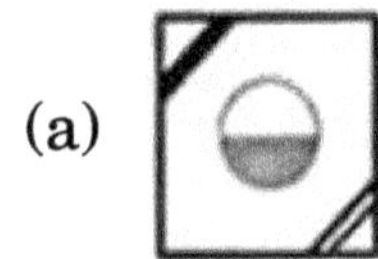   (b) 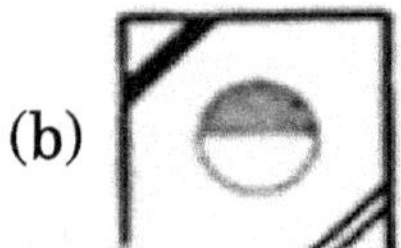   (c) 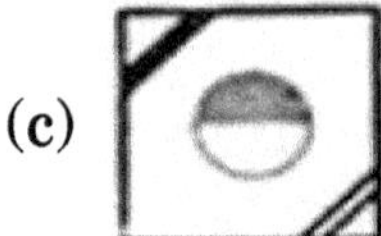   (d) 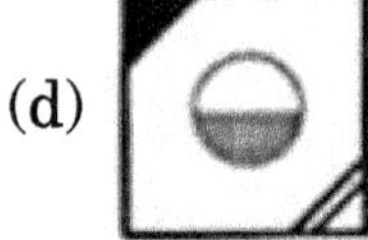

30. Which of the following options will complete the pattern in the given figure? **(2020)**

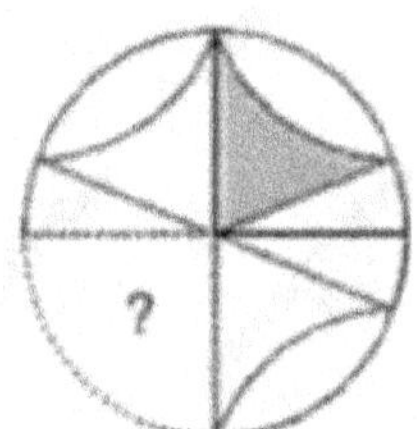

(a) 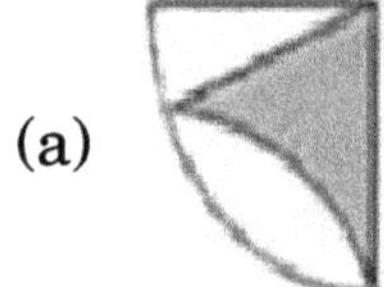   (b) 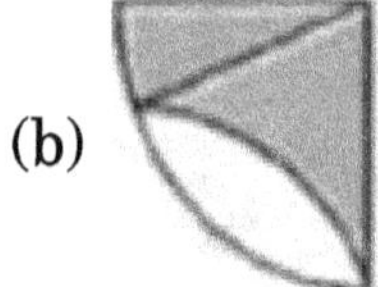   (c) 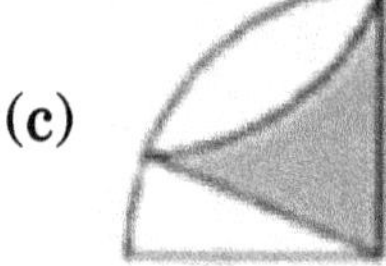   (d) 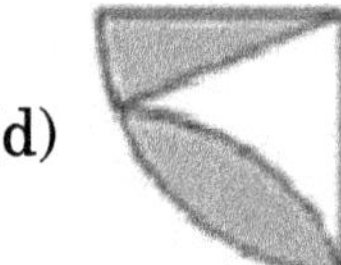

31. Which of the following options will complete the pattern in the given figure? **(2020)**

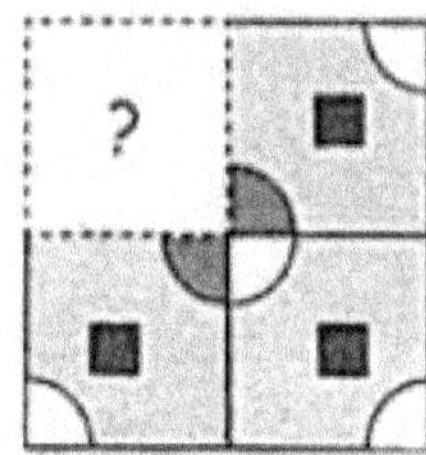

(a) 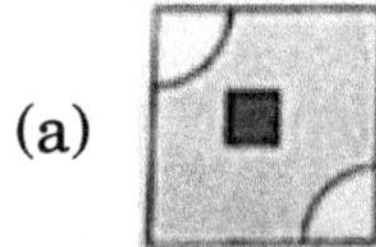   (b) 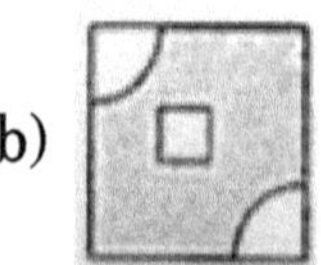   (c) 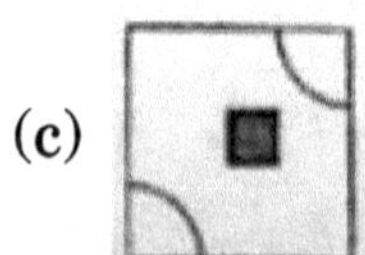   (d) 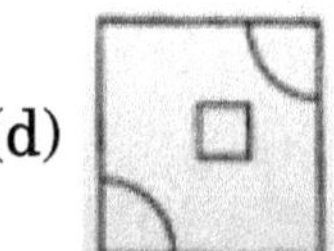

32. Select a figure from the options which will complete the pattern in the given figure. **(2022)**

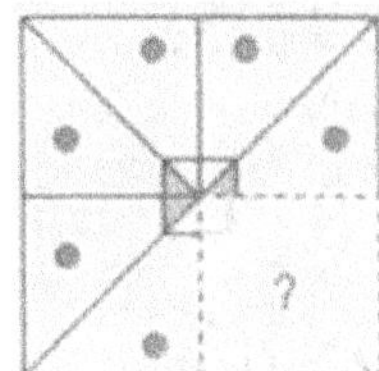

(a) 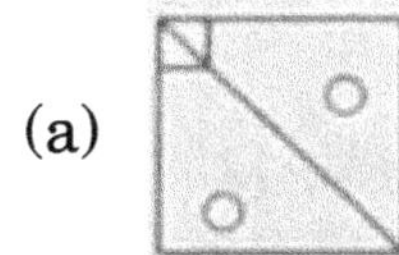 (b) 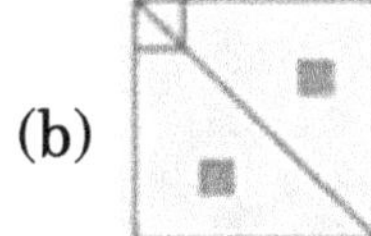 (c) 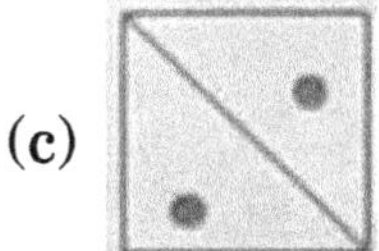 (d) 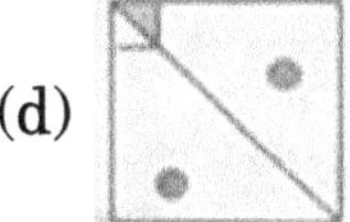

33. Find the missing terms in the given series. **(2022)**

(a) 28, 35   (b) 25, 28

(c) 28, 42   (d) 28, 32

LEVEL-2

1. This is the ________ view of the frog.

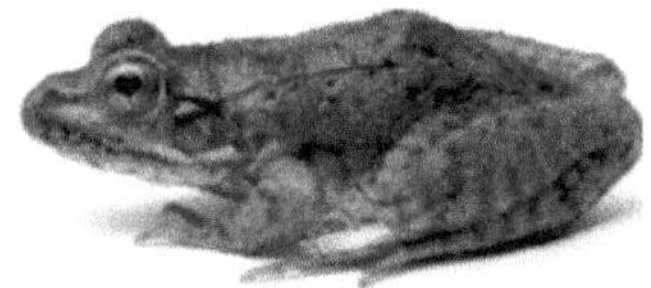

(a) Top view   (b) Front view   (c) Side view   (d) Back view

2. Identify the view of the given building below.

(a) Front view   (b) Side view   (c) Top view   (d) Back view

3. Identify which one of the following has a top view.

(a) 

(b) 

(c) 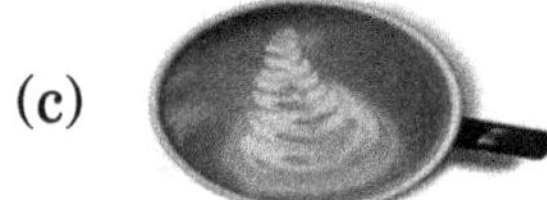

(d) 

4. Match the following objects with their respective sides of view.

Different sides of view	**Objects**
A Front View	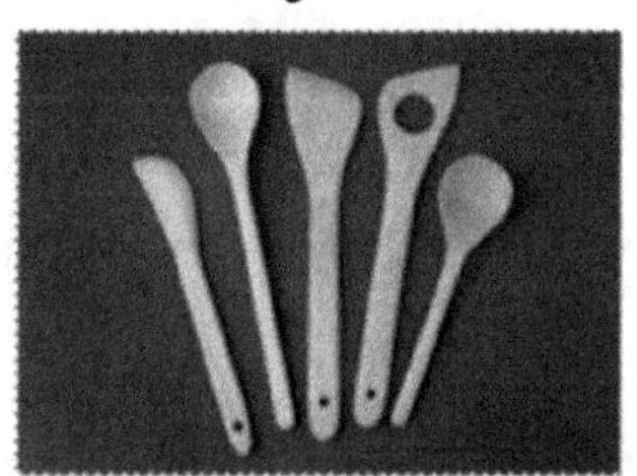 1
B Top View	 2
C Side View	 3

Codes:

	A	B	C
(a)	3	1	2
(b)	2	3	1
(c)	2	1	3
(d)	1	2	3

5. Identify the view of the given picture below.

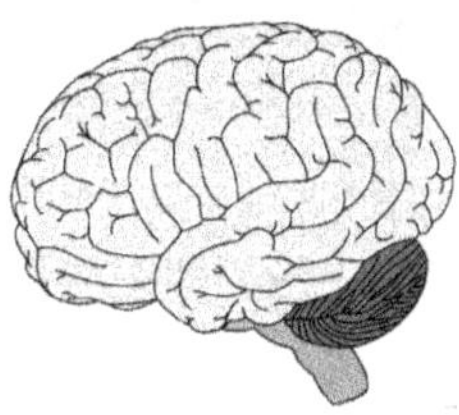

(a) Front view   (b) Side view   (c) Top view   (d) Back view

6. From which side the picture of the building has been captured?

(a) Front view   (b) Side view   (c) Top view   (d) Back view

7. Match the objects of the same sides of two different groups.

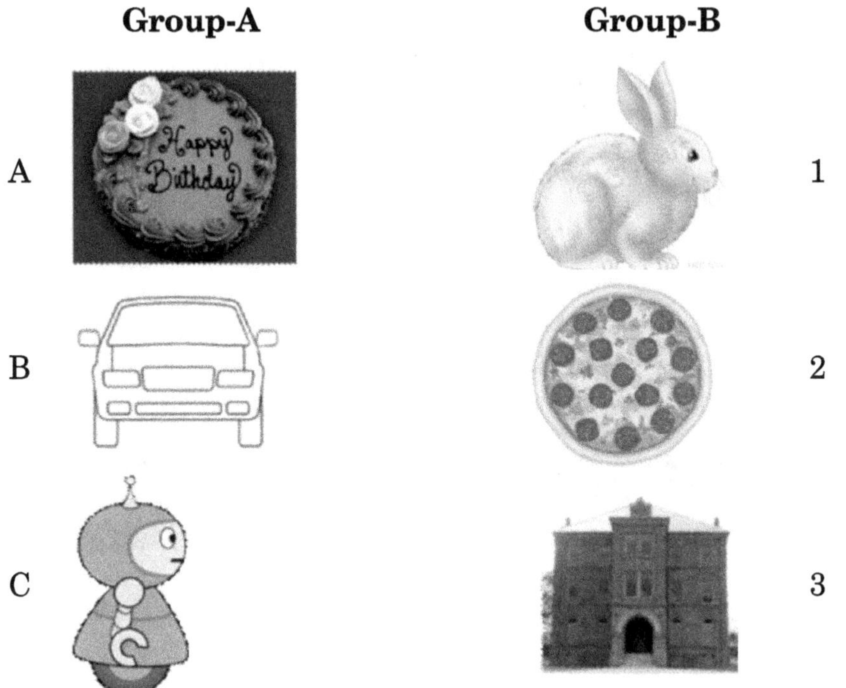

Group-A		**Group-B**
A		1
B		2
C		3

Codes:

	A	B	C
(a)	3	1	2
(b)	2	3	1
(c)	2	1	3
(d)	1	2	3

8. Fill in the blanks.

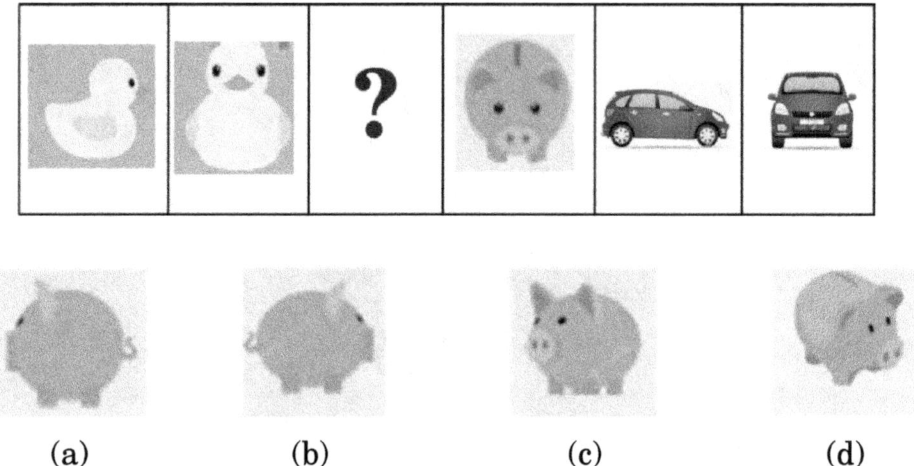

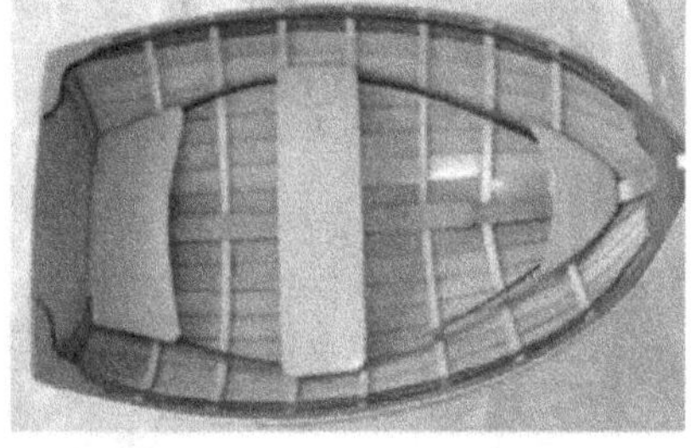

    (a)   (b)   (c)   (d)

9. This is the __________ view of a boat.

(a) Front   (b) Top   (c) Side   (d) Back

10. Identify the view of the train.

(a) Front view   (b) Top view   (c) Side view   (d) Back view

11. Read the following statements:

1.   We can see the side view of the ladybug.

2.   This is the side view of an aeroplane.

Now choose the correct option.
(a) 1 is true
(b) 2 is true
(c) 1 is false and 2 is true
(d) 1 is true and 2 is false

12. Choose the correct pair.

Group-A	**Group-B**

(a) 

(b) 

(c) 

(d) 

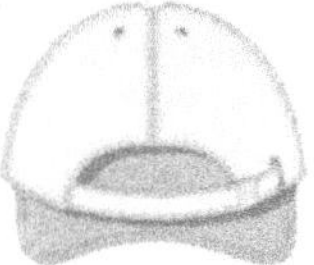

13. Identify the view of the fish.

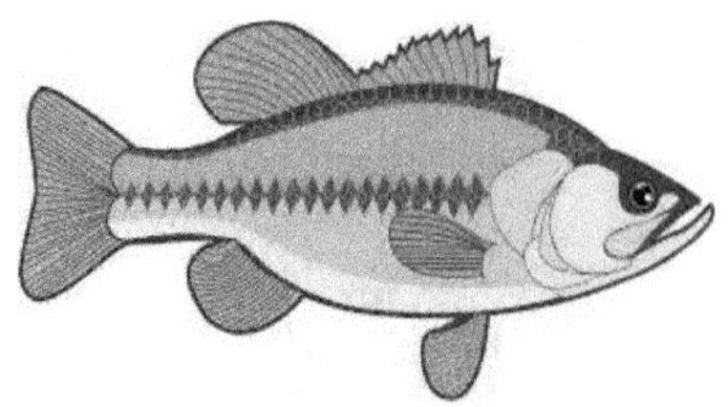

(a) Front view   (b) Top view   (c) Side view   (d) Back view

14. Three different views of a car are given below. Identify the views of each of them.

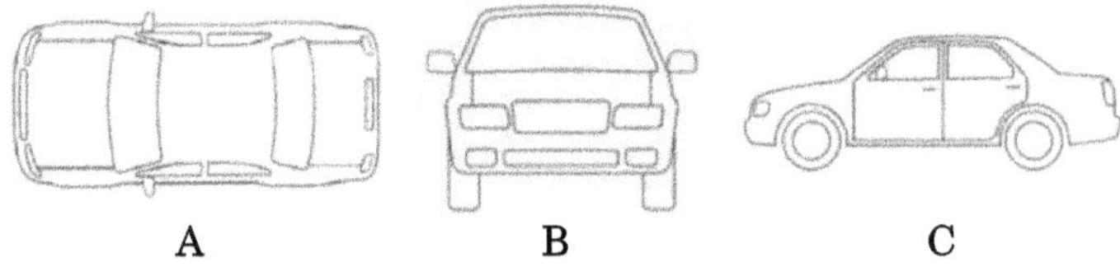

A   B   C

Codes:

	A	B	C
(a)	Top view	Front view	Side view
(b)	Side view	Top view	Front view
(c)	Front view	Side view	Top view
(d)	Side view	Front view	Top view

15. From which side the image of the T-shirt is captured?

(a) Top   (b) Front   (c) Back   (d) Side

16. This is the _________ view of the pool table.

(a) Top   (b) Front   (c) Back   (d) Side

17. Identify the view of the dog.

   (a) Top   (b) Front   (c) Back   (d) Side

18. Match the following.

List-A	**List-B**
A	 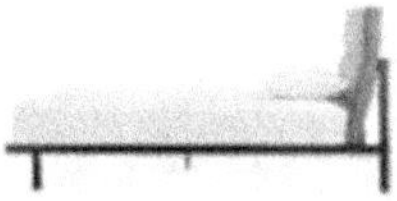 1
B	  2
C	  3
D	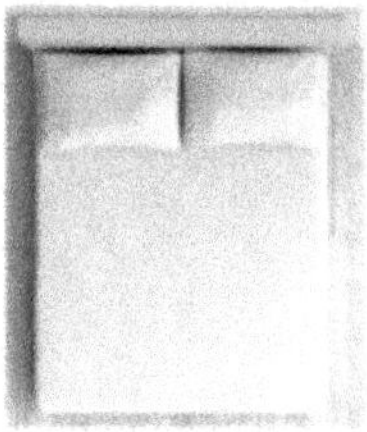  4

Codes:

	A	B	C	D
(a)	3	4	2	1
(b)	2	3	1	2
(c)	2	1	4	3
(d)	1	2	3	4

19. This is the top view of a __________ .

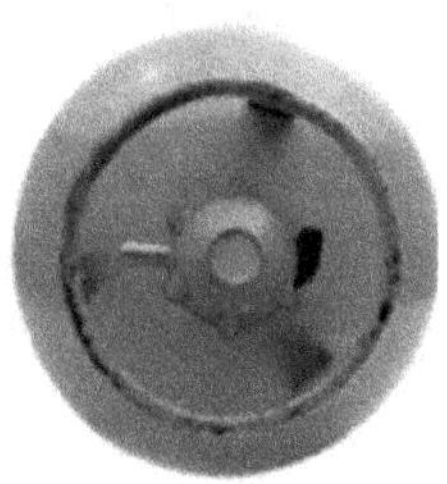

(a) Car Steering (b) Foot ball

(c) LPG Gas Cylinder (d) Water bottle

20. Fill in the blanks.

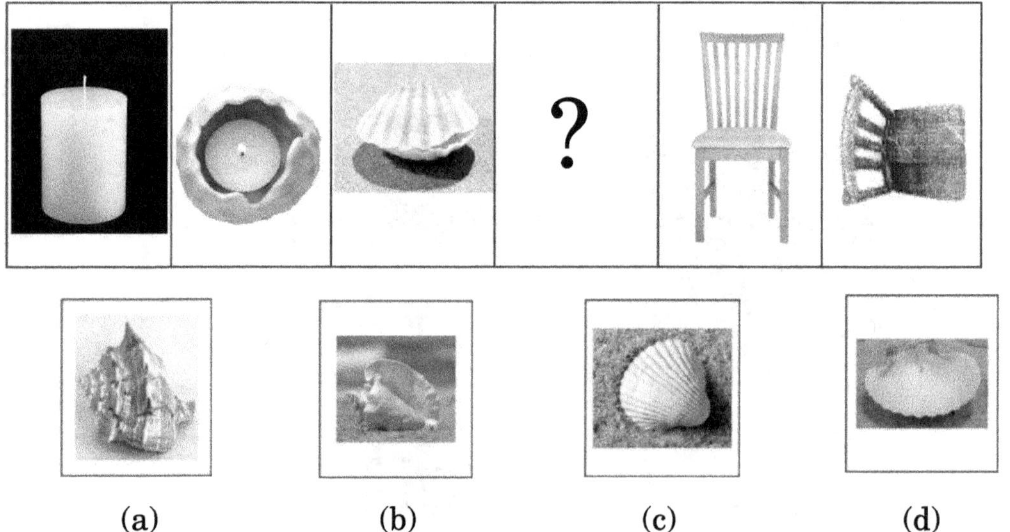

(a) (b) (c) (d)

21. Observe the pictures given below and answer the following questions.

(1)   (2)

1. Picture 1 is showing the side view of a cup.

2. Picture 2 is showing the front view of a match box.

Now choose the correct option

(a) 1 is true

(b) 2 is true

(c) 1 is false and 2 is true

(d) 1 is true and 2 is false

22. Choose the odd pair from the list given below.

Group-A   Group-B

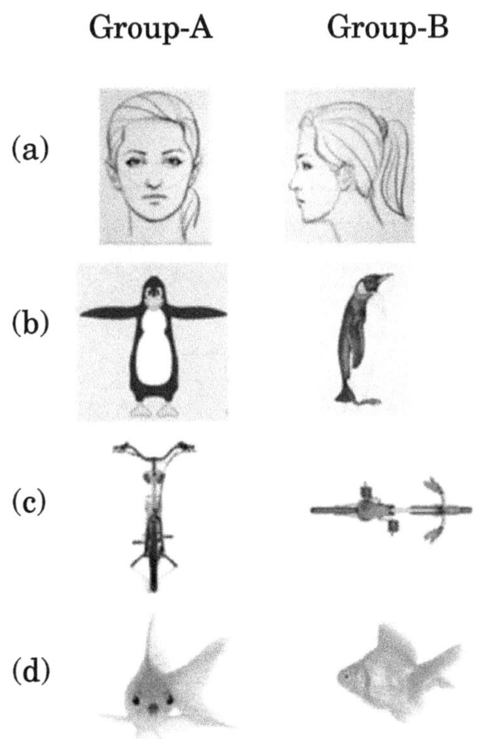

(a)

(b)

(c)

(d)

23. This is the _________ view of an elephant.

(a) Top   (b) Front   (c) Back   (d) Side

24. This is the _________ view of bridge.

(a) Top   (b) Front   (c) Back   (d) Side

25. Identify the view of each of them.

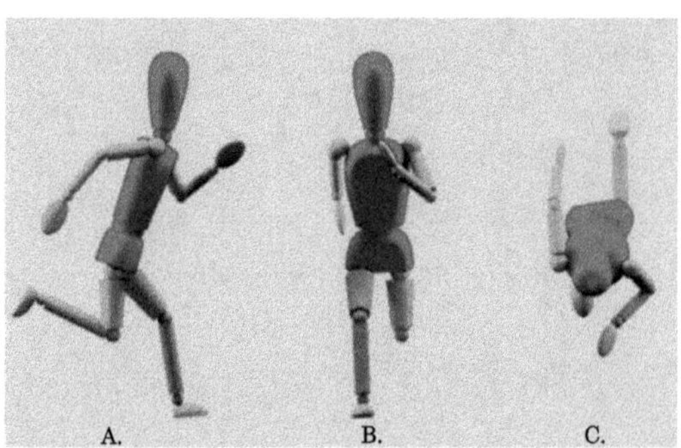

Codes:

	A	B	C
(a)	Top view	Front view	Side view
(b)	Side view	Top view	Front view
(c)	Front view	Side view	Top view
(d)	Side view	Front view	Top view

26. Match the following.

(A) Front view      1

(B) Top view      2

(C) Side view      3

(D) Back view   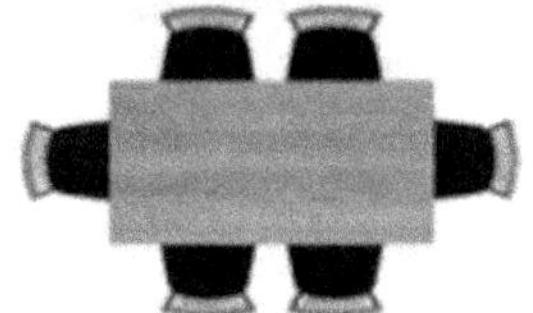   4

Codes:

	A	B	C	D
(a)	2	3	1	4
(b)	3	4	1	2
(c)	2	1	3	3
(d)	1	3	4	2

27. This is the _________ view of a wall clock.

(a) Top   (b) Front   (c) Back   (d) Side

28.

1. Picture 1 is showing the side view of a TV.

2. Picture 2 is showing the front view of a Refrigerator.

Now choose the correct statement.

(a) Both 1 and 2 are true

(b) Only 2 is true

(c) 1 is false and 2 is true

(d) 1 is true and 2 is false

29. Arrange the following letters to form a meaningful word.   (2022)

O	H	E	S	R
1	2	3	4	5

(a) 1, 4, 2, 5, 3   (b) 2, 1, 5, 4, 3

(c) 1, 3, 2, 5, 4   (d) 2, 5, 1, 3, 4

30. Find the missing number in the given pattern.   (2022)

(a) WXY   (b) WXZ

(c) VWX   (d) VXZ

Level-1

1. (a) The shadow in the picture is of hand.

2. (b) A-4, B-1, C-2, D-3

3. (b) The object in the shadow is a key.

4. (c) I am Nick.

5. (b) The shadow (X) resembles Guitar.

6. (b) (A) Owl, (B) Penguin, (C) Peacock, (D) Duck.

7. (b) The shadow of ant is missing.

8. (c) The 3rd one is not correctly matched.

9. (b) A-2, B-2, C-3, D-2.

10. (a) 1-Duck, 2- Cow, 3-Cock, 4- Pig.

11. (a) I am going to fit in the shadow of option (a).

12. (b) Option (b) is the exact shadow of the fish.

13. (b) A-4, B-1, C-2, D-3.

14. (d) 1-Cup, 5-Kettle, 4-Spoon, 3-Mug, 2-Glass.

15. (a) I am Mickey mouse.

16. (b) A-Lion, B-Rhinoceros, C-Elephant, D-Bear.

17. (c) Monkey is the animal whose shadow is given in the picture.

18. (b) The shadow of Ship is missing.

19. (b) 1-A, 2-B, 3-C, 4-C.

20. (b) A-4, B-3, C-2, D-1.

21. (b) A-4, B-3, C-1, D-2.

22. (c) Option (c) has correct shadow of a girl.

23. (a) Option (a) has the correct shadow of a parrot.

24. (b) A-3, B-4, C-1, D-2.

25. (b) Sandal doesn't have a matching shadow.

26. (b) B-2

27. (a) A-Apple, B-Pineapple, C-Mango, D-Grapes, E-Mulberry.

28. (b) A-3, B-4, C-1, D-2.

29. (a) 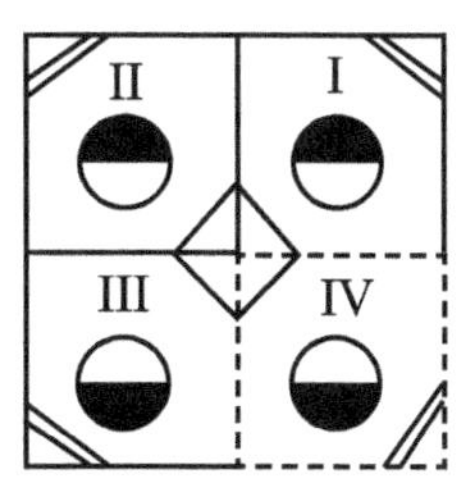
Missing part IV is same as part III.

30. (a)

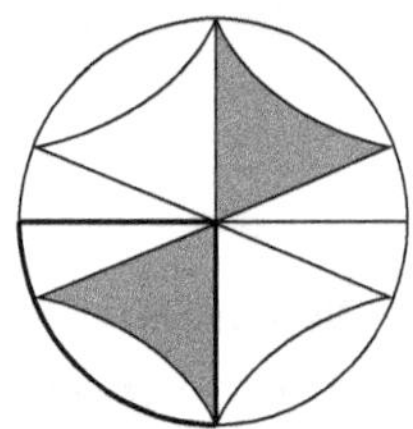

31. (a)

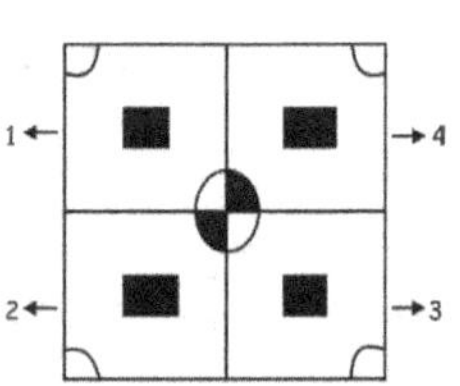

∵ 2 and 4 figures are Similar.

∴ 1 and 3 figures will be Similar.

32. (d)

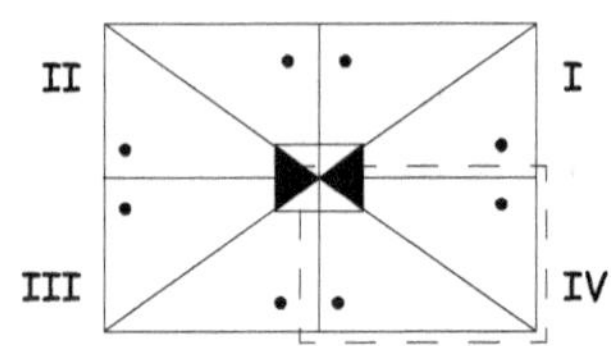

As II is mirror imager of I.
Similarly, IV is mirror image of III.

33. (c)

Level-2

1. (c) Side view.

2. (a) Front view.

3. (c) The object in option (c) has a top view.

4. (a) A-3, B-1, C-2

5. (b) Side view

6. (c) From the top view the picture has been captured.

7. (b) A-2, B-3, C-1.

8. (b) Option (b) is correct answer.

9. (b) The given image is the top view of a boat.

10. (c) Side view.

11. (c) 1 is false and 2 is true.

12. (d) The last pair is correct.

13. (c) This is the side view of the fish.

14. (a) A-Top view, B-Front view, C-Side view.

15. (b) Front.

16. (a) Top.

17. (d) Side.

18. (a) A-3, B-4, C-2, D-1.

19. (c) LPG Gas Cylinder.

20. (c) Option (c) is correct.

21. (d) 1 is true and 2 is false.

22. (c) The pair in option (c) is odd because it has the top view of a bicycle.

23. (b) Front.

24. (b) Front.

25. (d) A-Side view, B-Front view, C-Top view.

26. (b) A-3, B-4, C-1, D-2.

27. (d) Side.

28. (a) Both 1 and 2 are true.

29. (b)   30. (d)